T0269111

Security in Network Functions Virtualization

Series Editor
Guy Pujolle

Security in Network Functions Virtualization

Zonghua Zhang
Ahmed Meddahi

First published 2017 in Great Britain and the United States by ISTE Press Ltd and Elsevier Ltd

ISTE Press Ltd
27-37 St George's Road
London SW19 4EU
UK

www.iste.co.uk

Elsevier Ltd
The Boulevard, Langford Lane
Kidlington, Oxford, OX5 1GB
UK

www.elsevier.com

Notices

Knowledge and best practice in this field are constantly changing. As new research and experience broaden our understanding, changes in research methods, professional practices, or medical treatment may become necessary.

Practitioners and researchers must always rely on their own experience and knowledge in evaluating and using any information, methods, compounds, or experiments described herein. In using such information or methods they should be mindful of their own safety and the safety of others, including parties for whom they have a professional responsibility.

To the fullest extent of the law, neither the Publisher nor the authors, contributors, or editors, assume any liability for any injury and/or damage to persons or property as a matter of products liability, negligence or otherwise, or from any use or operation of any methods, products, instructions, or ideas contained in the material herein.

For information on all our publications visit our website at http://store.elsevier.com/

British Library Cataloguing-in-Publication Data
A CIP record for this book is available from the British Library
Library of Congress Cataloging in Publication Data
A catalog record for this book is available from the Library of Congress
ISBN 978-1-78548-257-1

Printed and bound in the UK and US

Contents

Preface

Software and networking industry is experiencing a rapid development and deployment of network function visualization (NFV) technology, in both enterprise networks and cloud data center networks. One of the major reasons for such a technological trend is that NFV has the capability of reducing capital and operational expenditures, thereby increasing networking service efficiency, performance, agility, scalability and resource utilization. Despite such well-recognized benefits, security remains to be one of the major concerns of network service providers that seriously impede the further development and deployment of NFV.

This book is therefore dedicated to investigating and exploring the potential security issues for NFV. It contains three major ingredients: (1) a comprehensive survey of the NFV framework and architecture, covering the significant advancements of NFV in both industry and academia; (2) a comprehensive threat analysis, with an objective to establish a threat taxonomy for NFV-enabled networking services and to identify the most essential security requirements; (3) comparative studies between traditional security functions and those that are tailored to NFV, such as: security management; identity and access management (IAM); intrusion detection and prevention system (IDS/IPS); network isolation and data protection. The first part is focused on NFV management and orchestration framework (MANO), examining those state-of-the-art NFV platforms and architectures. In the second part, based on the nine use cases proposed by ETSI, we classify them into five categories in terms of architecture and objective. For each use, we present a layer-specific threat analysis, and finally provide a holistic perspective on their attack surfaces. To address the identified threats, a set of corresponding security requirements are discussed. The third part studies the feasibility of implementing traditional security functions in NFV, by referring to the counterparts in three typical scenarios, i.e. IT, telecommunication and cloud.

This work is one of the first attempts to extensively discuss the security issues in NFV. We hope that it can serve as a basis or guideline for both academia researchers and industry practitioners to work together for achieving secure and dependable NFV-based network services.

Objectives

To better understand and identify the above promises and challenges, this book focuses on the following major tasks:

– Investigation of the impacts of NFV on traditional ICT services by carefully studying several NFV-based scenarios. These scenarios are used to analyze their specific security threats and identify the corresponding security requirements. Such a scenario-oriented threat analysis can finally lead to a comprehensive threat taxonomy, laying down a foundation to design NFV-based effective security mechanisms.

– Investigation of the impacts of NFV on cyber defense from a holistic perspective, covering security management and security service orchestration, as well as the basic security functions. More specifically, we analyze the gap between traditional implementation and NFV-based implementations of basic security functions: IPDS, IAM and encryption. We also study the feasibility of security service orchestration in the context of NFV.

To achieve these objectives, a very large set of technical reports, white papers, academia papers and project deliverables, as well as state-of-the-art proposals are reviewed and studied. Both case studies and comparative studies which are exploited and analyzed, from both academia and industry.

Audience

This book is primarily intended for engineers, engineering students, researchers or anyone working or interested in the field of networks and telecommunications (architectures, protocols, services) in general, and particularly software-defined network (SDN) and network functions virtualization (NFV)-based security services. It also targets network designers, architects and professionals who are involved in network management and administration.

To understand the concepts and technologies described in this book, it is desirable to have certain knowledge about IP networks, architectures and protocols.

Content

The book is organized as follows:

– In Chapter 1, we present an architectural framework of NFV, along with detailed descriptions of network management and orchestration. The purpose is to lay down a foundation to illustrate the use cases of interest in Chapter 2.

– Chapter 2 studies five specific NFV-based use cases, with an emphasis on examining their security threats, ultimately identifying their particular security requirements.

– Based on the threat taxonomy established in Chapter 2, from Chapter 3 to Chapter 7 we investigate the potential applications of several typical security mechanisms in NFV, including security management, identity and access management, intrusion detection and prevention, network isolation, and data protection.

– Finally, in the conclusion we discuss and summarize the key security challenges in NFV, while presenting some research perspectives.

Zonghua ZHANG
Ahmed MEDDAHI
September 2017

Introduction

I.1. Network functions virtualization

Adding a new service into today's networks becomes increasingly complex due to the proprietary nature of existing hardware appliances, the power consumption, the cost of maintenance and operations, as well as the complexity of network configuration when the network becomes larger. Many enterprises and service providers are seeking more effective techniques to speed up service deployment, reduce power usage and improve operational efficiency. In recent years, network function virtualization (NFV) and software-defined network (SDN) have emerged as novel networking technologies that offer promising opportunities to both cloud service providers (CSP) and cloud service customers (CSC). In particular, SDN and NFV can help to reshape their ICT infrastructures for saving hardware and deployment expenditure and reducing operation and management complexity, while improving network efficiency and performance and optimizing resource consumption [JAI 13]. One typical example is that telecommunication service providers can greatly improve their business continuity and agility, as well as the quality of service, with minimal operational cost and capital investments. As a result, time to market can be shortened, with increased economic profit.

In general, NFV technology aims at consolidating multiple network functions onto software, running on a range of industrial standard server hardware. As such, they can be easily migrated to various locations within the network, on demand, eliminating the need to install new equipment. The network services therefore become more agile and efficient, ultimately leading to lower CAPEX (capital expenditure, hardware acquisition and capital investment) and OPEX (operational expenditure), shorter time to market deployment of network services, better flexibility and better scalability. This also leads to the openness of the virtual device network, and the opportunities to test or deploy new services with lower risks [ETS 12, JAI 13, HAN 15]. According to Infonetics research, NFV and SDN markets will grow from less than $500 million in 2013 to over $11 billion globally in 2018 [INF 14]. In addition, a report of Analysys Mason shows that compound annual growth rate (CAGR) for cloud computing will grow more slowly compared to NFV and SDN technologies [ANA 14], with the rate 12%, 66% and 51%, respectively, as shown in Figure I.1.

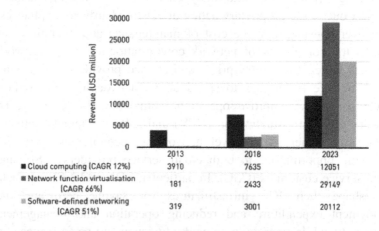

Figure I.1. *Software-controlled networking revenue by market segment, worldwide, 2013, 2018 and 2023, respectively [ANA 14]. For a color version of this figure, see www.iste.co.uk/zhang/networks.zip*

The major advantages of NFV can be summarized as follows, along with some brief analysis:

– Reduced CAPEX/OPEX: the platform transition from proprietary hardware to commodity standard hardware, together with the software or service migration from dedicated appliances to virtualized variants, significantly contributes to the simplified and automated operation, eventually reducing capital investment, while enhancing capacity utilization. The operational cost and complexity, as well as maintenance cost, can also be greatly reduced.

– Shortened time to market: this means deployment of new software and services more quickly and easily (from months to minutes), more scalable service creation, rapid prototyping and testing, remote and automated software updates, as well as flexible and adaptive network design tailored to particular business needs.

– Performance: NFV has great potential to eliminate performance bottlenecks in the network as traditional hardware appliances are moved to virtualized software. In particular, NFV relies on commodity hardware rather than proprietary systems and uses APIs to enable management, orchestration and automation of network services. However, as pointed out in [6WI 14], NFV may face two significant bottlenecks: software virtual switch (vSwitch) and virtualized network functions (VNFs).

– Reliability: it is generally believed that NFV can provide reliable network functions or services in which it usually creates multiple VNF instances in real time. However, as IETF points out, NFV may also have reliability issues; software failure at various levels, including hypervisors and virtual machines; hardware failure and instance migration, which may lead to unreliable network function instances. Thus, NFV deployment needs to ensure and deliver reliability comparable to traditional network appliances. For example, NFV can adopt a pooling mechanism to group together a number of instances that provide the same function [ZON 14].

In addition, the transformation from dedicated network function appliances to virtualized network functions instantiation enables NFV to provide network services with high *scalability*, *agility* and *efficiency*. The network operators are thus allowed to dynamically establish or realize a network with faster connectivity and quicker provisioning of service at lower prices. Furthermore, network operators are able to optimize the installation process of network deployment, to add new network functions easily and to dynamically control traffic flows based on network configuration and policy rules.

Despite those well-recognized advantages, security remains to be one of the major concerns when network services are migrated to NFV environment. In particular, the implications of security must be appropriately addressed in the context of NFV. For example, many enterprises do not have a clear understanding of virtualization security. Some users may believe that NFV will offer more security than traditional environment thanks to the isolation mechanisms of NFV, while others may think that security protection will not be significantly improved due to the complexity of software or service dependencies. The evolution of ICT has clearly indicated that a novel technology is always a double-edged sword from a security perspective. On the one hand, NFV brings many advantages, as aforementioned. On the other hand, novel security threats can potentially be introduced, and the resulting attack surface for an NFV-based network service can be even larger than its traditional counterpart. Therefore, the network service providers are expected to take extra precautions to ensure that the virtual infrastructure is sufficiently secure when physical appliances are migrated to virtualized environment.

In cloud datacenter networks, even though all those security processes and policies are well documented, and the personnel is well trained, there is still far too much information to be retained for manual processing. However, if security processes can be automated and implemented as part of the management and orchestration modules of NFV in cloud environment, a great deal of the potential problems can be mitigated. For instance, NFV allows the functional components to be controlled in a centralized way either through configurations or through network flows monitoring. Thus, it facilitates the systematic and consistent implementation of security policies. As aforesaid, the major advantages of NFV are to reduce CAPEX, OPEX, space and power consumption by decoupling network functions, e.g. Network Address Translation (NAT), firewall, Intrusion Detection System (IDS), Intrusion Prevention System (IPS), Domain Name Service (DNS), from the proprietary hardware through virtualization and software-based abstraction. As such, software workloads are no longer tied to a particular hardware platform, allowing a centralized control, with dynamic migration and deployment throughout the network, as needed. For example, the service providers can leverage NFV to install security applications such as anti-malware, data leakage prevention, firewall and remediation measures on network components. Thanks to the flexibility of NFV, security zones and traffic steering can be easily achieved in order to isolate compromised network elements from other appliances, thus containing the infection and propagation of malware. Also, the protection of data transmission between different network components can be improved.

I.2. Security challenges in NFV

It is unclear how NFV would fundamentally impact the landscape of cyber defense, how it can help to improve security management, and what kind of specific security risks it may introduce. In addition to the benefits proposed by NFV (highlighted in section I.1), the following issues require careful consideration:

– Overhead. During dynamic provisioning of NFV services, computation, storage and communication overhead will be incurred in virtual machine instances. Additional performance overhead could be introduced when network functions are frequently migrated from the dedicated hardware to the cloud infrastructure.

– Service provisioning. Considering the fact that different network functions may be located on both hardware and VMs, the process of service provisioning is complicated and must be sufficiently intelligent. In particular, in order to preserve the elasticity of service provisioning, the consolidation and migration of NFV should automatically and gracefully handle the workload and user demand.

– Interoperability. One of the key issues of NFV management and orchestration is the designing of standard interfaces between multiple virtual appliances, as well as the underlying legacy network equipment from different vendors, while avoiding the incurrence of significant costs in terms of integration or operation failures. Furthermore, the NFV deployment may involve hypervisor, hardware and software solutions from various cloud vendors, thus inevitably introducing compatibility issues.

– Troubleshooting. NFV management and orchestration needs to correlate information across heterogeneous entities, potentially increasing operational complexity despite the standardized interfaces, thus making it challenging to determine the root causes of service failures. For example, the end-to-end latency over NFV could be caused by NFV itself, the platforms that host virtualized functions, or any other components across the network. The interleaved dependency between those functional components makes it extremely challenging to infer the root causes of latency.

– Reliability. It is an important requirement for both network operators and service carriers to guarantee service reliability, strictly meeting with a service level agreement (SLA) when they are migrated to virtualized environment. However, the dependence on multiple components and utilization of commodity hardware introduce more complexity in achieving resilience for software-based implementations than in their hardware-based counterparts. For instance, moving NFV components from one commodity hardware platform to another requires service stability and continuity in terms of maximum packet loss rate, latency and failure recovery.

In addition to the above challenges associated with the performance of NFV, it is equally or even more important to identify the challenges of security. In particular, the implicit trade-off between NFV performance goals and security must be carefully studied, which is also a long-standing challenging issue for any other ICT scenarios. The ideal case is that service providers and network operators can ensure that all the implemented and deployed NFV instances and components are secure, which is however believed to be mission impossible in practice. Thus, a more realistic alternative, which is the traditional approach, is to conduct threat analyses for specific NFV scenarios and then enhance their security based on the identified security requirements. For example, European Telecommunications Standards Institute (ETSI) has proposed nine use cases [ETS 13b], including Network Functions Virtualization Infrastructure as a Service (NFVIaaS), Virtual Network Function as a Service (VNFaaS), Virtual Network Platform as a service (VNPaaS), VNF forwarding graphs, virtualization of mobile core network and IMS, virtualization of mobile base station, virtualization of the home environment, virtualization of CDNs (vCDN) and fixed access network functions virtualization. These use cases may vary in terms of security requirements and should be comparatively studied. *As a result, a comprehensive threat taxonomy can be established, helping service providers to deploy cost-effective security mechanisms according to their particular needs.* In fact, it has already been envisioned by security professionals and network operators that the attack surface of NFV could be very broad, covering hardware or firmware vulnerabilities, vulnerabilities of virtualized network functions, hypervisor vulnerabilities, orchestration vulnerabilities, or even policy violation due to administrative errors. More importantly, as the large-scale deployment of NFVs may cross different cloud datacenters and security domains, the frequent migration can bring a large set of challenges in specifying and enforcing security policies.

It therefore becomes clear that it is a significant and urgent issue that we provide a holistic yet fine-grained framework, covering both cloud infrastructure and virtual network applications and services, and that we carefully study the threats and security requirements of NFV-based services. More specifically:

– The attack surface of NFV-based network services is significantly enlarged due to the frequent migration of VM instances, dynamic formation or organization of virtual network zones, on-demand orchestration of software, and so on. Those factors collectively make it extremely difficult, if not impossible, to establish an in-depth defense line. An integrated security architecture, which should be fundamentally different from the ones proposed by the Cloud Security Alliance (CSA), is thus desirable in order to address those factors in a holistic way. One expected result is that the service-oriented, context-aware, high-level security policies can be effectively enforced to both coarse-grained and fine-grained PEPs (policy enforcement points).

– From a vertical (north-south) perspective, VNF-based network scenarios usually incorporate diverse system or service components ranging from infrastructure layer (high volume servers, switches and storage) to application layer (virtual network appliances, orchestrated models, service composition) to endpoint layer. For example, misconfiguration of a VM instance or hypervisor may eventually allow attackers to penetrate into the whole virtual network zone.

– From a horizontal (west-east) perspective, as each layer is composed of heterogeneous elements and involves multiple players, rigorous standardization efforts are needed. Despite the existing efforts such as OpenStack and OpenNaaS, the high reliance on additional software, the hypervisor and modules for management and orchestration makes the trust relationship between the service components, either hardware or software, hard to establish. In other words, it is challenging to securely and seamlessly incorporate the service components despite the availability of proprietary or open source APIs. More seriously, the complicated service dependencies make security policies hard to enforce at the most appropriate points. This requires the security mechanisms to be sufficiently agile, scalable and adaptive, protecting the assets both at rest and in motion.

– Either layered security mechanisms such as authentication and access control or security by design approaches must be able to optimally balance the trade-off between network performance goals, which are specified by SLAs and QoS metrics, and are essential security properties. For example, most telecommunication services are "real time" services; therefore, the adoption of security mechanisms should avoid introducing any latency. In other words, cost-effective security mechanisms are desirable in order to minimize service-related cost factors while preserving essential security properties.

On the other hand, as previously discussed, NFV, together with other new networking technologies such as SDN, potentially offers an opportunity to reshape the old-fashioned cyber defense. In particular, the traditional security functions, such as firewall, IPDS, NAT, IAM and authentication, can be transformed from dedicated hardware appliances to software-based instances. As a result, the deployment and operational cost, as well as the latency resulting from the whole lifecycle operation, can be significantly reduced. The performance of basic security functions, such as security monitoring, can be improved thanks to the centralized management enabled by NFV. Meanwhile, the barriers between different security product vendors can be broken, allowing scalable and flexible security service orchestration. Moreover, the orchestration of virtualized security functions potentially enables the construction of multi-layered defense lines, thus enabling security services to be deployed on demand. To achieve that, however, the enabling techniques and methods such as security APIs must be standardized. The gap between native security functions and their specific implementations in NFV must be thoroughly examined as well.

NFV Management and Orchestration

1.1. NFV Architecture: overview

The Internet grows exponentially with the proliferation of network devices, mobile terminals and users. However, the traditional TCP/IP model makes the Internet architecture struggle to cope with the increasing demand of computational resources and the performance of new applications such as multimedia content distribution, mobility and machine-to-machine (M2M) communications. Along with cloud computing, network function virtualization (NFV) and software-defined networks (SDN) have emerged as new networking paradigms which have the potential to significantly reduce the cost of network deployment and operation, along with providing flexibility, scalability and rapid deployment. In particular, NFV offers a new alternative for designing, deploying and managing networking services by decoupling the network functions from proprietary hardware appliances. Thus, their implementation and execution are made as software-based services. By decoupling the network control plane from the data plane, SDN allows programmable networks while enabling network service providers to have a better control over the entire network, thus providing a unified global view of the network while reducing network management complexity. In general, cloud computing, NFV and SDN complement each other and have mutual benefits.

1.1.1. *NFV framework and major components*

This chapter discusses NFV architecture and its key functional components. In particular, in order to facilitate the widespread adoption of NFV technology, ETSI has proposed an NFV management and orchestration (MANO) framework to develop production quality platforms with the expected service availability. Such a framework gives the ability to rapidly respond to failures, with simple provisioning of coherent and centralized views of NFV infrastructure [ETS 14a]. More specifically, MANO architecture is composed of four major functional blocks that are interfaced via reference points, as shown in Figure 1.1.

– *NFV Infrastructure (NFVI)*. This represents all the hardware and software resources that offer the virtualization environment on which VNFs are deployed. For example, physical computing, storage and networking can be virtualized in order to be shared between different network functions.

– *Virtualized Network Functions (VNFs)/Element Management System (EMS)*. VNFs are a collection of network functions that are implemented in software (e.g. deep packet inspection (DPI), firewall, load balancing) to run on a virtual environment, together with a collection of EMSs that perform configurations and basic management functionality for one or several VNFs.

– *NFV Management and Orchestration (MANO)*. This module plays an essential role in that it manages and orchestrates all the resources in the NFV environment, including computing, storage and networking.

– *Operating Support System/Business Support System (OSS/BSS)*. These are implemented by the VNF service providers to meet different business objectives (e.g. billing process).

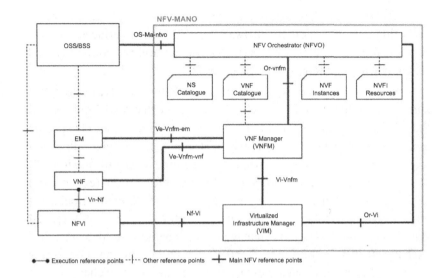

Figure 1.1. *ETSI NFV MANO framework [ETS 14a]*

1.1.2. *MANO reference points*

Figure 1.2 shows the reference points that constitute the interfaces between MANO functional components. In particular, the main reference points and execution points are represented using solid lines and lie in the scope of NFV, while the dashed line denotes reference points that are currently not yet available in NFV deployment and require extensions to handle NFV [ETS 13a]. In the following, we present the main reference points and their particular roles.

– Vi-Ha, which interfaces the virtualization layer (hypervisor) to the physical hardware for setting up an execution environment for VNFs. It facilitates the sharing of physical resources between network functions and collects resource state information for managing VNFs without relying on the hardware layer.

– Vn-Nf, which are essentially APIs provided by VNFI to VNFs executing on the virtual infrastructure. These interfaces provide functionality to specify the performance, reliability, portability and scalability that are required by each VNF.

– Nf-Vi, which serves as the interface between VNFI and VIM, and is particularly used to specify the capacity that VNFI provides to the VIM by accomplishing the following tasks [ETS 13a]: (1) specific assignment of virtualized resource in response to resource allocation requests; (2) forwarding of virtualized resource state information; (3) hardware resource configuration and state information (e.g. events) exchange; (4) requests for network service lifecycle management; (5) requests for VNF lifecycle management; (6) forwarding of NFV-related state information; (7) policy management exchanges; (8) data analytics exchanges; (9) forwarding of NFV-related accounting and usage records; (10) NFVI capacity and inventory information exchanges.

– Or-Vnfm, which is specified to send configuration information to the VNF manager, collect state information of the VNFs for network service lifecycle or send related resource requests (authorization, validation, reservation, allocation) by VNF managers.

– Vi-Vnfm, which is specified to request resource allocation by an NFV manager and exchange resource configuration and state information (events).

– Or-Vi, which is specified to request resource allocation by an NFV orchestrator and exchange resource configuration and state information.

– Os-Ma, which is specified to enable the interactions between the orchestrator and OSS/BSS systems that can hold useful information for NFV.

– Ve-Vnfm, which is used to request for VNF lifecycle management and exchange of configuration and state information.

1.2. Virtualized network function

This section discusses the essential components of virtualized network functions (VNFs).

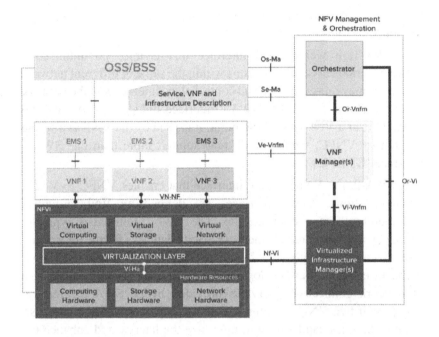

Figure 1.2. *ETSI NFV proposition for NFV architectural framework including the main functional blocks and reference points [ETS 14a]. For a color version of this figure, see www.iste.co.uk/zhang/networks.zip*

1.2.1. *VNF interfaces*

VNF refers to the fact that a traditional network function (switching elements, mobile networks node, traffic analysis, security) can be implemented and deployed on the NFVI and orchestrated by an NFV orchestrator and VNF manager [ETS 14a]. In particular, a VNF can be composed of one or more VNF components, communicating with other network functions (either physical ones or virtual ones) through well-defined interfaces, as shown in Figure 1.3. Based on ETSI MANO architecture, five interfaces are mainly used by VNF to exchange with the external world (VNF manager, VNF, PNF, end point, NFVI), while SWA-2 is particularly used between the VNF components (VNFC).

Basically, each interface is designed to perform a specific task, as explained as follows:

– SWA-1, a well-defined interface that enables communication between various network functions within the same or different network service. It may represent data and control plane interfaces of the network functions (VNF, PNF). The SWA-1 interface links two VNFs, a VNF and a PNF, or a VNF and an end point. It is used by the VNF as a whole and not by VNFC, while a VNF may support more than one SWA-1 interface [ETS 14c].

– SWA-2, the VNF internal interface that enables VNFC-to-VNFC communications. These interfaces are defined by VNF providers and therefore are vendor-specific. The SWA-2 interfaces typically specify performance requirements (capacity, latency) for the underlying virtualized infrastructure, which are therefore invisible for VNF users. In essence, they are logical interfaces that primarily make use of network connectivity services provided by an SWA-5 interface. However, if two VNFCs within a VNF are deployed on the same host, some techniques can be used to minimize the latency and enhance the throughput.

– SWA-3, which is used by VNF managers to perform lifecycle management (installation, scaling, termination) of one or more VNFs. The interface is typically implemented as a network connection (with assigned IP addresses).

– SWA-4, which is used by an EM to communicate with a VNF. In particular, it is used for the runtime management of a VNF based on fulfillment, assurance and billing. Although it is presented as an open interface, it is unlikely to use VNFs from one constructor and then EMSs from another vendor. Thus, it can be treated as a proprietary interface in real-world deployment.

– SWA-5, which corresponds to VNF-NFVI interfaces and describes the execution environment for a deployable instance of a VNF. As each VNFC maps to a virtual container interface of a VM, a set of interfaces may exist between each VNF and its underlying NFVI. Also, different types of VNFs (VNF forwarding graphs and VNF sets) potentially rely on a different set of NFVI resources (networking, computing, storage and necessary hardware) that are provided via an SWA-5 interface. In other words, the SWA-5 interface provides access to a virtualized slice of the NFVI resources allocated to a particular VNF.

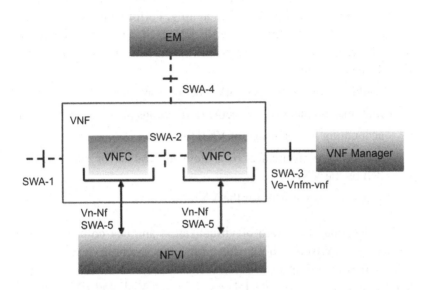

Figure 1.3. *The VNF interfaces [ETS 14a]*

1.2.2. *VNF scaling*

Elasticity is an important property for VNF, required for scaling one or more VNFCs depending on the workload. In particular, scale out/in is achieved by adding/removing VNFC instances, while scale up/down is achieved by adding/removing resources from an existing VNFC instance or instances.

As explained before, the NFV MANO components are essentially primary functions for managing and orchestrating network services in an NFV environment. They are systematically integrated through reference points or interfaces. However, in order to interoperate with existing OSS and BSS, other MANO functionalities are needed.

1.2.3. *Element management system (EMS)*

The purpose of element management systems (EMSs) is to achieve FCAPS (Fault, Configuration, Accounting, Performance and Security) management functionality for a VNF. EM exchanges information with VNFM through open reference point (VeEm-Vnfm). The tasks related to EM functions are:

– configuration for the network functions provided by the VNF;

– fault management for the network functions provided by the VNF;

– accounting for the usage of VNF functions;

– collecting performance measurement results for the functions provided by the VNF;

– security management for the VNF functions.

The EM may be aware of virtualization and can collaborate with VNFM to perform those functions that require exchange of information regarding the NFVI resources associated with VNF. It is not a requirement to have a 1:1 map between VNF and EMS and one single EMS may manage many VNFs.

1.3. Management and orchestration

This section is devoted to the discussion of NFV-MANO, i.e., virtual infrastructure manager (VIM), VNF manager (VNFM) and NFV orchestrator (NFVO).

1.3.1. *Virtual infrastructure manager (VIM)*

Virtual infrastructure manager (VIM) is composed of functions that are used to control and manage NFVI (computing, storage and network resources) of the domain infrastructure under the authority of the operator. This domain can consist of all resources within an NFVI-PoP (where an NFVI-PoP is a platform in which VNF is deployed), resources across multiple NFVI-PoPs, or a subset of resources within an NFVI-PoP. In particular, VIM handles the virtualization of physical hardware in the datacenter by collaborating with VM managers. Using a hypervisor, the VM manager enables the creation of multiple virtual computing, network, and storage elements. In fact, multiple VIMs within a single MANO are needed to perform the following tasks:

– orchestrating the allocation/upgrade/release/request of NFVI resources and managing association of the virtualized resource to the physical computing, storage, networking resources;

– performing root cause analysis of performance issues arising from NFVI;

– collecting fault information from infrastructure;

– collecting information related to capacity planning, monitoring and optimization;

– managing software images (add, delete, update, query, copy) as requested by other NFV MANO functional blocks (NFVO).

1.3.2. *Virtual network manager (VNFM)*

The VNF managers handle the deployment, configuration, lifecycle management, healing, upgrades and other element management of the VNFs. VNFMs may be deployed for each VNF or serve multiple VNFs. The major functions of VNFMs include:

– VNF instantiation such as VNF configuration if required by the VNF deployment template (e.g. VNF initial configuration with IP addresses before completion of the VNF instantiation operation);

– VNF instantiation feasibility checking, if required;

– VNF instance software update/upgrade;

– VNF instance modification;

– VNF instance scaling in/out and up/down;

– VNF instance assisted or automated healing;

– VNF instance termination;

– VNF lifecycle management change notification;

– management of the integrity of the VNF instance through its lifecycle;

– overall coordination and adaption role for configuration and event reporting between the VIM and the element management (EM).

The deployment and operational behavior of a VNF is defined as a template called a virtualized network function descriptor (VNFD) that is stored in the VNF catalog and fully describes the attributes and requirements necessary to realize or shape such a VNF. Then the NFV-MANO module uses a VNFD to launch instances of the VNF it represents and to manage the lifecycle of those instances, while NFVI resources are assigned to a VNF, based on the requirements specified in the VNFD.

1.3.3. NFV orchestrator (NFVO)

The orchestrator provides orchestration of NFVI across multiple VIMs and lifecycle management of the network services, including instantiation, scale in/out (known as elastic scaling), performance measurements, event correlation, resource management, validation and authorization for resource requests, and policy management. Resource orchestration manages and coordinates the resources under the management of different VIMs. NFVO coordinates, authorizes, releases and engages NFVI resources among different NFVI-PoPs or within the NFVI-PoP. This can be achieved by engaging with the VIMs, instead of the NFVI resource, directly through their northbound APIs. Network services orchestration manages and coordinates the creation of an end-to-end service that involves VNFs from different VNFM domains. The major functions of NFVO include:

– providing topology management of network service instances (known as VNF forwarding graphs);

– validating and authorizing NFVI resources requested by VNF managers;

– managing VNF instantiation in coordination with VNF managers;

– providing network service instantiation and lifecycle management (update, query, scaling, collecting measured performance results, event collection and correlation, termination).

There are four repositories of information associated with NFVO needed for the management and orchestration functions:

– Network services (NS) catalog: list of the usable network services. A deployment template for a network service in terms of VNFs and description of their connectivity through virtual links is stored in the NS catalog for future use.

– VNF catalog: database of all usable VNF descriptors. A VNF descriptor (VNFD) describes a VNF in terms of its deployment and operational behavior requirements. It is primarily used by VNFM in the process of VNF instantiation and lifecycle management of a VNF instance. The information provided in the VNFD is also used by the NFVO to manage and orchestrate network services and virtualized resources on NFVI.

– NFV instances: the list contains the details about network service instances and related VNF instances.

– NFVI resources: the list of NFVI resources utilized for the purpose of establishing NFV services.

1.4. Operating support system/business support system (OSS/BSS)

The OSS/BSS is the combination of various business support functions that are not explicitly included in the NFV-MANO architectural framework but are expected to exchange information with functional blocks in the framework. In particular, OSS/BSS functions may provide management and orchestration of legacy systems and have full end-to-end visibility of services provided by legacy network functions in an operator's network.

Theoretically, it is possible to extend the functionalities of existing OSS/BSS to manage VNFs and NFVI directly but that might be a vendor's proprietary implementations. As NFV is an open platform, managing NFV entities through open interfaces, as with those in MANO, is more meaningful. The existing OSS/BBS, however, can add a certain value to the NFV MANO by offering additional functions if they are not supported by a specific implementation of NFV MANO.

This is achieved through an open reference point (Os-Ma) between NFV MANO and existing OSS/BSS.

In particular, it is worth mentioning SDN, which enables the separation between the control plane and data or forwarding plane and allows one single control plane to monitor several data planes. While SDN and NFV are two different networking paradigms that can be deployed independently, there is clearly a potential added value by combining these two. For instance, SDN allows network devices to be programmable by an SDN controller through a southbound protocol or API (OpenFlow). Different from SDN, NFV aims to allow VNFs running on standard servers to be connected to the appropriate network at the appropriate place by taking into account necessary security policies and QoS management. Therefore, SDN can be seen as a network enabler for NFV by allowing users and orchestration software to dynamically configure the network, as well as the connectivity of VNFs. Along with SDN, NFV can provide a broard and unified software-based networking approach to abstract and control networking and network-based resources. Without SDN, NFV requires much more manual intervention, especially when resources outside the scope of NFVI are taken as a part of the network. For better illustration, Figure 1.4 represents the mapping between SDN components and ESTI NFV architecture, implying the following facts:

– SDN-enabled switch/network elements include physical switches, hypervisor virtual switches and embedded switches on the Network Interface Cards.

– Virtual networks are created using an infrastructure network, while an SDN controller provides connectivity between them.

– SDN controllers can be virtualized, running as a VNF with its EM and VNF manager. Note that there may be SDN controllers for the physical infrastructure, the virtual infrastructure and the virtual and physical network functions. As such, some of these SDN controllers may reside in the NFVI or MANO functional blocks.

– SDN-enabled VNFs include any VNFs that are under the control of an SDN controller, e.g. virtual router, virtual firewall.

– SDN applications, service chaining applications, can be VNFs.

– Nf-Vi interfaces allow management of the SDN-enabled infrastructure.

– Ve-Vnfm interfaces are used between the SDN VNFs, i.e. SDN controller VNF, SDN network functions VNF, SDN applications VNF, and their respective VNF managers for lifecycle management.

– Vn-Nf allows SDN VNFs to access connectivity services between VNFIs.

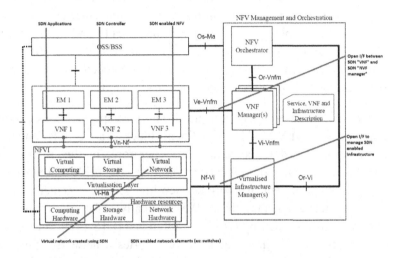

Figure 1.4. *Mapping SDN components with ESTI NFV architecture [ETS 14a]*

To summarize, the VIM and VNFM layers together provide the VNFs and resource lifecycle management capabilities. In particular, the NFVO provides the lifecycle management around the virtual network services. NFV MANO covers the orchestration and lifecycle management of physical and software resources that support the infrastructure virtualization and the lifecycle management of VNFs. It is used to manage and orchestrate all the virtual resources including computing, networking, storage, and VM resources. It is also focused on the virtualization of specific management tasks in the NFV framework and integrating with OSS/BSS in an existing network management framework. However, the orchestration of work flow processes is an essential part of NFV, as many of the benefits and characteristics of NFV are difficult to achieve.

1.5. MANO functional requirements

The nature of NFV facilitates the creation and deployment of new service more rapidly or dynamically. However, this may require a new set of management and orchestration functions to be added to the current model of operation, administration, maintenance and provision. As discussed previously, NFV management and orchestration (MANO) framework plays an essential role to manage the infrastructure and orchestrate the resources needed by the network services and virtualized network functions (VNFs).

In order to have a clear concept of interface specifications exposed between the NFV-MANO functional blocks, a set of functional requirements need to be addressed. Therefore, in this section, we specify functional requirements required by the NFV-MANO (VNF lifecycle management, network service lifecycle management, virtual resource management, etc.). We basically take the functional requirements specified by ETSI as a reference [ETS 15a]. They can be categorized into three general categories: network functions virtualization orchestration (NFVO), VNF manager (VNFM) and virtualized infrastructure manager (VIM).

1.5.1. *Functional requirements for NFVO*

Functional requirements for NFVO can be classified into 14 subcategories:

1) Virtualized resource management:

- The NFVO supports the orchestration of actions related to virtualized resources managed by one or more VIMs.

- The NFVO supports the capability to mitigate conflicts in resource allocation when conflicting resource requests occur.

- The NFVO supports the capability to provide deployment-specific configuration information for virtualized resources related to network services.

- For VNF-related resource management in indirect mode, the NFVO supports the capability (1) to request the VIM with virtualized resource management for VNF instantiation, scaling and termination; (2) to invoke resource management operations toward the VIM as requested by the VNF manager (VNFM); (3) to receive notification regarding the resource being allocated/released from specific VNF instances, as well as events and relevant fault reports related to those resources; and (4) to request the VIM affinity and anti-affinity policies for the VNF's virtualized resources.

- For VNF-related resource management in direct mode, the NFVO supports the capability to provide appropriate information about VIM to enable the VNFM to access the VIM.

- The NFVO supports the capability to issue requests to the VIM in order to allocate resources needed for the connectivity of network services, to identify current resource allocation associated with a particular network service instance and to update current resources allocated to the network service instances or release resources that had been allocated to network service instances.

- The NFVO supports the capability (1) to query the VIM about resources that are allocated for the connectivity of VNF forwarding graphs of specific network service instances; and (2) to receive notifications of the resources that are allocated/released from specific network service instances, as well as events and relevant fault reports related to those resources.

- For resource reservation management, the NFVO supports the capability (1) to request creation, query, update and termination of virtualized resource reservation; (2) to consider affinity and anti-affinity rules for resource reservation management; (3) to receive change notification regarding virtualized resource reservation; and (4) to provide the VNFM resource reservation identification information.

- For resource capacity management, the NFVO supports the capability (1) to maintain information regarding the virtualized resource capacity, its usage at different granularities and levels, and resource zones available on the connected VIMs; (2) to query information about resource zones managed by the VIM, and about NFVI-PoP administered by the VIM; (3) to retrieve information regarding the virtualized resource capacity at different granularities and levels; (4)

to synchronize periodically and automatically virtualized resource capability information on demand; (5) to configure thresholds for setting virtualized resource capacity shortage alarms at different granularities and levels; (6) to notify about virtualized resource capacity shortage; and (7) to receive the notification from VIM related to the changes of NFVI capacity information.

- For resource performance management, the NFVO supports the capability (1) to invoke the virtualized resource performance management operations on the virtualized resources for the network services it manages; (2) to receive performance information related to virtualized resources for the network services it manages; and (3) to map the network services and the received performance information related to virtualized resources.

- For resource fault management, the NFVO supports the capability (1) to collect fault information related to the virtualized resources assigned to the managed network services; (2) to correlate the virtualized network resource fault information with the managed network service that is impacted; and (3) to request corrective operations on virtualized network resources from VIM for further performing network service healing.

- For resource information management, the NFVO supports the capability (1) to collect information on virtualized resources that can be consumed in a VIM or across multiple VIMs; (2) to forward the information about resource shortage to the operating support system (OSS) as soon as it becomes available in the NFVO; and (3) to receive the notification regarding changes of the information on consumable virtualized resources.

- For network forwarding path management, the NFVO supports the capability (1) to request management of network forwarding paths; (2) to provide or update the classification and selection rules applied to a specific network forwarding path instance; and (3) to receive the classification and selection rules applied to a network forwarding path from an authorized entity.

- For quota management, the NFVO supports the capability (1) to request the VIM to create, change, delete and query the quota for the user of the virtualized resources; (2) to receive change notification regarding virtualized resource quotas; and (3) to provide VNFM the information on available quotas applicable to this VNFM.

- For permitted allowance management, the NFVO supports the capability (1) to maintain and enforce permitted allowance at various granularity levels (VNFM, VNF, network service); (2) to reject any granting requests from VNFM that would cause the corresponding permitted allowance to be exceeded; (3) to manage the overall consumption of resources across all the permitted allowances; (4) to notify its resource consumption; (5) to provide notification when permitted allowance reaches its limit; (6) to process a request for permitted allowance extension or permitted allowance reduction; and (7) to arbitrate conflict in permitted allowance consumption.

2) VNF lifecycle management:

- The NFVO supports the capability to process notifications about VNF lifecycle change.

- The NFVO supports the capability to grant lifecycle management requests.

- The NFVO supports the capability to validate the lifecycle operation requests that are submitted, using information specified in the VNF packages.

- The NFVO supports the capability to request changing the state of a VNF instance.

- The NFVO supports the capability to query the status of ongoing lifecycle management operation.

- The NFVO supports the capability to query information about a VNF instance.

- The NFVO supports the capability (1) to request the instantiation of a VNF instance (VNF instantiation); (2) to request the expansion/contraction of the capability of a VNF instance (VNF scaling); and (3) to request the termination of a VNF instance (VNF termination).

3) Network service lifecycle management:

- The NFVO ensures the integrity of data related to the network service instances against loss and corruption, from hardware/software failures and against data tampering by unauthorized parties.

- The NFVO supports the capability to use the deployment information from the network service deployment template (network service descriptor) for network service lifecycle management.

- The NFVO supports the capability to notify about events related to network service lifecycle changes, such as the start or the result of lifecycle procedure.

- The NFVO supports the capability to manage the instantiation of network service instance (network service instantiation), to manage the expansion/contraction of a network service instance (network service scaling), to manage the update of network service instance (network service updating), and to terminate a network service instance (network service termination).

4) VNF configuration management:

- The NFVO supports the capability to invoke a request to set initial configuration parameters or update configuration parameters for a VNF instance.

5) VNF information management:

- The NFVO supports the capability to manage VNF packages.

- The NFVO supports the capability to verify the integrity and authenticity of the VNF packages.

- The NFVO supports the capability to verify the presence of all the mandatory information in the VNF package and their compatibility with the standard for this information.

- The NFVO supports the capability to validate the integrity and authenticity of the VNF descriptor (VNFD) in the package.

- The NFVO supports the capability to notify about the onboarding of the VNF package.

6) Network service information management:

- The NFVO supports the capability to manage the network service deployment template.

- The NFVO supports the capability to verify the integrity of the provided network service deployment template.

- The NFVO supports the capability to verify that all the mandatory information in the network service template is present and complies with the standard for this information.

- The NFVO supports the capability to report information related to the operation result of network service template.

- The NFVO supports the capability to perform version control of onboarded network service deployment templates.

- The NFVO supports the capability to receive runtime data related to network service instances creation.

7) Network service performance management:

- The NFVO supports the capability to manage performance of network services.

- The NFVO supports the capability to notify about the availability of performance information for the managed network services.

8) VNF fault management:

- The NFVO supports the capability to request VNF healing to the VNF manager (VNFM).

- The NFVO supports the capability to collect notifications about alarms on a VNF instance, as a result of state change in the virtualized resources used by the VNF.

9) Network service fault management:

- The NFVO supports the capability to provide notifications of fault information and notification of changes related to the managed network services.

- The NFVO supports the capability to perform automated or on-demand healing on the managed network services.

- The NFVO supports the capability to notify about errors during network service lifecycle procedure.

10) Infrastructure resource management:

- The NFVO supports the capability to collect the information about NFVI-PoPs, such as network connectivity endpoints and geographical locations.

11) Security consideration:

- The NFVO supports the capability to validate the received message from an authenticated and authorized user.

- The NFVO supports the capability to verify the integrity of the received message.

- The NFVO supports the capability to encrypt the sent message or decrypt the received message using a negotiated key and algorithm to/from an authenticated and authorized user.

12) Software image management:
- The NFVO supports the capability to distribute the software images to one or more VIMs.
- The NFVO supports the capability to query the VIM for information on the software images.
- The NFVO supports the capability to invoke software image deletion requests to VIM that are distributed by the NFVO and managed by VIM.
- The NFVO supports the capability to invoke updating of the user-defined metadata for the selected software images, distributed by the NFVO and managed by VIM.

13) NFV acceleration management:
- The NFVO supports the capability to request VIM for allocation and release of necessary acceleration resources to meet the acceleration capability requirements of the VNFs.
- The NFVO supports the capability to retrieve acceleration capability requirements of the VNF from the VNF deployment template.
- The NFVO supports the capability to receive/query acceleration capability information from VIM.
- The NFVO supports the capability to select a VIM that has enough available acceleration capabilities to support the acceleration capability requirements for the VNF.

14) Multi-tenancy:
- The NFVO supports the capability to manage network service tenants, infrastructure tenants, and the mapping of such infrastructure tenants to the VIM.
- The NFVO supports the capability to assign onboarded VNF packages and network service deployment templates to one or more network tenants.
- The NFVO supports the capability to onboard VNF packages and network service deployment templates for a tenant.

- The NFVO will allow a tenant to instantiate VNFs and network services using VNF packages and network service deployment templates, or share VNF packages and network service deployment templates.

- The NFVO supports the capability to limit operations only to the service and infrastructure resource group, assigned to the requesting tenant.

1.5.2. Functional requirements for VNFM

Functional requirements for VNFM can be classified into 10 subcategories:

1) Virtualized resource management:

- The VNFM has the capability to provide deployment-specific configuration information for virtualized resources related to VNF instances.

- The VNFM should be capable of maintaining the mapping between a VNF instance and the virtualized resources.

- The VNFM should be able to request resource allocation for VNF instances that meet the requirements specified by the VNF providers.

- For VNF-related resource management in indirect mode, the VNFM supports the capability (1) to request to NFVO the management of virtualized resources needed for VNF instantiation, scaling and termination; and (2) to invoke resource management requests towards the NFVO in order to allocate resources that meet the requirements specified by the VNF provider.

- For VNF-related resource management in direct mode, the VNFM supports the capability (1) to request from the VIM the management of virtualized resources needed for VNF instantiation, scaling and termination; (2) to query the VIM about the resource being allocated to VNF instances it managed; (3) to receive notifications regarding the resources being allocated/released from specific VNF instances, as well as events and relevant fault reports related to those resources; (4) to request allocation and update of resources in the different resource commitment models; (5) to request the VIM affinity and anti-affinity policies for the VNF's virtualized resources; (6) to use resource reservation identification information obtained from the NFVO to request allocation of virtualized resources for a VNF; and (7) to obtain appropriate information to enable the VNFM to access the VIM.

- For resource reservation management, the VNFM supports the capability to receive change notification and query information regarding virtualized resource reservation.

- For resource performance management, the VNFM supports the capability (1) to invoke virtualized resource performance management operations on the virtualized resources for the VNF instances it manages; (2) to receive performance information related to the virtualized resources for the VNF instances it manages; and (3) to map VNF instances with the received performance information related to the virtualized resources.

- For resource fault management, the VNFM supports the capability (1) to collect fault information related to the virtualized resources assigned to VNF instances it manages; and (2) to correlate the virtualized resource fault information with impacted VNF/VNFC instances it manages.

- For resource information management, the VNFM supports the capability (1) to query the information regarding consumable virtualized resources that can be provided by the VIM; and (2) to receive notifications regarding the changes in the information on consumable virtualized resources that can be provided by the VIM.

- For quota management, the VNFM supports the capability (1) to query information on the quota that applies to VNFM/VNFs it manages; (2) to receive change notification regarding the quota constraints that apply to VNFM/VNFs it manages; and (3) to receive information from the NFVO on available quota applicable to this VNFM.

2) VNF lifecycle management:

- The VNFM supports the capability to notify about events related to the VNF lifecycle changes, such as the start of the lifecycle procedure, the end and the result of the lifecycle procedure including errors.

- The VNFM supports the capability to notify about the type of VNF lifecycle change, the addition/deletion of VNF components, and the changes on virtualized resources associated to VNFCs as a result of VNF lifecycle change.

- The VNFM supports the capability to notify about virtual networks and connection points that are added/deleted as a part of the VNF lifecycle operation.

- The VNFM supports the capability to validate the lifecycle operation requests it processes, using the information specified in the VNF package.

- The VNFM supports the capability to change the state of VNF/VNFC instances.

- The VNFM supports the capability to use the deployment information from the VNF deployment template (VNF descriptor) for the VNF lifecycle management.

- The VNFM supports the capability to provide the status of ongoing VNF lifecycle management operations in response to a query.

- The VNFM supports the capability to request operation granting before executing the VNF lifecycle operation procedure.

- The VNFM supports the capability (1) to manage the instantiation of VNF instances (VNF instantiation); (2) to manage the expansion/contraction of the capacity of VNF instances (VNF scaling); and (3) to terminate a VNF instances (VNF termination).

3) VNF configuration management:

- The VNFM supports the capability to set initial configuration parameters or update configuration parameters for VNF/VNFC instances.

4) VNF information management:

- The VNFM supports the capability to obtain details of the available VNF packages of managed VNFs.

- The VNFM supports the capability to receive notifications as a result of onboarding of VNF packages and of changes in package states.

- The VNFM supports the capability to receive runtime data related to VNF instance creation.

- The VNFM supports the capability to provide information on the mapping relationship between the VNF instances and associated virtualized resources in response to the query.

5) VNF performance management:

- The VNFM supports the capability to notify about the availability of VNF performance information.

6) VNF fault management:

- The VNFM supports the capability to provide notifications of virtualized resources and notifications of changes-related fault information on the managed VNFs.

- The VNFM supports the capability to provide virtualized resource-related fault information on the VNFs it managed.

- The VNFM supports the capability to notify about alarms on VNF/VNFC as a result of the state changes in the virtualized resources.

- The VNFM supports the capability to request corrective operations on virtualized resource to VIM in order to perform VNF healing.

- The VNFM supports the capability to perform automated and on-demand VNF healing on the managed VNFs.

7) Security consideration:

- The VNFM supports the capability to validate the received message from an authenticated and authorized user.

- The VNFM supports the capability to check the integrity of the received message.

- The VNFM supports the capability to encrypt the sent message and decrypt the received message using the negotiated key and the algorithm to/from an authenticated and unauthorized user.

8) Software image management:

- The VNFM supports the capability to query the VIM for information of the software images.

9) NFV acceleration management:

- For VNF-related resource management in direct mode, the VNFM supports the capability to request to the VIM the allocation and release of necessary acceleration resources to meet the acceleration capability requirements on the VNFs.

- For VNF-related resource management in indirect mode, the VNFM supports the capability to request to the NFVO the allocation and release of necessary acceleration resources to meet the acceleration capability requirements of the VNFs.

- The VNFM supports the capability to retrieve acceleration capability requirements of the VNF from the VNF deployment template.

10) Multi-tenancy:
- The VNFM supports the capability to manage VNF tenants.
- The VNFM supports the capability to limit operations only to the service resource groups assigned to the requesting VNF tenant.

1.5.3. *Functional requirements for VIM*

Functional requirements for VIM can be classified into six subcategories:

1) Virtualized resource management:
- The VIM supports NFVI resource management within its responsibility area.
- The VIM supports the capability of resource reservation management.
- The VIM supports the capability of quota-based resource management.
- The VIM supports the capability to correlate allocated and reserved virtualized resources with changes in underlying hardware/software resources due to the maintenance, operation and management of NFVI.
- The VIM supports the capability to notify about changes in allocated and reserved virtualized resources.
- The VIM supports the capability to enforce affinity and anti-affinity policies for NFVI resource management.
- The VIM supports the capability to receive the virtualized resource management requests from the VNFM and/or NFV orchestrator (NFVO) and conduct the corresponding resource management operations.
- For resource reservation management, the VIM supports the capability (1) to manage resources according to different resource commitment models (reservation model, quota model and on-demand model); (2) to ensure that resources are allocated or updated from a resource reservation when processing virtualized resource allocation

or update requests; (3) to infer information about reservation that is applicable by using input information received with the allocation or update request; (4) to map the applicable resource reservation by using other information such as user/tenant identification; (5) to consider affinity and anti-affinity rules for resource reservation management; and (6) to notify the change regarding virtualized resource reservation.

- For resource capacity management, the VIM supports the capability (1) to collect and maintain information regarding the capacity of the managed NFVI; (2) to provide information related to available, allocated, reserved and all virtualized resource capacity; (3) to provide the notification of the changes related to the capacity of the managed virtualized resource; and (4) to provide information about resource zones in the managed NFVI, as well as information about NFVI-PoP it manages, such as network connectivity endpoints and geographical location.

- For resource performance management, the VIM supports the capability (1) to collect performance information related to virtualized resources; (2) to notify about performance information that is allocated on the virtualized resource; and (3) to provide virtualized resource performance management in response to the request.

- For resource fault management, the VIM supports the capability (1) to collect fault information related to virtualized resources; (2) to notify about the fault information that is allocated on virtualized resources; (3) to notify about changes in fault information on virtualized resources; (4) to perform automated or on-demand corrective operations on virtualized resource failure; and (5) to provide fault information on virtualized resources that are allocated in response to a query.

- For resource information management, the VIM supports the capability to provide information on virtualized resource and notify about changes of information on virtualized resources that can be consumed within its responsibility area.

- For resource configuration management, the VIM supports the capability to configure management of individual or a set of related virtualized resources using specific deployment configuration information received.

- For network forwarding path management, the VIM supports the capability (1) to manage network forwarding paths including creating, updating and deleting a network forwarding path; and (2) to provide fault notification about the virtualized resources associated with specific network forwarding path instances.

- For quota management, the VIM supports the capability (1) to reject virtualized resource allocation requests, causing a quota to be exceeded; (2) to create, update and delete resource quota for the user of the virtualized resources; and (3) to provide information on the resource quota and notify about changes of the information on the resource quota for the user of the virtualized resources.

2) Infrastructure resource management:

- The VIM supports the capability to collect performance information and fault information related to the software and hardware resources within the NFVI.

- The VIM supports the capability to correlate fault information on virtualized resource with fault information related to the underlying software and hardware resources used within the NFVI.

3) Security consideration:

- The VIM supports the capability to validate that the received message is from an authenticated and authorized user.

- The VIM supports the capability to verify the integrity of the received message.

- The VIM supports the capability to encrypt the sent message or decrypt the received message using the negotiated key and the algorithm to/from an authenticated and authorized user.

4) Software image management:

- The VIM supports the capability to manage software images as requested.

- The VIM supports the capability to verify the integrity of the software images.

- The VIM supports the capability to manage multiple versions of software images.

- The VIM supports the capability to provide the information on the managed software images.

5) NFV acceleration management:

- The VIM supports the capability to manage the NFV acceleration resources.

- The VIM supports the capability to retrieve feature-related information provided by the NFV acceleration resources.

- The VIM supports the capability to provide acceleration capability information to NFVO.

- The VIM supports the capability to translate the acceleration capability requirement (bandwidth value) into the acceleration resource context (number of FPGA blocks).

6) Multi-tenancy:

- The VIM supports the capability to manage infrastructure tenants.

- The VIM supports the capability to identify software images assigned to an infrastructure tenant and images shared among infrastructure tenants.

- The VIM supports the capability to allow an infrastructure tenant to instantiate virtual resources using its own private software images or shared software images.

- The VIM supports the capability to limit operations only to the infrastructure resource groups assigned to the requesting infrastructure tenant.

1.6. State of the art and development trends

In order to get a clear overview about the technological advantages of NFV over the traditional networks from an industrial perspective, a comparative analysis between the two models from a business perspective is provided. The results are summarized in Table 1.1. In particular, the perspectives and visions of different leading companies are analyzed and compared. Table 1.2 specifically addresses the impact of NFV technology on the current network infrastructure, on telecommunication service provisions, and on the products that can be designed in order to be incorporated into NFV.

Business Benefits	Network Functions Virtualization (NFV)	Traditional Network
Low cost	1) Minimize hardware expenditure, software development cost and time to market 2) Cost saving on electricity consumption and hardware maintenance 3) Space saving in datacenter	1) Specific hardware equipments performing specific network functions 2) The amount of hardware increases when network infrastructure gets large
Flexible network function deployment	1) Migrate function from dedicated hardware to virtual machine via software-based approach 2) New service rapid deployment, installation and provision	1) Legacy networks lack of sufficient automation. 2) Network architectures based on purpose-built network appliances with manual and complex configuration and proprietary systems interfaces 3) Longer time for deployment
Highlighted elastic scalability	1) Agile and flexible scaling up/down of network capacity as demand changes 2) Rapidly adapt new services to meet user's changing needs	1) Network infrastructure depends on IP addresses to identify and locate server; it works fine for static network where each physical device is identified by IP addresses but it is extremely difficult for large-scale networks 2) Poor capacities scaling
Management and orchestration	1) Resource optimization and load balancing 2) Handle virtualized resources through appropriate abstracted services 3) Rapid scaling and efficient allocation of server resources on the fly 4) Automate orchestration in action and reduce operational cost without downgrading reliability 5) Simplify service chain provisioning, making it easier and cheaper to spin up applications in enterprise and service provider networks	1) Lack of effective automated resource allocation and configuration; each networking device needs to be configured separately 2) Closed and proprietary setup make it complex and difficult to manage when the number of network functions are increased 3) Requires dedicated administrators to maintain network traffic load balancing. Does not allow users to design flexible strategies based on actual network conditions 4) All requests are passed through a single piece of hardware; any failures will cause collapse of the entire service

Lightweight built-in security mechanisms	1) Allow additional security with lower cost 2) Rapid deployment of software-based virtual security appliances 3) Easy creation, management, and customisation of security zones 4) Automated virtual firewall placement, dedicated software firewall on demand, and update security rules remotely	1) Specific security devices such as firewall, IPS, IDS are used to prevent attacks. Attack may happen if network operators fail to activate the corresponding security function or specify appropriate security policies 2) Difficult to test, monitor and troubleshoot a service across multiple vendor hardware platforms

Table 1.1. *Comparative analysis between traditional network model and NFV model*

Companies	Objectives	Perspectives
Alcatel-Lucent [LUC 13]	1) Operational and capital expenditure (OPEX and CAPEX) saving 2) Increase automation, simplify operation, and agile business solutions	*Motivation:* 1) The nature of operations and business management will change; network functionalities will move to real time management-based service solutions 2) NFV may introduce new security concerns, but automation through tools provided by NFV enables service providers to address these concerns effectively and further improve security 3) NFV has the ability to continuously optimize resource allocation based on the results of sophisticated analytics-based algorithms 4) Constituting NFV may need to take QoS requirements into account, while interconnection of network functions is a complex arrangement that requires additional networking considerations not generally found in the IT world

		Architecture: 1) Alcatel-Lucent CloudBand's product provides a carrier-grade management and orchestration function to support lifecycle management and NFV PaaS services 2) CloudBand provides a platform for NFV that consists of *CloudBand management system* to optimize and orchestrate cloud resources among network services, and *CloudBand node* to provide computing, storage, switching hardware, hypervisors and cloud resources control software for large-scale deployment 3) CloudBand integrates five differentiators for successful NFV implementation including orchestrating distributed datacenters, leveraging the network, automating the cloud node, managing application lifecycles, open and multi-vendor support
		Business model: 1) To achieve NFV benefits, Acatel-Lucent depicts several evolutionary stages (virtualized, cloud, automated lifecycle management, and auto-optimization) that service providers may have to consider 2) Alcatel-Lucent works with processor and hypervisor supplier to improve the capabilities that enable low latency processing in a virtualized infrastructure 3) Alcatel-Lucent is a leader in NFV that has deeply analyzed the impact of virtualization on reliability, availability and operation to assist operators transitioning to NFV

		4) Alcatel-Lucent is a market leader for an NFV solution that addresses computation, storage and networking aspects of NFV infrastructure 5) Alcatel-Lucent's bold NFV road map including virtual EPC, IMS and LTE RAN helps mobile network operators become more efficient, resposive and innovative
		Remark: 1) Alcatel-Lucent continually improves its portfolio using technical insights gained from customer collaboration, NFV open source project contribution, and industry standards like ETSI NFV
Intel [INT 13, INT 14]	1) Reduce equipment, operational costs and time to market for new services 2) CAPEX and OPEX saving 3) Shorten development and test cycles, and improve operational efficiency	***Motivation:*** 1) Flexible networking architecture that enables network operators to react more quickly to evolving market landscape 2) Provide tailored services and connectivity with secure separation of application execution environments 3) A multi-layer network and multi-vendor SDN-based end-to-end service orchestration and an NFV management solution is essential to connect NFV, running in the datacenter, to the end user and operationalizing it in a service provider network
		Architecture: 1) Intel, Red Hat, Dell, Cyan and Connectem collaborate to deliver a proof of concept (PoC) that demonstrates a novel NFV-based orchestration solution for operator's cloud-based mobile Evolved Packet Core (EPC)

		2) EPC consists of Serving Gateway (S-GW), Packet Data Network (PDN), Gateway (P-GW), Mobility Management Entity (MME), Policy and Charging Rules Function (PCRF) that run on commodity resources 3) Intel provides Data Plane Development Kit (DPDK) tools to optimize vSwitch and improve NFV performance running on cloud-based datacenter resources 4) Intel DPDK libraries provide commonly used functions like queue, buffer mangement, and packet flow classification such as memory manager, buffer manager API, queue manager API, flow classification API
		Business model: 1) Intel developes capabilities that fall into three categories: workload consolidation strategy, virtualization performance optimization, and switching performance optimization 2) Intel's architecture provides operators with a standard, reusable, shared platform for SDN and NFV applications that is easy to upgrade and maintain 3) Intel reference designs can help to reduce development time
Huawei [HUA 14]	1) NFV technology can help to reduce network CAPEX and OPEX and improve operational efficiency 2) Help to deploy or support new network services with agility and low cost	***Motivation:*** 1) With radical change in business model, new technology like NFV will have a tremendous impact on CSP business models, network design, and implementation 2) NFV plays an important role in centralizing and optimizing network management, flexible resource allocation, and dynamic deployment of network assets

		3) Need to investigate NFV proofs of concept related to the transition from hardware to software
		4) Network and data security operations and business continuity management are mission critical issues; they require more investigation to help transform their operations
		Architecture: 1) So far, six of Huawei's applications for open source project initiation have been approved by OPNFV projects [OPN 15] that include three controller nodes and two compute nodes [HUA 15]
		2) Huawei successfully deployed first commercial NFV-based voice over LTE network (VoLTE) in Europe through the use of virtualized IP multimedia subsystem (vIMS)
		Business model: 1) Huawei actively works with standardization organizations, open source communities, and partners across industry chains to build an open and mature ecosystem toward ICT transformation
		2) Huawei leads the implementation of the continuous integration (CI) project, OpenStack-based VNF Forwarding Graph (SFC) project, and ONOS Framework project, etc.
		3) Most of Huawei's core network products support virtualization and are ready for commercial use
		4) Huawei aims to deploy a virtualized multiple service engine (vMSE) solution for NFV architecture to provide an open platform for third parties to quickly deploy value-added service (VAS) within the network

		Remark: 1) Huawei leads an active research in cloud computing technologies and participated in NFV discussion in ETSI NFV ISG 2) Huawei has made significant technical contributions to NFV group specification by providing VNF standard, virtualized software/hardware design, management/operation
HP [HP 14c, HP 14b]	1) Optimize operational expenses (OPEX & CAPEX) 2) Accelerate time to market, improve business processes, and deliver business agility 3) Automate operations to reduce the cost and time to deliver IT services with open development platform	Motivation: 1) From technology perspective, NFV introduces a new abstraction resulting from the indirection between network functions and resources; it adds complexity and requires additional orchestration 2) NFV enables communications service providers (CSPs) to reset the cost base of their network operations and creates flexible service delivery environments they need 3) NFV enables significant benefits through deployment of virtualized network applications on shared infrastructure, and it brings additional benefits through IT like layering and purchasing decisions
		Architecure: 1) The HP architecture underpinning NFV is based on the requirement from industry drivers, the HP vision and ETSI 2) The functionality includes NFV application, NFV orchestrator, and virtualized NFV infrastructure to allow customers to add new functions and flexible work with specific tools. 3) The NFV application is provided by network equipment providers, independent software vendors, and HP

		4) The NFV orchestrator is a set of portfolios that can be deployed either as stand-alone modules or a layered solution; the modules are fulfillment, a common data model, service management, and policy management 5) The virtualized NFV infrastructure includes storage, networking, and its element managers that may embed automated processes to support physical and virtualized resources
		Business model: 1) HP offers an open NFV architecture, establishes operational IT support services at the heart of NFV management and orchestration, and defines NFV-related standards 2) HP aims to provide a complete foundation for network equipment providers (NEPs) to move their network applications to NFV through the HP OpenNFV program, and provide a proof of concept (PoC) catalog for all NFV deployment 3) HP aims to identify a set of key building blocks for NFV solutions including operation support systems, VNFs, VNF manager, management and orchestration, compute and network virtualization, SDN and cloud controller, servers, storage, networking, and converged infrastructure management
		Remark: 1) HP is actively involved in many standard organizations (ETSI, ONF, IETF, ATIS, ODCA, and OPNFV) 2) HP's commitment to NFV through the introduction of a commercial virtual services router (VSR)

		3) HP's CloudSystem product supports the NFV infrastructure as a service (IaaS)
Ericsson [ERI 14]	1) Increase service agility and enable better asset utilization 2) Lower costs for managing services and networks	*Motivation:* 1) NFV helps achieve security and integrity through separation and isolation 2) The security and policy configuration associated with network functions may have to be provisioned on a large number of switches and other network functions 3) The complexity of network configuration dynamically increases when the number of network elements increase
		Architecture: 1) Ericsson's NFV offers coverage of the entire range of ETSI-defined architecture blocks [ERI 15b] including - NFV infrastructure offerings (Ericsson Cloud System, Ericsson SDN offering) - NFV management and orchestration offerings (Ericsson Cloud Manager, Ericsson Network Manager) - Virtual network functions (Ericsson virtual evolved packet core, Ericsson virtual IMS, Ericsson virtual router) - Cloud transformation services (Ericsson cloud transformation services)
		Business model: 1) Ericsson collaborates with other industry players to bring NFV to an industrial scale, provide a full suite of virtualized network applications, an execution platform, NFV orchestration and management, combined with consulting and system integration services

		2) Ericsson OPNFV certificate program is designed to support customers and partners to certify their NFV solution 3) Ericsson's NFV solution strategy is based on horizontal, open and programmable design principles as a solution to interact, reshape telecom network architecture, enable new business and revenue streams to be explored
		Remark: 1) Ericsson is a platinum member of OPNFV (open platform for NFV) [OPN 15] 2) Primary authors of OPNFV project's report are from Ericsson; this project works closely with ETSI NFV ISG to drive consistent implementation of open and standard NFV reference platform 3) Ericsson is also a key contributor in other open source initiatives such as the OpenDaylight and OpenStack projects
Cisco [CIS 15b]	1) Reduce overall costs per unit of workload 2) Reduce the dependence on dedicated, specialized physical devices	***Motivation:*** 1) Today, the virtualization aspect of NFV lacks clarity on how to integrate the virtual functions with the existing network components, and lacks direction on how to create multiple function services 2) Service providers face the quandary of deploying the most cost-effective virtualization solutions 3) Systematic approaches to understand how the entire solution stack might interact (tradeoffs) and standardized test methods do not yet exist

		Architecture: 1) Cisco provides open architecture and offers two platforms which are *Cisco Evolved Services Platform (ESP)* [CIS 14c] and *Cisco Evolved Programmable Network (EPN)* [CIS 14a] - The Cisco ESP is a software suite that lets customers automate their services delivery; it has the software building blocks including automated service delivery, launching of new services rapidly, and slashing of network operation costs - The Cisco EPN helps customers deploy a highly secure infrastructure for network, computing and storage; it works together via open APIs with the complementary Cisco ESP to help transform and deploy new services with reduced costs
		Business model: 1) Cisco intends to provide architectural and technical direction of network architecture, service design, and strategy plan for service providers and enterprise operators 2) Cisco has developed a modular software platform to address management and orchestration requirements for NFV and a broad spectrum of additional services 3) Cisco and Intel have joint interests in the fundamentals of NFVI to pursue optimal performance
		Remark: 1) Cisco delivers industry-leading NFV orchestration solutions 2) Cisco implementation for NFV management and orchestration through the Cisco ESP and EPN

Nokia Networks [NET 15]	1) Reduce CAPEX and OPEX, and increase business agility 2) Reduce the requirement investment by consolidating network functions to commodity hardware	*Motivation:* 1) From an economic perspective, the rapid developement of cyber crime has a negative economic impact 2) The introduction of SDN/NFV introduces security challenges with the separation of the control and forwarding plane, ensuring security of the north and southbound APIs, and control authentication 3) With the advent of ETSI NFV, it is obvious that in the future, most network functions and network elements will be implemented as cloud-based solutions; this may help customers avoid security breaches and allay their concerns by installing techniques to measure the state of security
		Architecture: 1) Nokia Networks introduces the telco cloud solution based on NFV architecture with a three-layered approach: - The virtualized infrastructure layer - The application and application management layer - The service management layer 2) Four dimensions in building the telco cloud: - Network function virtualization (NFV) - SDN in mobile networks - Cloud enhancement of the RAN - End-to-end management and orchestration
		Business model: 1) Nokia Networks aims to provide operators with an open source-based cloud to meet reliability and availability requirements and accelerate their transition to NFV deployment

		2) Nokia Networks offers a comprehensive set of security products and helps security consulting expertise create operator-specific optimal solutions such as virtual firewalls, virtual tenant networks, security zones, mutual authentication, and traffic encryption 3) Nokia Networks has conducted exhaustive research and applied stringent testing to ensure that the telco cloud can meet high performance and high security demands of carrier-grade operation 4) Nokia Networks collaborates with different partners to offer telco cloud solutions compliant with ETSI NFV principles 5) Orange and Nokia Networks teaming up on Telco Cloud aim at leveraging the benefits of virtualization applied to IMS (IP multimedia core network subsystem) for operator business models and network architecture
		Remark: 1) Nokia Networks together with Alcatel-Lucent, Brocade, Cisco, Huawei, Intel and Red Hat are collaborative authors of OPNFV project's report, whereas Ericsson and Intel are the primary authors 2) Orange and Nokia Networks have achieved one of the first voice calls in a fully virtualized IMS experimental environment 3) There is Open Platform for NFV (OPNFV) [OPN 15] which is a new open source project that aims to accelerate the evolution of NFV by establishing a carrier-grade, integrating open source reference platforms from different vendors, and ensuring consistency among multiple open source components to test and fulfill development gaps

Portugal Telecom Inovacao [INO 15]	1) Aims to increase operational efficiency, overcome the huge CAPEX and OPEX costs imposed by network appliances 2) Aims to increase agility in new service launching	*Motivation:* 1) Mature NFV/SDN propositions from network providers need proof of concept (PoC) initiatives to evaluate NFV/SDN technology 2) Many use cases are required to fulfill a sequence of multiple network functions 3) The next generation operating support system (OSS) will have the capacity to manage and orchestrate IT and network virtual functions in a single management platform
		Architecure: 1) There is T-NOVA project (network functions as-a-service over virtualized infrastructure) [TNO 14] that aims at promoting the NFV concept by introducing a novel enabling framework as value-added services (ETSI NFV ISG use case #2) 2) It designs and implements an integrated management architecture including orchestration platform, automated provision, management, monitoring and optimization of VNFs over network/IT infrastructure 3) T-NOVA NFaaS platform for the service provider's customer consists of two components: *a connectivity service* and *a set of associated network functions* 4) A connectivity service to manage connectivity component (e.g. network links with specific capacity and QoS) and establish virtual networks (vNets) where required

		5) A set of associated network functions to handle and control traffic flows in network packet payload processing according to customer needs 6) T-NOVA is an integrated project co-funded by the European Commission; the consortium comprises 18 partners including PT Inovao, Intel, HP
		Business model: 1) PT Inovacao aims to define business strategy by integrating NFV/SDN in its network evolution road map 2) PT Inovacao aims to consider the scenario where network functions are spread across a network of datacenters and micro datacenters to optimize cost, customer experience, resilience and network load 3) PT Inovacao's perspective on evolution to the cloud paradigm can be split into three phases (virtualized IT and network functions, converged automated lifecycle management, and integrated network and IT management)
		Remark: 1) PT Inovacao, which is a telecom software/hardware vendor, works SDN/NFV concepts into its portfolio of products by collaborating with operators and relevant vendors to reach the best architecture and solutions 2) PT Inovacao participates in several international R&D projects in NFV/SDN domains

Table 1.2. *Industrial perspectives about NFV*

2

Use Case Driven
Security Threat Analysis

In this chapter, we consider the use cases proposed by ETSI NFV ISG Use Cases document [ETS 13b] as a basis on which to selectively redefine five representative use cases, with focus on the NFV infrastructure, for the purpose of analyzing the technical challenges that the network operators may encounter in the process of migrating legacy network services to NFV. Based on the understanding of objectives and architectures of the specific use cases, we conduct threat analyses on them and further identify their security requirements.

2.1. NFV Infrastructure as a Service (NFVIaaS)

Infrastructure as a Service (IaaS) is one of the three fundamental service models of cloud computing; the others are Platform as a Service (PaaS) and Software as a Service (SaaS). Basically, IaaS is defined as the capability to provide access to processing, storage, and fundamental computing resources in a virtualized environment. The users can use the provided resources to run specific applications, on which they have control while not taking care of the underlying network infrastructure. NFV Infrastructure as a Service use case aims at providing an approach with which to map the cloud computing service models IaaS and NaaS as elements within the the NFV infrastructure when it is provided as a service.

2.1.1. *Overall description*

The NFV infrastructure aims to provide the capability, resources or functionality for building a virtualized environment in which network functions can be executed. This NFVIaaS approach can greatly expand a carrier's coverage in terms of locations, for providing and maintaining services at a large scale, while reducing or avoiding the physical network assets. It also impacts significantly the reduction of the cost and complexity in terms of deploying new hardware or leasing fixed services.

NFVIaaS provides computing capabilities that are comparable to an IaaS cloud computing service as a run time execution environment, as well as supporting the dynamic network connectivity services that may be considered as NaaS (Networking as a Service). Therefore, the architecture of this use case combines IaaS and NaaS models as key elements in order to provide network services within the NFV infrastructure. Service providers can either use their own NFVI/cloud computing infrastructure or leverage another service provider's infrastructure to deploy their own network services (VNFs). Based on NFVIaaS, the computing nodes will be located in NFVI-PoPs such as central offices, outside plants, specialized pods, or embedded in other network equipment such as mobile devices. The physical location of the infrastructure is largely irrelevant for cloud computing services, but many network services have a certain degree of location dependence.

To better understand how an NFVIaaS can be performed, we may refer to Figure 2.1, which illustrates an NFVIaaS supporting cloud computing application, as well as VNF instances, from different service providers. As the figure shows, service provider 2 can run VNF instances on the NFVI/cloud infrastructure of another service provider 1 in order to improve service resilience and to improve the user experience by reducing latency and to perfectly comply with regulatory requirements. Service provider 1 will require that only authorized entities can load and operate VNF instances on its NFV infrastructure. The set of resources, e.g. computing, hypervisor, network capacity and binding to network termination, that service provider 1 makes available to service provider 2 would be constrained. Meanwhile, service provider 2 is able to integrate its VNF instances running on service provider 1's NFV infrastructure into end-to-end network service instance, along with VNF instances running on its own NFV infrastructure. It is obvious that as the NFVIaaS of the two service providers are distinct and independent, the failure of one NFVIaaS will not affect the other.

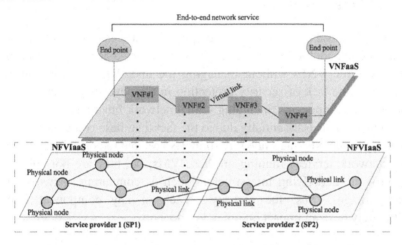

Figure 2.1. *NFV infrastructure as a service. For a color version of this figure, see www.iste.co.uk/zhang/networks.zip*

Moreover, non-virtualized network functions can coexist with the VNFs regarding this case. Alternately, virtualized network functions from multiple service providers may coexist within the same NFV infrastructure. NFV infrastructure also provides appropriate isolation between the resources allocated to the different service providers, thus VNF instance failures or resource demands from one service provider will not affect the operation of another service provider's VNF instances.

To summarize, this model provides basic storage and computing capabilities as standardized services over the network, whereas the storage and network equipment are pooled and made available to the users. The capabilities provided to the users are the processing, storage, networks and other fundamental computing resources, by which the users are able to deploy and run arbitrary network services. In doing so, the users do not manage or control the underlying infrastructure, but they are capable of controlling their deployed applications and can arbitrarily select networking components to accomplish their tasks.

2.1.2. *Threat analysis*

The purpose of NFVIaaS is to provide basic storage and other fundamental computing resources to the users, who are allowed to run their specific VNFs without managing the underlying infrastructure. However, the lack of security protection in this layer will affect other layers and components, including virtual network functions and virtual appliances. This is essentially due to the fact that these components are built upon the NFVIaaS layer. Also, users are able to control VMs and the network services running on these VMs, but they are not able to control the underlying infrastructure such as computing, networking and storage. Thus, the security breach of any component will ultimately have an impact on other components.

Generally, NFVIaaS is sensitive to all of the threats that are raised by traditional and standard IT environments. Considering the fact that for service providers, all applications within the tenants are considered as black boxes running on the provided virtual infrastructure, the tenants are expected to carefully secure their network service applications. In [CAN 15], the authors pointed out that the major security issues in the cloud environment are: insecure interface APIs, shared resources, data breaches, malicious insiders and misconfiguration issues. Also, in [DAW 10], the authors identified the security vulnerabilities that may occur in the infrastructure environment, which are related to Service Level Agreement (SLA), utility computing, cloud components, computer hardware, virtualization platforms, and network and Internet connectivity. As the IaaS of the cloud and NFVIaaS have many characteristics in common, the security threats existing in the IaaS of the cloud can also occur in NFVIaaS, which threats are specifically discussed as follows.

– Insufficient context in Service Level Agreement (SLA): SLA is a contract between a service provider and the end user that documents a required level of service, service negotiation, monitoring, enforcement, and guarantee an acceptable level of QoS. SLA contract definition and negotiation stage are important to determine the benefits and responsibilities of each user; any misinterpretation will affect system security and expose users to vulnerabilities. The NFVIaaS service providers are therefore expected to rigorously enforce the security policies in SLA and make them explicitly understandable by their users.

– Inconsistent service composition: the process of NFV IaaS-enabled service composition may involve different layers. The lower layer may offer the services to the next layer, which then may also offer the service to its upper layer. If one layer fails to provide sufficient security protection, the infrastructure and those related network service components could become attractive attack targets. For example, the attackers may manage to access the network services without being authorized, and then take further control of other unauthorized network services, or even subvert the policy rules to achieve their malicious objectives. In such multiple-layer architectures, the system is deemed to be complex and requires holistic security management.

– Data breach on service components: as NFVIaaS is always integrated together with many heterogeneous cloud components, security issues may arise due to some data breach and side channel attacks. For example, when one VM component intends to access data from other VM components, such as using the shared processor's cache to access the data of other VM components which run on the same physical host, data loss can happen. It is also worth noting that most data breach attacks in the cloud environment are due to the web applications, whose permissions are poorly configured in the clouds.

– Malicious insiders: in [MAR 07], the authors identified that over 70% of attacks on sensitive data and resources are caused by insider attacks. Also, in [CAN 15], the author found that 8% of reported data breaches were a result of insider thefts. In a public or hybrid cloud model, remote insider threats would also occur. This means that a remote administrator of the NFV cloud provider can directly access the tenant's data and potentially perform illegal operations. Similarly, the malicious insider, such as an employee of the cloud service provider, could have complete access to the company resources and the users' information. One of the root causes of such insider threats is that service providers do not strictly enforce security policies, manage their hardware devices and train employees. Clearly, if security guidelines are not completely complied with and security policies are not appropriately enforced, the insiders will be granted opportunities to achieve their malicious goals.

– Lack of transparent monitoring: NFVaaS allows a service provider to run VNF instances in an NFV infrastructure, which is provided as a service by different service providers. While network service performance and service deployment can be improved, the limited control over the underlying infrastructure that belongs to the third party may cause security threats. Specifically, the service providers have the ability to deploy their services globally, but they are not able to monitor all data transaction processings within the NFV environment, especially for the underlying infrastructure owned by another service provider. Therefore, the lack of transparent monitoring allows attackers to penetrate the victim's system, perform illegal activities and further gain complete control over the VNF instances without being noticed.

– Security issue in virtualization platforms: virtualization plays a fundamental role in cloud computing, enabling multiple network services to be aggregated into a single hardware platform by virtualizing the computing resources, and creating a new abstraction layer to hide management complexities of the physical computing platform. The security issues associated with this virtualization platform can be classified into two main categories: (i) security threats sourced from the local host and (ii) security threats sourced from other parties.

- Security threats in the local host: these security threats include sniffing, communication interceptions and process modifications of VMs. Specifically, the purpose of sniffing is to intrusively gather the information, such as application content, protocol meta data, traffic headers and traffic patterns. Also, the communications between the VM components and the host could be intercepted, e.g. attackers may exploit some useful features in the VM components, such as the option for shared information, to allow sensitive data to be transferred between malicious programs in the VM components and the host [KIR 07]. More critical is the fact that, when a host is taken over by compromising its kernel processes, all the VM components will be put at risk.

- Security threats originating from other parties: the security threats related to traffic sniffing, communication interception and process modification are similar to the first case, but they are usually caused by other VM components or by external machines. First, the malicious VM components can monitor other VMs' memory resources and access other VMs' virtual disks allocated in the host. Second, unlike physical network machines which are connected via a dedicated communication channel, VMs in virtual networking are linked to the host machine by a virtual switch. The attacks such as packet sniffing and Address Resolution Protocol (ARP) poisoning could occur between VMs. As for communication interception between VMs, it depends on how those machines will be deployed. For example, sharing resources between VMs can allow the malicious VM to access other victim VMs through shared memory, network connections and other shared resources without compromising the hypervisor layer. Furthermore, the misconfiguration of a hypervisor may allow a single VM to consume all the available resources which are allocated to multiple VMs running on the same physical machines, thus eventually causing DoS attacks.

– Insecure interface APIs: the interfaces play a vital role in the NFV infrastructure, facilitating the integration and communication of different VNF instances. As previously discussed in the Introduction and as shown in Figure 1.1, a set of interfaces is widely used by VNF instances to execute network services on virtual infrastructures, and they can be classified into several types, performing different functionalities:

- virtual network function interfaces to physical hardware (VI-Ha), which is used between the platform and underlying hardware to allow decoupling of software from hardware.

- interfaces used by VNF instances to execute on the virtual infrastructure (Vn-Nf).

- interfaces between the virtual infrastructure and the VIM (Nf-Vi) are used for managing the NFVI virtualized resources as well as consistency in the platform.

- interfaces from the VIM to the VNF manager and orchestration system (Or-Vi and Vi-Vnfm) are used to provide the ability for application management systems and orchestration systems to interact with the virtual infrastructure manager.

However, insufficient and inadequate knowledge of the interface design and implementation may result in vulnerabilities. For instance, an adversary may pose as a black hole and embed malicious code into the interfaces in order to gain access to the victim's system, without being detected by either service providers or users.

– Network and Internet connectivity vulnerability: although NFVIaaS spans multiple geographical sites to reduce the latency and damage from unpredicted disasters, such an infrastructure may face conventional vulnerabilities of the Internet and network connections, e.g. port scanning, IP spoofing, Distributed Denial-of-Service (DDoS) and man-in-the-middle (MITM) attacks. More critical is the fact that, the long implementation and verification period makes DDoS mitigation in an NFV cloud environment a real challenge.

– Shared resources: NFV enables ubiquitous, convenient and on-demand access to a shared pool of computing resources across multi-tenancy through virtualization. However, shared physical resources, such as hard disks, RAM, CPU cache, GPUs and other elements, are not naturally well-designed to support multi-tenancy requirements. This may create security breaches and lead to information leakage. It has already been found [CAN 15] that one vulnerability in core components like hypervisors can eventually lead to the compromise of the entire cloud infrastructure and services. Also, the inappropriate resource isolation mechanism can allow an attacker to exhaustively use the shared resources. In particular, if attackers combine this advantage with network-based DDoS attacks, they could prevent other tenants from accessing their critical resources.

As already discussed, for the service model NFVIaaS, a pool of computing, storage and networking resources is shared by multiple VNF instances and managed in a collective manner using policy-driven processes. The creation of virtual environments to allocate hardware resources among a large number of distributed VNF instances should be achieved at the virtualization layer. It is therefore very important to understand the security threats and vulnerabilities that may occur at this layer. In [HUA 12], the security impacts of virtualization were discussed, along with the software vulnerabilities that could be targeted. Due to the software-based approach used by VNF, there have been a number of vulnerabilities that can lead to an entire compromise of the farm hosting the VMs. In the following, we will specifically address the threat analysis of the virtualization infrastructure.

– Hyperjacking: the hyperjacking attack aims at subverting the existing hypervisor or injecting a rogue hypervisor into the NFV infrastructure. Due to the fact that the hypervisor runs at the most privileged ring level on a processor, it would be extremely hard, if not impossible, to detect suspicious activities running over the hypervisor. Regular security measures are ineffective because the operating system cannot be aware of the VMs that have been compromised. If the rogue module is injected or attackers gain access to the hypervisor, all components connected to the compromised hypervisor can be manipulated. Additionally, the compromised hypervisor can control the VMs running on top of the same host and monitor their network traffic.

– VM escape: VM escape enables an attacker to run malicious code on a VM to break out and interact directly with the hypervisor. This exploitation gives attackers access to the host OS and all the other VMs running on that host. To achieve their objective, the attackers can leverage the vulnerability or misconfiguration of the host OS and penetrate the virtualization layer. Although there is no incident report, the VM escape is considered as one of the most serious threats to VM security.

– VM hopping: VM hopping allows an attacker to move from one virtual instance to compromise other virtual instances that reside in the same physical hardware, by exploiting vulnerabilities in either the virtual infrastructure or the hypervisor. For example, assuming that an attacker is interested in virtual machine A, where he gets no access privilege the attacker can then manage to penetrate virtual machine B which is on the same host OS as A, and ultimately gain access to A. One of the prerequisites is to obtain the IP addresses of the target VM, so that the attacker can break the isolation control through the internal network bridge.

– VM DoS: the general purpose of virtualization is to share physical resources among multiple VMs, with the objective to improve the utilization of physical resources. In [HUS 13], the authors discussed virtual machine vulnerabilities caused by the VM DoS attack, which is a major threat considering the fact that multiple VMs are running on the same host. As a DoS attack aims at exhausting all the available resources, a successful DDoS attack can impact all the other VMs running on the same compromised host. In practice, the attack could be easily achieved by exploiting the hypervisor's misconfiguration.

– VM-based rootkits: in [KIN 06], the authors evaluated a new type of malicious software that can gain qualitatively more control over VMs, called a *Virtual Machine-Based Rootkit (VMBR)*. Specifically, the VMBR exploits known security flaws and installs a Virtual Machine Monitor (VMM) underneath an existing operating system, such as Windows and Linux. As such, the attackers can gain complete control of the target OS without being detected, meanwhile controlling all the hardware interfaces. This type of attack is hard to detect and remove, because its state cannot be accessed by security software running in the target OS.

2.1.3. *Security requirements*

Security threat analysis allows us to carefully identify the security requirements, so that appropriate security hardening schemes or countermeasures can be developed. The major security requirements are given as follows.

– Data encryption and leakage protection: data stored in datacenter storage across the infrastructure are considered as confidential data and need to be closely monitored. Thus, verifying whether the data have been accessed by the authorized users or not, or observing who is accessing the information, how this information has been accessed, from which location and if this information has been manipulated (e.g. forwarded to another user or copied to another site) are critical issues. To solve these problems, access control and up-to-date right management services are necessary for authenticating and authorizing users before gaining access to the information. This is possible through the creation of restriction or policy rules for this information and then the deployment of those policies without user intervention.

Moreover, to protect data during transit, an encryption scheme such as Transport Layer Security (TLS) or Internet Protocol Security (IPSec) are widely applied. Typically, the TLS and IPSec mechanisms are used to protect the links between two communication entities, by using certificates as the credentials to prevent these kinds of attacks. These mechanisms can also be used to protect the new interfaces introduced by NFV scenarios [HUA 14]. Disk or storage encryption needs to be considered to ensure that all the confidential data in the storage have already been encrypted. Thus, this solution can prevent not only storage attacks but also offline attacks. Also, network administrators need guarantees that all communications to host OS and VMs in the NFV infrastructure are encrypted to keep end user communications safe and secure. Again, this can be done using SSL/TLS or IPSec.

– Security monitoring and intrusion detection: the limited visibility and controllability over the underlying infrastructure make the attack surface unbounded. To combat the risks, such as malicious insiders and anomalous behavior, security monitoring and intrusion detection are considered as important tools which are used to detect threats, identify suspicious events and mitigate security attacks over the NFVIaaS layer.

– Authentication and authorization: in order to prevent unauthorized access, robust authentication and authorization methods are required. As the first process, authentication provides a way of identifying a user, typically by having a unique set of criteria (e.g. user name and password) before access is granted.

– Logical network segmentation: a restrictive and well-planned network configuration should be applied in an NFVIaaS environment. Some existing techniques, which are related to logical network segmentation such as the VLANs mechanism, offer isolated segments to prevent external VMs from sniffing or monitoring internal traffic. Also, security zoning offers a group of components with the same protection policy, in order to protect their communication from attacks. It is an effective strategy for reducing many types of risk, especially when we consider the permeability of existing networks.

– Trusted Virtual Domains (TVDs): TVDs are another kind of security requirement which aim to figure out security issues in the NFVIaaS layer. By means of the TVD concept, each VM has to trust each other based on a common security policy before starting its communication. In general, TVDs have been proposed by [CAB 07, CAT 10] to provide confinement boundaries, create secure communication and maintain security among the TVD's members. Thus, the TVD is considered a promising concept to improve security in virtualization platforms. In addition, the discussion on TVDs may encompass (1) Trusted Virtual Datacenter (TVDc) [BER 08], to manage security in datacenter virtualization through the use of access control schemes, and (2) Trusted Cloud Computing Platform (TCCP) [SAN 09], to ensure the confidentiality and integrity of computations that are outsourced to NFVIaaS services.

Moreover, the following security requirements are recommended to mitigate the security threats that might be caused by virtualization layers.

– Regular VM updates and patches: virtualization is a prime target for security breaches and attacks. Therefore, in order to minimize vulnerabilities and mitigate security risks from these virtualized attacks (e.g. hyperjacking, VM escape, VM hopping and VM Dos), it is important to keep regular VM updates and patches. Keeping VMs patched can help to maintain a stable virtual host environment. This practice needs to be applied not only to normal OS patches but also to all supporting software and workloads that are being deployed. Some examples of main locations for hypervirsor patches that are provided by virtualization vendors are Microsoft Hyper-V update list [MIC 10] and VMware patch download [VMW 15].

– Defense in depth: nowadays, many enterprises deploy layered defense solutions to mitigate security risks, but hardware virtualization in NFVIaaS makes such solutions complicated and bewildering. For example, if one VM is compromised, then all the other VMs that are part of the virtual network can be compromised. To ensure that the virtualization layer has been properly operated without any attack interruption, and that it has been maintained with complete layered security, the defense in depth solution is highly expected to identify resource assets, identify potential attacks, and deploy effective security solutions to combat these attacks.

– Security of host OS: one solution that is recommended to defend against attacks in VMs is to deploy the Intrusion Detection System (IDS) on the host OS [GAR 03] to monitor and intercept events from the VMs. This solution is known as Virtual Machine Introspection (VMI). IDS on host OS has been widely accepted as a secure model for monitoring the system, and it is difficult for the attacker to compromise the IDS even though he or she has complete control of the VM.

– Defending against VM-based root kits: it is believed Virtual Machine-Based Rootkits (VMBR) are fundamentally more difficult to detect than traditional malware, as their state cannot be accessed by the security software. Nonetheless, a VMBR gives signs of its presence that an Intrusion Detection System can observe. In [KIN 06], the authors classify the detection techniques into two categories: (i) the detection system running under the VMBR and (ii) the detection system running above the VMBR.

– Security software under the VMBR: the best way to detect a VMBR is to access a layer that is not controlled by the VMBR. Detectors that run under the VMBR can observe the state of the VMBR and can read the physical memory and look for signatures or anomalies that indicate the presence of the VMBR. There are various ways to do this, such as:

- using secure hardware: for example, Intel's LaGrande [INT 13], AMD's platform [AMD 03] and Copilot [PET 04] are products of secure hardwares, which are used to develop and deploy low-layer security software and can run beneath a VMBR;

- booting from a safe medium such as a CD-ROM, USB drive or network boot server: this boot code can run on the system before the VMBR loads and can also view the VMBR disk state;

- using a secure VMM: a secure VMM gains control of the system before the OS boots: although it cannot be used to stop the VMBR, it does retain control over the system and could easily add a check to stop the VMBR from modifying the boot sequence.

Additionally, other low-level techniques such as secure boot [ARB 97] could also be applied to ensure the integrity of the boot sequence and prevent a VMBR from gaining control over the target OS.

– Security software above the VMBR: running detection software below a VMBR is the best way to detect the VMBR. Unfortunately, to the best of our knowledge, in [KIN 06] the authors do not suggest an appropriate solution, instead exploring the question of whether software running above the VMBR can detect its presence. The authors analyze the possible perturbation that a detector could notice when running inside the VMs. For example, using the time differences of machine resources (e.g. CPU time, memory, disk space and possibly network bandwidth) to detect the VMBR attack by comparing the actual running time with wall-clock time.

2.2. Virtual Network Platform as a Service (VNPaaS)

Thanks to NFV, the service providers can provide a suite of infrastructure and applications as a platform – a platform on which the enterprises can develop and deploy their own network services and applications that are customized to their business purposes.

2.2.1. *Overall description*

In cloud computing, Platform as a Service, or PaaS, is defined as the capability of the service providers to offer computing platforms to the users. Thus, they can deploy their applications or services by either using predefined service templates or using certain orchestration functions. To do that, the toolkit of the networking infrastructure is provided by the service providers for conveniently developing, deploying and managing network applications. In particular, VNFs can be part of the platform for creating virtual networks, so that enterprise users can use them to develop their own virtual network, based on their particular needs.

The VNPaaS is similar to the VNFaaS, but differs mainly in the scale of the service and programmability or scope of control provided to the users. The VNPaaS provides a larger scale service of virtual networks rather than a single virtual network function. It provides the enterprises with the capability to introduce their own VNF instances; however, the VNFaaS is limited to configuring the set of VNF instances made available by the service provider. For example, VNFaaS is considered as an email server and as a VNF instance in scope of the NFV, while the VNPaaS is considered as a hosting service provider that provides an installation of an email server without any configuration. The enterprises have full administrative control over this email server, in which they can apply all configurations based on their needs with potential support from the hosting service providers. Additionally, the enterprise might deploy other VNF instances connected to the email server to allow advanced configuration (e.g. spam protection, DHCP, DNS, proxy or caching services).

The type of services supported on the VNPaaS can range from a simple firewall service for a single enterprise to a whole business communication suite based on an IP Multimedia Subsystem (IMS) network for a third party. A service may either be orchestrated out of existing services, deployed as new elements or implemented as a combination of both.

To summarize, the services provided by the VNPaaS allows the enterprise to place certain services on a virtualization platform including firewall, DHCP, DNS, proxy, caching, email or communication services. Through the VNPaaS scenario, the enterprises may get a pre-configured service with a basic set of configurations for further modifications based on their own control and deployment. Figure 2.2 depicts an example of sharing network resources according to the VNPaaS use case, whereas the hosting service provider owns the infrastructure and re-sells shared infrastructure resources to the third parties. Enterprises may deploy a standalone VNF instance that does not have any connection with other VNF instances in the hosting service provider's network, but that might have a connectivity with the enterprise corporate network. It is also possible to deploy VNF instances which are connected to other VNF instances, hosted by the service provider's network. In addition, there is the orchestration interface for each entity, which is used to specify policy rules and further communication among the VNFs and service providers.

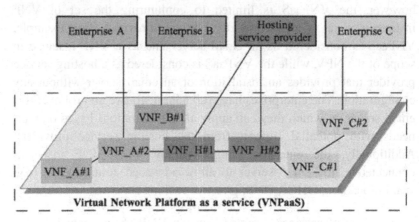

Figure 2.2. *VNPaaS architecture model, an example of sharing network resources. For a color version of this figure, see www.iste.co.uk/zhang/networks.zip*

2.2.2. *Threat analysis*

The major difference between VNPaaS and VNFaaS is the scope of services and control scale. In particular, the VNPaaS provides the capability of the users to deploy their own VNF instances as per their particular needs. As a result, the threats in the VNFaaS can also appear in the VNPaaS, including management and control plane attacks, vulnerabilities in orchestration and management modules, lack of transparent monitoring, insecure application programming interfaces, shared technology vulnerabilities, multi-tenancy vulnerability and privacy data leakage. As of all these security threats and the relevant security requirements have already been discussed in the previous use case, in this section, we aim to focus on the threats that uniquely occur in the VNPaaS.

Specifically, the VNPaaS model gives most of the resource and security control to the users, while the service providers only preserve the fundamental security of the underlying infrastructure, such as firewalls, servers and storage. The threat vectors are therefore significantly multiplied, including at least default application configurations, flaws in the Secure Socket Layer (SSL) protocol, insecure access permissions to the infrastructure, malicious insiders and lack of interoperability.

– Exploiting default application configurations: in a VNPaaS scenario, the users usually run their applications or services upon the infrastructure with a basic set of configurations, potentially leading to backdoor attacks. For example, the firewall deployed with default administrator login credentials can easily be hacked. More seriously, the attacker can modify the configuration rules and let malicious traffic go through. From a security standpoint, most of the default configurations are usually not secure, because the default settings tend to have a basic configuration for authentication, encryption, authorization or any other type of security control.

– SSL/TLS implementation flaws: in a VNPaaS scenario, the SSL/TLS is used to achieve secure communication between the entities. Despite the significance of using the SSL/TLS in the cloud environment, the flaws and vulnerabilities resulting from misconfigurations have become an attractive target in the hacking community. As a matter of fact, many attacks targeting theoretical and practical weaknesses have been identified and exploited. For example, attacks on PKI and handshaking protocol have been reported in [MEY 13]. Specifically, the attackers can alter the *ClientHello* message sent by the initiator of the connection, manipulating or completely replacing the cipher suite. Also, the nonce used by the SSL/TLS can possibly be predicted and compromised, as the generation of nonce relies on predicable values such as current time, current process ID and process ID of the parent process, which are vulnerable to brute force attacks.

– Insecure data access: there is no fundamental difference from the threats of data leakage in the previous use cases. The sensitive data at the virtual infrastructure could be compromised due to improper

configurations on permission settings or access control policies. In particular, the following cases may happen:
- improper enforcement of security policies;
- improper update of security policies or data access procedures;
- insecure communication channels between two entities.

– Malicious insiders: the threat of a malicious insider has been previously identified. Due to the lack of transparency of the operational process and procedure in the NFVPaaS model, malicious insiders are difficult to prevent. For example, a hosting service provider may perform an unauthorized access and collect confidential data from his user assets without user permission. With inadequate transparency, the insider threats cannot be overlooked.

– Lack of interoperability: the VNPaaS provides a large set of services and powerful control to the users with which to manage and orchestrate their particular services. However, the diverse computational resources and sophisticated isolation of the workloads for different operators may lead to security breaches. In particular, if the platform resources are not accessed and managed with standard solutions, or the security mechanisms are not applied to separate workloads in appropriate ways, the Quality-of-Service could seriously downgrade, even leading to malicious attacks.

– Side channel attacks: side channel attacks typically occur when hardware leaks information to potential attackers. This attack may target the weakness of implementation of the cryptographic algorithms. In fact, the cryptographic algorithms may be sufficient enough to prevent the attacks, but software implementation flaws and bugs could make cryptographic algorithms become vulnerable to side channel attacks. Also, the attackers may use the signals leaked from side channels during the system's normal execution to reveal the secret information. This type of attack is hard to detect. For example, in [ZHA 14], the authors present an example of a side channel attack on the shared CPU in a PaaS cloud environment. At the first step, adversaries seek to arrange a malicious instance to run within a different container on the same host OS as the target victim and then extract confidential information such as a secret of interest from the target victim using this break point.

In addition, security threat analysis is also possible based on the virtualization layer, as already mentioned in the previous use case. This is essentially due to the concept of the VNPaaS that provides the underlying infrastructure and shares network resources. The VNPaaS allows enterprises' services to be deployed based on the enterprises' needs. As a result, security threats and vulnerabilities that occur at the virtualization layer (e.g. hyperjacking, VM escape, VM hopping, VM DoS and VM-based root kits) could also impact business operations and security performance in the VNPaaS environment.

2.2.3. *Security requirements*

The threat analysis indicates that the use cases VNFaaS and VNPaaS have a large set of security threats in common. In addition to these security requirements for the use case VNPaaS, some security issues caused by default or improper configurations, SSL/TLS implementation flaws and insecure data access need to be carefully studied.

– Hardening default configurations: based on the previous analysis, default configurations can leave backdoors for the attackers, and so their hardening can prevent a large set of attacks. To do that, the network operators need to be well-trained, so as to obtain solid knowledge and deep understanding of the VNPaaS service components. In particular, it is an essential and important step for the network operators to carefully check the security configurations of specific applications or services with the predefined security policies before running them. The comprehensive threat models and taxonomy are certainly helpful.

– Securely deploying and configuring SSL/TLS: as the SSL/TLS plays a vital role in the network infrastructure and it has become an attractive target to the attackers, special attention must be given to its deployment and configurations. For example, weak cipher suits, cryptographic algorithms or random number generators should be avoided. The applications running over the SSL/TLS should be carefully examined to avoid introducing configuration errors or even security vulnerabilities. The three major hardening measures suggested in [RUB 13] must be carefully considered: (i) perfect forward secrecy, (ii) strict transport security and (iii) public key pinning.

- Perfect forward secrecy: the service providers need to preserve prefect forward secrecy for SSL/TLS sessions, ensuring that a session key derived from a set of long-term keys cannot be compromised even if one of the long-term keys is compromised.

- Strict transport security: this must ensure that the users always establish connections using the SSL/TLS session, while the connections with expired server certificates must be denied.

- Public key pinning: the SSL/TLS server needs to force the browsers to only trust those certificates issued by particular Certificate Authorities (CAs).

– Always enforcing AAA and access control: to effectively protect the cloud data, the network services and applications running in the VNPaaS must adopt granular security policies and mechanisms. This involves clearly identifying and specifying the relationship between permission rules and authorization policies and strictly enforcing the specific actions and security controls on the particular objects or assets. More specifically,

- authentication: in the NFV framework, authentication and authorization are applied to ensure that only authenticated VNF instances from authorized service providers are allowed to execute;

- authorization: in general, authorization determines who can access the objects based on the predefined policy rules and security enforcement. In this use case, role-based access control and federated access control can be employed for authorization purposes;

- accounting and traceability: effective monitoring schemes should be deployed to keep a record of events occurring on the platform, while historic operations or events of critical resources should be accountable and traceable for forensic analysis.

– Enhancing interoperability: as a general trend, today's enterprises are migrating their services to the cloud infrastructure. However, without industry-wide cloud standards, vendors tend to create proprietary cloud services based on their unique software stacks, resulting in service lock-in and incompatibility with others. It is therefore important to create a common matrix of interoperable VNFs and NFVI, covering both standalone VNF instances, functions and platforms. In fact, it is well-recognized by the community that one of the grand challenges for the long-term adoption of the NFV is the interoperability between the NFV elements, while OpenStack is one of the ongoing attempts to achieve the goal.

– VNPaaS tenant isolation: the VNPaaS aims to increase server utilization and reduce operational costs. It also supports multi-tenancy, meaning that the VNPaaS is able to run multiple users' instances on the same operating system. Therefore, isolation between tenants is essential for enhancing security in the VNPaaS environment. In [ZHA 14], the authors divided tenant isolation into three different types, which are as follows:

- runtime-based isolation: some Platform-as-a-Service hosting network service applications owned by multiple tenants in the same process, provide isolation with application run times. Multiple tenants therefore may share, for example, the same Java Virtual Machine (JVM) environment and be isolated only by JVM runtime security mechanisms;

- user-based isolation: A more widely used isolation technique is the traditional user-based isolation within the host OS. Each tenant runs as a non-privileged user on the host OS, and the network service instances are a set of processes run by that user. Basically, the host OS provides a certain level of memory protection, in order to prevent illegal memory access across instance boundaries, while correctly configuring Discretionary Access Control (DAC) in the system such as Unix to prevent cross-tenant file access;

- container-based isolation: the main limitation of user-based isolation is the unrestricted use of computer resources by individual instance. This has been relatively and recently addressed with the advent of Linux containers as implemented by using the Linux-VServer [VSE 17], OpenVZ [OPE 15b] and LXC [LXC 14]. However, the LXC has been merged into mainstream Linux kernels. In addition, containers are groups of processes that are isolated from other groups via distinct kernel namespaces and resource allocation, and are also called *control groups or cgroups*. An example of an open source project such as Docker containers [DOC 13] has been adopted by several platforms as a service's offering. It builds on top of LXC to facilitate the management of Linux containers;

– defense-in-depth approaches: there is the possibility that the VNPaaS may generate vulnerabilities which attackers can exploit. To mitigate these risks, it is important to consider the defense-in-depth approach. Traditional defense-in-depth applies to a business company that has full control of its IT infrastructure, from physical servers to the networks. In terms of the VNPaaS environment, hosting service providers let tenants develop, test, deploy or run any number of network service applications on the VNPaaS. This also allows tenants to change the behavior of network service applications or reconfigure network traffic paths to make them work well on the VNPaaS. However, only hosting service providers who own the network fabric have the ability to control and manage their underlying infrastructure, while tenants have limited control of the VNPaaS infrastructure. As the result, defense-in-depth approaches need to be classified into four phases of the lifecycle [MYE 14] as follows:

- Asset identification phase: identifying assets is the first step toward building defense-in-depth. This phase is used to identify the user, cloud, data and hardware assets. For example, user assets include developers, testers, policy makers and SLA managers, and cloud assets include VNPaaS providers and the type of Infrastructure as a Service on which the VNPaaS is running.

- Adversaries identification phase: this phase is used to identify the possible adversaries there might be (e.g. private individuals and terrorist groups) in order to examine how adversaries are likely to attack the system. For example:

- Adversaries may passively monitor communication between VNPaaS developers, testers, policy makers and business analysts without revealing their presence.

- Adversaries use social engineering to steal or access the VNPaaS hardware assets.

- Adversaries flood cloud resources with excessive packets, resulting in DoS to the VNPaaS.

- Adversaries may maliciously insert malware into the VNPaaS.

- Adversaries directly attack the management and control the plane used to control the VNPaaS network traffic.

- Layers of defense phase: after completely identifying assets and adversaries, this phase is about security solutions for different attacks. Two examples are given as follows:

- In order to combat passive attacks, secured firewalls and access control within the VNPaaS are required.

- In order to combat insider attacks, secure access control and personnel security mechanisms are required to protect physical and virtual resources from unauthorized access.

– Review phase: this focuses on periodically reviewing defense-in-depth because new types of attacks may emerge, calling for additional defense mechanisms. It is important to recheck frequently when user requirements have changed or when security services are out of date.

2.3. Virtual Network Function as a Service (VNFaaS)

More and more services are deployed by enterprises, at the edge network (CPE). The cost of dedicated standalone appliance-per-feature is significant and not flexible, while delay and complexity in terms of service deployment and maintenance are increased. The increasing virtualization capabilities driven by NFV can meet the growing user requirements and reduce the aforementioned complexities and costs. In particular, NFV has great potential to bring cloud velocity to network service providers, by enabling specific network services such as routers, load balancers, firewalls and packet gateways, which can be carried out on virtual machines rather than on dedicated hardware.

2.3.1. Overall description

Moving network service functionality from the purpose-built platform to a commodity hardware environment provides cloud computing capabilities such as NFVI. Rather than investing its own capital on deploying the network infrastructure, the enterprise can seek the NFVI service, which provides advanced networking features including service and resource elasticity, high availability and network function mobility from one physical and geographical location to another. In this use case, the enterprise is defined as the user of the service who is able to manage and control the application only from a configuration perspective, without being able to control and manage the underlying infrastructure. The service provider can then scale the

NFVI resources allocated to the VNF instances, in response to increase in the usage of the VNFs. Making the VNF functionality available to the enterprise as a service is comparable to cloud computing (Software as a Service).

To date, the most prevalent transition models from the physical to virtualized network service include Virtual Network Functions as a Service (VNFaaS), VNF forwarding graphs, virtual Evolved Packet Core (vEPC), virtual Customer Premises Equipment (vCPE), virtual Radio Access Network (vRAN), virtual Content Delivery Network (vCDN), virtual Set-top Box (vSTB) and virtual Residential Gateway (vRGW). The architecture of representative models are discussed below. An overview of the VNFaaS is shown in Figure 2.3.

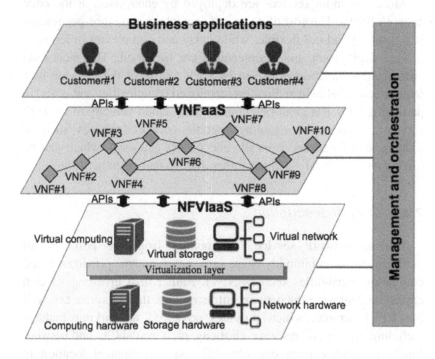

Figure 2.3. *The overall concept of NFVIaaS and VNFaaS. For a color version of this figure, see www.iste.co.uk/zhang/networks.zip*

2.3.1.1. *Virtual Network Function as a Service*

Pre-NFV service provider networks include a Provider Edge (PE) router typically shared by a high number of users located in the service provider cloud, whereas a Customer Premises Equipment (CPE) router is used exclusively by a single user. With VNFaaS, the virtualization of the enterprise may include virtualization of the CPE function (vCPE) in the service provider cloud, and virtualization of the PE function (vPE) where the virtual network service functions and core-facing PE functions can be executed in the service provider cloud. These two steps are independent and may be deployed separately. However, scale savings that can be done through CPE virtualization are significantly greater when compared to PE virtualization. This is essentially due to the fact that PE routers can be shared by a large number of users while a CPE router is used by a single user. For this reason, vCPE may take place first to provide the largest benefits for both enterprise users and service providers. The vPE may be carried out at a later stage to complete the transition to a fully virtualized NFV solution.

Typically, the service provider is responsible for deploying, configuring, updating and managing the operations of the vCPE and vPE with supplementary Service Level Agreement (SLA) to provide service availability and service baselines across the VNFaaS layer. Figure 2.4 presents the VNFaaS scenario, which demonstrates co-existence and interoperability of virtualized and non-virtualized enterprise CPE functions.

Examples of functionalities provided by vCPE include routing, VPN termination, QoS support, stateful firewall, IDS/IPS, DPI, NG-FW, WAN Optimization Controller (WOC), and so on. The vCPE functionality may be located in various sites.

The vPE is hard to deploy short term, mainly due to high throughput requirement. Nevertheless, vPE can improve the scalability of virtual network services, through dynamic resizing or allocating of virtual resources. The service provided by vPE includes IP VPNs, Virtual Private LAN Service (VPLS), Ethernet Virtual Private Network (EVPN), pseudo-wire services and more.

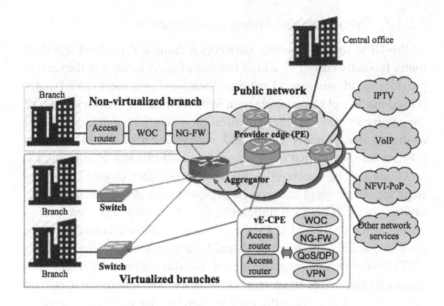

Figure 2.4. *Non-virtualized CPE and virtualized CPE*

In addition, there are a number of network functions that can be deployed today within enterprise networks, such as Access Router (AR), Provider Edge (PE) router, enterprise firewall, Next Generation Firewall (NF-FW), enterprise WAN Optimization Controller (WOC), DPI, IPS and network performance monitoring.

Some examples from industrial use cases related to the virtual enterprise CPE have been proposed by [AMD 15]. The objective is to create an enterprise solution of virtual enterprise services e.g. firewall, DDOS, network connectivity and VPN creation, which are mainly based on Juniper Virtualized Network Functions. This use case implements a full NFV topology including OpenStack CMS [OPE 17, ERI 15a] and Contrail Cloud Platform [OPE 15a] for VNF's establishment and service chain creation, as it aims to provide a full end-to-end security service. At the same time, the T-NOVA project [TNO 14], which is an integrated project co-funded by the European

Commission with the participation of eighteen partners, also proposes an integrated top-down NFV system architecture for the provision of the VNFaaS (ETSI NFV ISG use case #2). This is performed in order to facilitate the involvement of various actors in the NFV scene and to attract new market entrants through T-NOVA's establishment of an NFV Marketplace, whereas network services and functions by several developers can be published and brokered. Users can browse and select the services and virtual appliances that best match their needs, through the negotiation of associated SLAs under various billing models.

2.3.1.2. *VNF forwarding graphs*

A forwarding graph is one example of an end-to-end Virtual Network Function as a Service, which is defined as the sequence of network functions that a packet traverses, as shown in Figure 2.5. VNF forwarding graphs are analogous to the connection of existing physical appliances via cables and they provide the logical connectivity between virtual appliances (e.g. VNFs). Benefits of VNF forwarding graphs include offering of resource sharing across functions and reduction of delays in deployment and upgrading. Also, the addition of new features with less complexity of VNFs' configuration and easy deployment in the enterprise's network are other key benefits.

This use case provides a more complex structure associated with VNF forwarding graphs as the objective is to enable migration from existing physical network functions to their equivalent in virtualized environment and to enable the implementation of new functions. Therefore, the service provider needs to define and develop network services at an abstract level and then deploy them in instances with respect to particular NFVI resources. The services should include identification of VNFs' types, the relationships between these VNFs and the interconnection (forwarding) topology along with related management and dependency relationships.

The VNF forwarding graphs have standardized and published interfaces, which may include layer 1, layer 2, layer 3, layer 4 and layer 7 according to the OSI model. The role of VNF forwarding graphs encompass logical parts and several entity relationships that can be divided into two perspectives, which are the logical view and physical view of VNF forwarding graphs.

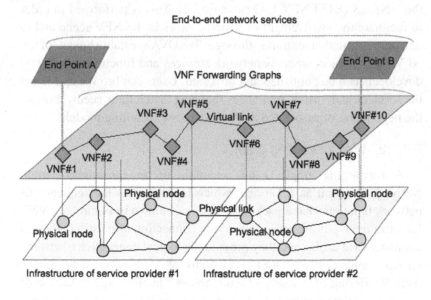

Figure 2.5. *Forwarding graphs of VNFs and end points. For a color version of this figure, see www.iste.co.uk/zhang/networks.zip*

The logical view of VNF forwarding graphs can be divided into four main parts: physical network function, physical network logical interface, packet flow and NFV network infrastructure.

– Physical network function: the overall services of the physical network function, such as physical access, backbone network and standalone VM, that cannot be virtualized for deploying, managing and operating considerations by a service provider.

– Physical network logical interface: the boundary between a VNF forwarding graph and physical network function is specified by the network service provider through a physical network logical interface. The physical network logical interface may be based upon fields in the packet header (e.g. source and destination of packets entering).

– Packet flow: the net outcome that contributes to the overall service, in which the number of packet flows in certain groups may pass to the same path through the VNF forwarding graph or differ in each direction depending on the services' configuration.

– NFV network infrastructure: the NFV network infrastructure provides connectivity services between the VNFs (that implement the forwarding graph links) and VNF nodes as controlled by the NFV management and orchestration. They also provide functions such as traffic classification, tunnel encapsulation, traffic steering and some forms of load balancing.

The physical view of VNF forwarding graphs consists of physical network association, physical network port, network forwarding path and virtual machine environment.

– Physical network association: this associates the relationship between the NFV network infrastructure and a physical network port on the physical network function. The relationship is known by management and orchestration at the boundaries between VNFs and physical elements.

– Physical network port: the physical network port on a physical network function or a physical network switch/router, or a physical NIC.

– Network forwarding path: the sequence of hardware/software switching ports and operations in the NFV network infrastructure as configured by management and orchestration that implement a logical VNF forwarding graph link, connecting with logical interface of the VNF node (e.g. VNIC on a VM). The VNF forwarding graph information describes the characteristics of these links.

– Virtual machine environment: this describes the characteristics of the compute, storage and networking environment as configured by management and orchestration. However, information related to configuration of VNF forwarding graphs is determined by the VNF provider and network service provider.

VNF forwarding graphs offer several benefits that can cope with the limitations of existing physical appliance forwarding graphs. Some of these benefits are as follows:

– Efficiency: different network services can share resources across functions.

– Resiliency: in some cases, backup functions can share hardware resources and network capacities in the NFV infrastructure.

– Flexibility: VNF forwarding graphs provide rapid deployment for creating, removing and upgrading network services. This is essentially due to the software-based functions.

– Complexity: virtualized switching functions and VNF configurations can also implement forwarding graphs in a more straightforward and efficient manner, and VNF forwarding graphs can also reduce configuration complexity.

– Deployability: virtualized functions and switching are less complex to deploy in the enterprise's network.

2.3.1.3. *Virtualization of CDNs (vCDNs)*

Virtualization of CDNs is another example of network services that can be provided as VNFaaSs. Due to the growth of today's video traffic, one of the major challenges for main network operators is to define new mechanisms to meet the QoS and on-demand content service requirements coming from the end users. NFV technology can help to increase the amount of content to be stored rather than constrain content delivery using local storage.

Many current deployments of CDNs are based on dedicated physical appliances, are relied on hardware based appliances and are deployed side-by-side for different purposes. These come with a number of limitations, such as follows:

– The dedicated physical devices and servers from several parties introduce a certain complexity with a cost for the network operator.

– Dedicated hardwares have limited and inflexible designs to react to CDN changes such as new content formats, protocols, device types and content protection requirement.

– The average peak utilization and resiliency of CDN nodes for dedicated purposes from different partners is low, such as low usage of dedicated hardware appliance and CDN servers during weekdays or business hours. Also, it is hard to react dynamically in case of unforeseen capacity and needs.

– The dedicated CDN nodes may require some value-added services to improve security and optimize performance from the outsourcing of a partner's solution instead of having their own solutions.

Integrating CDN nodes into operator networks can be a cost-effective way to answer the challenges of video traffic delivery. Producing content streaming of storage nodes close to the end users can be cost-effective in terms of upper network links, equipment, and allowing media to deliver with high bandwidth and a more reliable quality. Virtualized CDN covers potentially all components of the CDN, with a first impact on cache nodes, in order to achieve an acceptable performance in terms of throughput and latency. Regarding the objectives, virtualized CDNs aim to improve resource allocation for efficient use during weekdays and business hours. And so, the sharing capacity for all contents' delivery appliances and the operational process of resources for harmonizing, replacing or adding new services in content delivery, can be facilitated through software-based appliances.

The concept of virtualized CDNs was designed in order to combine multiple components, such as cache nodes and CDN controllers. The CDN controller selects a cache node or a pool of cache nodes to answer the end user request, and then redirects the end user to the selected cache nodes. The cache node answers the end user request and delivers the requested content to the end user. The CDN controller is a centralized component, while the CDN cache nodes are distributed within the network.

The virtualized CDN potentially covers all the components of CDN, whereas physical CDN cache nodes can be replaced by virtual appliances (VNFs), as shown in the Figure 2.6. A variety of services can be implemented by the loosely coupled software components, which are either virtualized or non-virtualized. Thus, the CDN controller controls the cache nodes deployed on virtualized and non-virtualized server instances in parallel. Possible scenarios of coexistence:

– Deploying virtualization on centralized cache nodes and deploying a dedicated physical cache node, which requires a deeper network distribution for operational reasons.

– Centralized cache clusters that require high performance, can run on dedicated physical servers, while others can run on virtualized cache nodes.

– For such a migration scenario from non-virtualized to virtualized, the legacy cache nodes can be kept in dedicated physical devices until their hardware life cycle is completed (e.g. operational efficiency is reached by adding new capacity to the virtualized CDN).

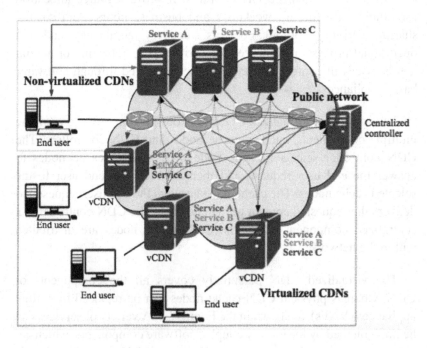

Figure 2.6. *Principle of the deployment of different vCDN cache nodes in a virtualized environment*

2.3.1.4. *Virtualization of the home environment*

The availability of high bandwidth access and the emergence of NFV technology facilitate virtualization of the home environment by requiring only simple physical connectivity, and low cost and low maintenance devices at the customer premises. NFV technologies become ideal candidates to support computation workload in the home environment with minimal cost and improved time to market, while new services can be introduced as required or needed. Therefore, benefits derived from avoiding installation of new equipment would be amplified if the home environment is considered with the appropriate NFV approach.

This use case aims to provide some main benefits, such as increasing the bandwidth demand between the home and the network, making cost savings on Set-top Box (STB) and Residential Gateway (RGW), avoiding constant maintenance and upgrading the Customer Premises Equipment (CPE), and carrying out remote diagnostics of home devices. Also, Quality of Experience (QoE) is improved through functionalities and mobility that provide remote access to all contents and services, with smooth services and less cumbersome services, as not only the dependency on the CPE functionality but also the user installation process are limited.

Without home virtualization, all services are received by the RGW, converted to a private IP address, and delivered inside the home network via either a Point-to-Point Protocol Over Ethernet (PPPoE) tunnel or IP Protocol over Ethernet (IPoE). NFV technology facilitates virtualization of services and functionalities' migration from home devices to the NFV cloud. Figure 2.7 presents the coexistence between virtualized and non-virtualized home devices. The original devices (such as RGW and STB) have been maintained and replicated to virtualized devices (vRGW and vSTB respectively). Each one performs different functionalities.

RGW can be virtualized as the following target scenario:

– Connectivity: such as

- the DHCP server, to provide private IP addresses to home devices;

- Network Address Translator (NAT) router, to provide routing capabilities to the home by converting the home addresses to one public IP address;

- Application Level Gateway (ALG), to allow application-specific routing behavior; and

- Point-to-Point Protocol over Ethernet (PPoE), to connect to the Broadband Remote Access Server (BRAS).

– Security: such as

- firewall, antivirus and IPS, to provide protection to the home environment;

- parental controls, to allow control of web content delivery;

- port mapping, to allow translation entry by mapping the protocol port on the gateway to the IP address and the protocol port on the private LAN; and

- VPN server, to provide remote access to the LAN user.

– Management: such as

- Web GUI, to allow subscriber management and

- statistics and diagnostics.

Also, the STB can be virtualized as the following target scenario:

– User interface and connectivity: such as

- remote user interface server, to allow the same look and feel to a big variety of home devices, including user interface automatic negotiation to provide better user experience, and

- middle ware client, to provide an interface for existing middle ware servers to query information.

– Media streaming: such as

- media server, to expose all media inventory;

- video on demand, to provide interfaces for existing content platforms;

- streaming methods, to serve and deliver video and audio content over the Internet;

- multi-screen, to support various and simultaneous screens of varying resolution and formats; and

- media cache, to support caching of different content types and formats.

– Management and security: such as

- Web GUI, to allow subscriber management;

- encryption, to support different encryption schemes for cached content; and

- shared content, to provide a user with access to its contents for any virtualized home.

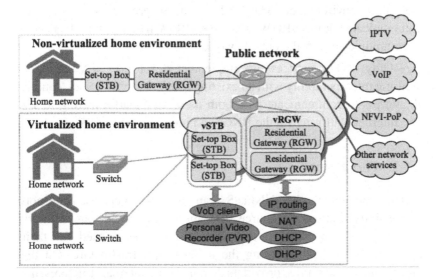

Figure 2.7. *The differentiation between virtualized and non-virtualized home environments*

Based on this use case, RGW and STB are the main candidates for virtualization. Virtualization of the home environment drives a deployment change due to the virtualized devices that have been moved from the home to the operator network and from the private IP space to the public IP space. However, it is possible for virtualized home devices to coexist with non-virtual home devices, as present in the following examples.

– Only vRGW would be implemented in the NFV network to provide a private IP address to the home, while it is directly connected to some services such as IPTV and VoIP.

– Both vSTB and vRGW are implemented. The vSTB uses a public IP address to communicate with the vRGW and its service platforms (e.g. IPTV or Internet platforms via BNG).

– Both vSTB and vRGW are virtualized and physically connected to the Broadband Network Gateway (BNG). This use case emulates the home environment. The vSTB uses a private IP address to communicate with its vRGW, while the vRGW uses a public IP address to communicate with the outside world.

– Only vSTB services are implemented for the NFV network, assuring interoperability with an existing RGW. The vSTB uses a public IP address to communicate with both its service platforms (e.g. IPTV and Internet platforms via the BNG) and home-located RGW.

2.3.2. Threat analysis

On one hand, the VNFaaS can improve network transport connectivity, optimize resource allocation and provide an arbitrary selection of computational and storage resources needed for their applications, without handling the underlying infrastructure. On the other hand, as the service providers do not expose internal structures, the tenants may have limited visibility and controllability over the network resources. Also, the fluctuations in activities or demands of adding and deleting network services in real time can hardly be implemented by the legacy network infrastructure. These intrinsic limitations lead to significant security threats, which are analyzed in the following:

– Attacks on management and control plane: thanks to the decoupling between the software implementation and hardware platform of network devices enabled by NFV technology, various networking functional components can be deployed into a virtual machine within the service provider's datacenter, simply as a piece of software-based instance. As such, the VNFaaS moves network functions and services to the virtualization environment and gives operators the capability to manage network assets from a central control point. On this aspect, SDN technologies have the potential to be seamlessly integrated, as the SDN controller, NFV management and control planes are considered as the brain of all operations, including VNF creation, configuration, management and provision, as well as monitoring network services and their components and devices. However, the management and control plane could become a single point of failure and an attractive attack target. Its availability, integrity and authenticity must be well-protected, as any compromised operation may lead to the failure of the entire system. For example, DDoS attacks can make the control point hardly available to the legitimate users. More seriously, if the attackers can gain access to the control point, the entire network service will be under control. The attackers can freely reconfigure network services, disrupt data paths, monitor data transaction and further acquire the confidential and sensitive information of the victims. And so, the attack surface of the NFV management and control plane could be comparable with that of SDN controllers.

– Vulnerabilities in orchestration and management modules: in addition to provisioning and managing virtual networking features, NFV management and orchestration modules can control the connectivity between VNFs and create the relationship between VNFs and physical elements. They can also specify logical and physical interconnection points between the NFVI and physical network functions, maintain a sequence of network forwarding paths, and address the entire service chaining process. NFV management and orchestration offer rapid configuration, dynamic service deployment and operational cost reduction. However, the lack of consistency on how to manage and orchestrate the functional modules leads to security threats. In particular, many NFV vendors implement network services independently, with a lack of sufficient collaboration among other NFV vendors. Such service fragmentation brings significant challenges to enforcing network-level security policies that are applied to diverse functional components, as any inconsistency will potentially be exploited by the attackers for launching attacks.

– Lack of control and monitoring: as we previously discussed, the lack of control and monitoring can lead to security threats to the NFVIaaS. This issue can occur in the VNFaaS as well, due to the fact that the tenants are not able to monitor all data transaction processing within the NFV environment, especially in the underlying infrastructure. For example, the tenants have no visibility on how data are accessed, how it is performed, how network services are deployed in physical machines or even how the data are transferred over the network links. Without transparent monitoring of such processes, the attackers can manage to harvest confidential data or modify them for malicious purposes without the awareness of VNF providers and tenants. More seriously, the malicious insiders can gain complete control over the VNFs services, including both physical and virtual assets.

– Insecure service and application programming interfaces: the NFV architectural framework clearly shows that functional components are identified and communicate with each other via interfaces. Those interfaces are widely used by applications to execute network services on virtual infrastructures, or communicate with VNF managers and orchestration systems. Generally, these interfaces are specified to ensure interoperability between different service components to facilitate multi-vendor implementation environments, e.g., the orchestrator and Virtual Infrastructure Manager (VIM), orchestrator and Virtual Network Function Manager (VNFM) and VNF and NFVI. Considering the prevalence and significance of these interfaces, adequate knowledge about their implementations, deployment and operation are necessary. The security and trust concerns must be carefully taken into account in the the entire life-cycle, as any implementation errors or misconfiguration can expose the interface to attacks. For example, an adversary can manage to embed malicious codes into the interfaces in order to escalate his or her privilege, which then grant their access to those valuable network assets.

– Threats resulting from multi-tenancy: one of the salient features of the NVF is physical resources sharing among multiple tenants through the software virtualization layer. The shared resources are disk partitions, CPU caches and Graphic Processing Units (GPUs) among others. The concept of sharing makes a tenant's resource stack essentially exposed to security threats, primarily because those hardware elements are not designed with strong isolation properties for multi-tenant architectures. By design, a tenant should be completely unaware of its neighbor's identity, security profile, and intention. However, a malicious tenant can manage to run their VM instance next to the victims', sniff the communication between the tenants on the same hypervisor, and to even subvert their operations. Also, the confidential data sitting in the common storage hardware have the potential to be compromised due to loose access management or even targeted attacks.

– Data loss and information leakage: as in other use cases, the VNFaaS also suffers from data loss and information leakage due to inappropriate access control mechanisms and weak data protection schemes. The root cause of this security threat is the cross-layer, ranging from the virtualized network service to the platform and infrastructure, including the management and orchestration layers. Both data in transit and data at rest can be compromised. For example, when the data are migrated from static physical servers to virtual volumes, the storage administrator needs to reassign or replicate the tenants' information across the datacenter without incurring service interruption. Any misconfiguration or operation mistake may lead to the exposure of the tenants' identity information.

2.3.3. Security requirements

Based on the analysis of potential security threats of the NFVaaS, we identify the following security requirements, which can be fulfilled and implemented according to the particular use cases:

– SLA enforcement: as indicated in [KYR 13], the SLAs provide the fundamental ground for service providers and end users to regulate their interactions. In particular, SLAs are not only part of a quality initiative to improve user focus, service delivery and organizational performance, but they also help to provide a clear framework for service delivery, monitoring performance and service quality and supporting continuous improvement. As proposed in [DUF 05], integrating security parameters into the service level specification can help to improve SLA management more efficiently, as the service providers can define network policies to ensure that there is an adequate amount of resources for the needs of both security and QoS. This also enables VNF service providers to provide security as a service to their users, making the services achieve desirable security properties without deploying and managing security mechanisms locally.

– User authentication, authorization and accounting (AAA): in the use case VNFaaS, regardless of particular implementation architectures such as NFVIaaS, VNFaaS, VNPaaS, and VNF Forwarding Graphs, AAA mechanisms should be applied to at least two layers: the network infrastructure to identify the tenants and the network function layer to identify the actual users. As such, only authorized VNF instances provided by authenticated service providers are allowed to be executed. In fact, ETSI NFV security and trust guidance [ETS 14b] have addressed the privacy issues in authentication and security accounting in the NFV, including the generation and validation of identity tokens, the exchange of identities, as well as the attributes that need to be validated in multi-layered, multi-tenant environments. Some examples related to AAA mechanisms are as follows:

   - authentication of VNF images:
   - authentication of tenants which intend to access the NFV management and orchestration functional blocks;
   - authentication between the different functional blocks: intra-domain/intra-domain, intra-domain/inter-domain; and inter-domain/ inter-domain; and
   - authentication of all operational interfaces between different functional blocks.

– Security monitoring: as in the cloud, the status of infrastructure, network services and events in the use cases of the VNFaaS are hardly observable. Thus, effective security monitoring mechanisms can help to increase the transparency of VNFaaS functional components, obtain visibility into the network events and activities of interest, so as to enable logging and accounting functions for forensics and anomaly detection. For example, in [ZHA 15], the authors have proposed a scheme called *CloudMonatt* to monitor different aspects of security health. Also, in [MEN 13], *Monitoring as a Service (MaaS)* was proposed to deploy network state monitoring at different levels of the cloud services. A trusted monitoring framework for virtualized cloud platforms was proposed in [ZOU 13] to offer guaranteed framework integrity.

– Protection of data in transit: as other use cases, the traditional security mechanisms such as SSL/TLS and IPsec should be used to encrypt network traffic between two communication entities in order to prevent man-in-the-middle attacks. But their deployment relies on the effective key management infrastructure, as well as the correct implementations and configurations of different service components from different service providers. In addition, although the traditional encryption techniques can be used to protect data operation and communication from being compromised by adversaries, more advanced encryption schemes such as homomorphic encryption [ZHO 08, LAU 12] are more desirable in VNF environments, especially for service orchestration. However, the currently available schemes can be considered only if the computational resource is ample and if the network services are not time critical. In [NET 14], a *CrytoFlow Cloud Solution* was proposed by Certes Networks, with an objective enhancing the encryption and policy enforcement of vCEP and vCFNet for supporting the NFV and other virtualized environments. In particular, CryptoFlow aims to create fully secure, tunnel-less VPNs to protect sensitive data traffic over the virtualized network, allowing enterprises to set and control their own data protection policies and encryption keys without third parties. The solution also permits data traffic to be fully segregated to protect sensitive data, control data flow and other critical data in motion.

– Enforcement of service dependency and end-to-end management: a traditional network infrastructure has a one-to-one relationship between a network service and a set of dedicated physical resources. This straightforward relationship becomes significantly complicated in the NFV infrastructure, as a network service can be supported by a number of VNFs that are running on several VMs. And also, a single VNF can support a number of distinct network services, or a group of VNFs can support a single network service running on a number of distinct physical servers. As a result, end-to-end management systems need to support a three-tiered network model based on many-to-many relationships among network services, virtualization infrastructure and physical infrastructure. Clearly, enforcing the strong and consistent security and management policies between the VNFs is extremely important to ensure service chaining and their inter-dependency. For example, a service chaining architecture was proposed in [BRO 15], with the objective developing a set of architectural building blocks to enable network operators to create a service topology and instantiate a service function path across the network. It covers the placement of network functions, service chain management, diagnostics and security models.

– Security management, orchestration, and automation: as a matter of fact, a huge number of virtualized devices such as vCPE, vCDN, vRGW and vSTB can be deployed in NFV environments. To perform network service chaining where multiple VNFs can be used in sequence to deliver a service, the NFV provides an additional set of management and orchestration functions that can be added to the current model for supporting various network services (such as NFVI, VNFs, VNF forwarding graphs, virtual links and physical network functions), while maintaining virtualized resources. These functions require the security mechanisms to be automated, on demand, friendly interfaced and agile, so that they can be quickly deployed at various security Police Enforcement Points (PEPs), either across platforms or in the same NFV environment. Clearly, the major purpose of security management, orchestration and automation is to ensure secure and fast service delivery, improving end user experience. For example, an interactive topology map of all network services e.g., firewalls, routers, subnets and zones, can be automatically generated in order to provide application-centric solutions for managing complex policies across network security services and other related security infrastructures.

– Network isolation and segmentation: in both VNFaaS and VNPaaS use cases, a large number of VNF instances are created in the NFV environment, so that the infrastructure service providers have to ensure the security of data, transactions and communications resulting from VNF executions. In particular, network isolation and segmentation play a significant role in achieving the goals. As a matter of fact, NFV has certain security isolation and segmentation characteristics, such as separating virtual networks from the underlying physical infrastructure through traffic encapsulation, providing security zones for a group of VNF instances that have common security policies. These benefits can help the service provider to preserve data confidentiality and integrity.

2.4. Virtualization of mobile networks

As a matter of fact, today's mobile networks are populated with a large variety of proprietary hardware appliances. NFV has a significant potential to reduce network complexity and the cost of ownership by leveraging standard virtualization technology to consolidate different types of network equipment. Thus, it is possible to create innovative implementations of third party network applications by unlocking the proprietary boundaries of current mobile core networks or IP Multimedia Subsystems (IMSs) and virtualizing different mobile network systems into mobile-based stations. As such, NFV can help to increase data rates, improve the QoS, reduce operational complexity and increase processing capability such as call controls for VoIP.

2.4.1. *Overall description*

This use case aims at applying the NFV to mobile networks by consolidating different mobile network services into the virtualization environment, such as the mobile core network and mobile base station. If we consider the Evolved Packet Core (EPC) as the latest core network architecture for cellular systems, IMS can rely on the cloud communication platform to improve the VoLTE performance and other components related to mobile services. Also, the Radio Access Network (RAN) and Evolved Node B (eNodeB)-based stations can help to achieve resource sharing and dynamic allocation, as well as power reduction.

This section covers the architectures of several virtualized mobile networks, including virtualization of the mobile core network, IMS and mobile-based stations.

2.4.1.1. *Virtualization of mobile core network and IMS*

The architecture of the NFV over the mobile core network can scale dynamically, according to its specific resource requirements (e.g. capable to increase the resources for a specific VNF instance without impacting other VNF instances). According to this use case, a set of

VNFs (e.g. S/P-GW, Mobility Management Entity (MME)) can be scaled independently according to their specific resource requirements. For example, it allows flexible resources adding at data planes without affecting the performance of the control plane and vice versa.

Some examples of mobile core network functions and IMS network functions that can be virtualized as part of this use case are as follows:

– For mobile core network functions:

- EPC core and adjunct network functions, as Mobility Management Entity (MME), PP-GW and Policy and Charging Control Function (PCRF);

- 3G/EPC interworking network functions, as Serving GPRS Support Node (SGSN) and Gateway GPRS Support Node (GGSN).

– For IMS network functions, mainly Media Gateway Control Function (MGCF), Application Server(AS) and Interrogating/Proxy/ Serving Call Session Control Function (I/P/S-CSCF).

In fact, NFV-based virtualized mobile networks can coexist with non-virtualized ones, as illustrated in Figure 2.8. As most of the existing mobile core networks are not based on the NFV, network operators should be able to choose NFV deployment according to their migration plan. In particular, it is possible to virtualize only a fraction of the components or network functions in mobile networks, allowing network operators to deploy a set of virtualized core network functions, besides the non-virtualized ones. The virtualized network functions can be used for specific services or devices on demand. When the traffic exceeds the capacity of the non-virtualized network, the virtualized ones can be created dynamically, in real time.

Also, in order to achieve service continuity and availability, it is important to ensure resiliency for both control plane and data plane. As virtualization enables network functions to be decoupled from underlying hardware, new resiliency schemes can be developed by taking advantage of the portability of VNF instances, such as VM relocation and replication. Network operators should consider the design policies, to take into account the interactions between the non-virtualized and the virtual mobile cores. Nevertheless, there is no need for operators to know whether it is a virtual network function or a non-virtualized network function.

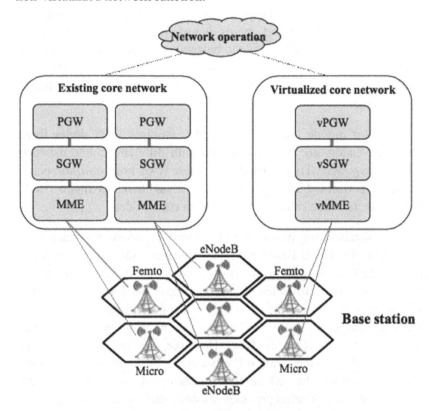

Figure 2.8. *Example of coexistence between virtualized and non-virtualized mobile core networks*

2.4.1.2. *Virtualization of mobile-based stations*

Mobile network traffic is significantly increasing according to the demands and needs generated by the use of mobile applications. As the emerging cellular network system, 3GPP LTE (third generation partnership project long-term evolution) specification leads to increased data rates, QoS, low complexity and cost reduction of the radio access and packet core. The virtualization mobile based station aims to consolidate different mobile network systems into based station virtualization, leverage IT virtualization technology, at least a part of the radio access network (RAN) nodes onto standard IT servers, storage and switches. It is expected to provide some benefits such as lower carbon footprint and energy consumption, thanks to dynamic resource allocation and traffic load balancing, simple management and operation processes and faster times in reaching the market. In addition, it aims to unlock the proprietary boundaries of mobile-based station nodes.

In major mobile operator's networks, multiple RAN nodes from multiple vendors are usually operated with different mobile network systems (e.g. 3G, LTE and WiMAX). These RAN node utilizations are typically performed in lower capacities than their maximum. Each RAN node resource cannot be shared with other nodes.

Virtualization for mobile-based stations is essentially related to RAN and virtualized Based Stations (BSs) necessary for overcoming the limitations of traditional RAN nodes while leveraging more efficient resource utilization. The centralized RAN technology with virtualization facilitates the aggregation of resources onto a centralized virtualization environment and optimization of resource utilization among different physical BSs. However, inside a RAN node, purpose-built hardware can still exist since all baseband processing functions cannot be efficiently implemented on software-based stations. BS virtualization provides resource sharing, dynamic resource allocation and power limitation. BS virtualization requires baseband radio processing using IT virtualization technology to perform virtualized real-time processing with high performance for signal processing capacity. Figure 2.9 presents an illustration of mobile-based station virtualization.

This architecture allows for the cohabitation of virtualized and non-virtualized network functions. The virtualized mobile-based station should support the partial deployment scenario that takes into account different functions and elements of the RAN part for different mobile network systems. For example, when the virtualized tranditional eNodeB cooperates with non-virtualized eNodeB, it requires a standardized X2 interface for inter communication, or when the virtualized Base Band Unit (BBU) pool cooperates with non-virtualized eNodeB, it also requires a standardized X2 interface for further communication.

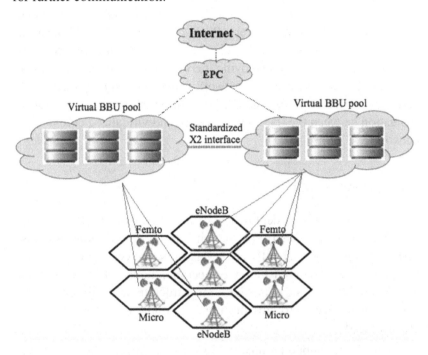

Figure 2.9. *Virtualization of the mobile-based station by using the centralized Baseband Unit (BBU) pool*

Some commercial companies such as NEC Corporation and NTT DOCOMO inc. [NEC 13] propose interoperable solutions for mobile networks that use virtualized EPC to improve telecom connectivity and enable fast delivery of new telecom services. The tests show that NEC's vEPC successfully operated on a virtualization platform, built by each partner, to achieve the mobile core network solution, based on the NFV and virtualized infrastructure. Also, NEC's vEPC solution achieves the NFV on a virtualization infrastructure running on a commercial off-the-shelf Intel server. NEC has also conducted joint testing of vCPE for in-home communication devices with Telefonica and has bolstered its effort toward SDN/NFV.

Another solution proposed by Nokia Solutions and Networks (NSN) with a leading global operator [SOL 12] aims to demonstrate the viability and feasibility of core virtualization and cloud management. A Proof of Concept (PoC) to identify the requirement for cloud computing in the mobile core network has been deployed. This PoC aims to focus on deploying network elements in the cloud, monitoring performance of network elements and dealing with hardware failures. Also, the NSN solution shows a comparative evaluation between the traditional network and virtualized core mobile network.

2.4.2. Threat analysis

The large increasing deployment of mobile broadband IP networks result in a large variety of security threats and vulnerabilities. These threats appear at different levels or interfaces such as service components level, administration or operation boundaries and between VNF component instances and NFV infrastructure. In the following, the main threats, specific to virtualization of mobile networks [MAC 13], are discussed:

– Attacks to mobile terminals: Most of the network traffic between mobile devices in the wireless APN is IP traffic. As most of the mobile devices are still relatively unprotected, attackers can gain access to the mobile networks. For example, a compromised mobile device can extensively scan other locally adjacent peers for consuming the limited spectrum. A compromised mobile device may allow attackers to perform automated scanning and sniffing. Also, the attackers can exploit mobile devices to launch DDoS attacks in order to make network services unavailable.

– Attacks to eNodeB/Femtocell/Microcell: To reduce the operational cost, many service operators and carriers are adopting virtualization technology, not only at the radio edge, in the mobility management infrastructure, but also in the core network. These hardware platforms and software components are capable of optimizing resources utilization while reducing operational costs. However, virtualization introduces vulnerabilities to the mobile networks. For example, a common eNodeB (4G base station) may use a virtualized Linux operating system instead of a custom operating system, which is explicitly hardened and more secure. If a virtualized eNodeB is compromised through the commercial hypervisor or operating system of the application (radio) software, the entire process will be compromised also. As eNodeB is considered as a trusted device, the attackers can exploit it and navigate to other internal devices, including management infrastructure. Similarly, if virtual radio edges are compromised, the overall network management infrastructure can be taken over by the attacker. Regardless of specific strategies, the attackers can eventually manage to disrupt network services or cause outages once they have penetrated into the network infrastructure.

– Attacks to IMS: It has been identified that a large variety of potential attacks can be launched in IMS core networks, primarily including the following:

- DoS or DDoS attacks: IMS can be overwhelmed by a tremendously large number of spoofed packets, originating from either a single location or multiple locations. The purpose of such attacks is to quickly exhaust the resources of IMS and make it fail to provide services to its legitimate users;

- fraud attack: this attack can occur in IMS in many different ways. For instance, an attacker can gain access to the IMS by hacking the interfaces or specific APIs, then further masquerades other users and acts as a gateway between the Public Switched Telephone Network (PSTN) and IMS.

– Lack of interoperability: Current mobile networks are mainly deployed with physical network functions and purpose-built hardware devices. Not all of them can adapt to the virtualization environment due to the built-in proprietary protocols. For example, RAN nodes are usually implemented on purpose-built hardware, because the baseband processing functions cannot be efficiently implemented on software. Considering this fact, an alternative solution is to make virtualized and non-virtualized network functions co-exist in the network. However, such heterogeneous mobile network environments involve sophisticated management tasks which can lead to challenging security issues. In particular, the lack of interoperability may allow the attackers to penetrate the mobile nodes, disrupt network services and gain complete control over the whole management infrastructure.

– Traffic interception: In virtualized mobile networks, the attackers can also snoop and intercept legitimate traffic, as in traditional mobile networks. As identified in [MAC 13], many types of traffic can be intercepted in mobile networks, such as the edge cache traffic and phone calls. More specifically, the attackers can manipulate the frequently requested content that is stored at the edge of the mobile network or they can track and intercept VoLTE traffic. Moreover, the attackers can intercept data communication incoming to and outgoing from the Internet.

– Loose access control: Location and access record are sometimes treated as privacy for mobile cloud subscribers. In the virtualized mobile networks, the entire network services are migrated to the cloud infrastructure, leading to security threats that are inherited from the underlying infrastructure. And so, as traditional access control methods are often insufficient, limited confidentiality for controls, not only exposes the data to additional vulnerabilities, but also causes violation of security policies, regulations or contract terms.

– Insecure content and media delivery: The number of mobile device users has grown sharply, as have the number of mobile attacks, in number and sophistication. Attackers are motivated to steal data, identities and intercept corporate IMS services. As in virtualized environments, the data are stored in the public infrastructure and frequently accessed by multiple users. A variety of threats and potential attacks are possible, without sufficient protection schemes for both data (stored and in transit).

2.4.3. Security requirements

Based on the threat analysis, we provide a set of corresponding countermeasures to defend against or mitigate the potential attacks:

– Security by design in virtualized mobile-based stations: As all those mobile network endpoints, including mobile station and mobile devices, cannot be fully trusted, it is important for service providers to design a secure infrastructure, from the top layer (business application services) to the lower layer (NFV infrastructure). Additional security services for each layer need to be well-defined with appropriate security solutions.

– Security service on demand: In general, the virtualized infrastructure provides a kind of shelter for network protection, but it still needs to maintain open connections for external users. In addition to the security mechanisms that are tailored for hypervisors or other virtualization technology, some examples of security services such as firewalls, IPS/IDS and DPI can be used to mitigate the risks.

– Virtualization transparency to network control and management: As other virtual networks, the virtualization of mobile networks also require confidentiality assurance when data are processed over untrusted cloud infrastructure. In other words, the data should remain confidential and be disclosed only with the users' permission. Since the users differ in privileges, data access must be individualized and restricted to authorized users. In particular, data protection in an untrusted environment normally can be achieved by using the following schemes:

- security policy enforcement: one of the benefits of NFV is to enable the users and service providers to enforce centralized policies to improve control over traffic flow, as well as network programmability and payload elasticity. An example of policy enforcement is discussed in [GIO 15], with a focus on establishing the baseline architecture that is capable of orchestrating and facilitating a rapid deployment of diverse VNFs. In particular, the policies are used to define the behavior of entities within a managed environment of the NFV infrastructure;

- authentication and authorization: basically, authentication and authorization are used to verify the user's identity, for their privileges or rights to access to the target resources, and then their permissions are granted accordingly. For example, the role-based access control or attribute-based access control can be candidate mechanisms;

- security zoning and segmentation: in the NFV, security zoning and segmentation services are provided to allow network service appliances to be effectively managed in a secure environment. More specifically, security levels can be specified to differ in the zones, for example between the Internet edge security zone, client systems security zone and network services security zone;

- security monitoring and forensics: security monitoring plays an important role in detecting threats and mitigating attacks in network virtualization. The monitoring scope can cover network traffic, VNFs, as well as other activities that may pose security threats. This is one of the basic requirements of the network service management system to ensure end-to-end service monitoring on the virtualized resources (VNF instances), while allowing frequent and real-time interactions;

- encryption: to protect data confidentiality and integrity, encryption schemes are always applied to the data that are outsourced to the (untrusted) networks. However, in a multi-tenant environment, an additional key management layer is necessary for generating, managing, distributing and revoking the cryptographic keys.

2.5. Fixed access network functions virtualization

It is well-known that the major performance bottleneck generally occurrs at the network access. For the wireline fixed access network, most of the prevalent broadband access technologies are based on Digital Subscriber Lines (DSLs), and network equipment is normally owned and operated by a single organizational entity. Considering the fact that virtualization can support multi-tenancy, more than one organizational entity can be assigned with a dedicated partition of a virtual access node. As a result, the virtualized broadband access node enables the co-location of wireless access nodes from different organizational entities in a common NFV platform framework (e.g. common NFVI-PoPs) for reducing the deployment costs and the overall energy consumption.

2.5.1. *Overall description*

This use case aims to provide low cost, minimal power consumption, automated provisioning and limited hardware complexity at the remote node by moving this complexity to operate at the head end, while improving the degree of future proofing through centralized software updates. Energy consumption can be reduced at different stages or level, when deploying access to the NFV:

– node level, where the energy can be reduced through power adjustable components, low power components and complexity reduction;

– link level, where the energy can be reduced by dynamic adaptation of different operational parameters and sleep modes;

– network level, where the energy can be reduced by selecting and forcing nodes/links to a sleep mode, under particular conditions and through resource consolidation, cooperative relaying and green routing.

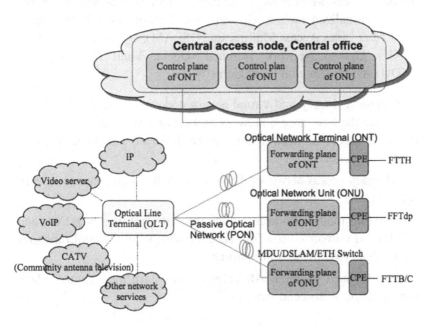

Figure 2.10. *An example of the access network function virtualization: the forwarding plane is separated from the control plane, while the control plane runs at the central office. For a color version of this figure, see www.iste.co.uk/zhang/networks.zip*

Access network functions virtualization is applied initially to the hybrid fiber DSL node, such as fiber to the cabinet (FTTcab) and fiber to the distribution point (FTTdp), which is deployed as a layer 2 functionality, as shown in Figure 2.10. The network elements and control plane functionalities can be separated and run in the NFV platform, in which the control functions are deployed in the central office. An NFV abstraction layer is used to facilitate the control and functional distribution of the centralized network setup configuration. This layer enables high level configuration through the control of centralized network functionalities, by providing abstraction flows and services definitions, that can be used by service providers to transform their network service configuration into a concrete parameter configuration for further consolidation of various network functions in the access network. The target network functions in access nodes that can be virtualized include Optical Line Termination (OLT), Digital Subscriber Lines Access Multiplexer (DSLAM), Optical Network Unit (ONU), Optical Network Terminal (ONT), Multi Dwelling Unit (MDU) and Distribution Point Unit (DPU).

Moreover, legacy and virtual access nodes can coexist in order to mutualize the fiber access network and service platforms. In addition, the fixed access network nodes can be deployed into three different models, as follows:

– Legacy access networks: Each network function contains its own control plane.

– Hybrid mode: The access node supports both legacy (xDSL and FTTH) and virtualized (FTTdp) access nodes, whose control functions are implemented in the central office.

– NFV-based solution: All access nodes have their control plane virtualization at the central office.

As such, access network function virtualization could require a heterogeneous set of resources, an abstraction layer and a common northbound interface to hide the complexity. Access network function virtualization provides rich interfaces, shared by different access technologies. Additionally, it provides a single platform for different applications, user and tenants. Service providers can share a pool of managed connectivity resources that can be dynamically allocated and combined, to deploy on demand services, across different users. As a result, broadband resources utilization is more efficient, facilitating the emergence of new business models.

2.5.2. *Threat analysis*

Although access network functions virtualization provides additional benefits to support multi-tenancy in terms of low cost, minimizing power consumption and provision automation, they are still faced with threats and vulnerabilities. This section addresses all the possible threats:

– Control plane attacks: The concept of the fixed access network virtualization aims to shares the fiber backhaul, power connection and associated centralized computational resources by moving the control plane to operate and manage at the central office. This is correct in terms of configuration; hence, the administrator can easily configure access network nodes remotely, reduce time consumption and is flexible in adding new network services or scale network capacity on the fly. However, controlling and managing all services at one point in the central office may raise the single point of failure and control plane attacks. This control plane is considered to be the brain of all operations. If attacks and vulnerabilities occur inside the control plane, then the entire network services are affected. In case the control plane is compromised, attackers can disrupt the data path. For example, altering the traffic flow, reconfiguring the access network nodes or re-changing policy rules.

– DoS/DDoS attacks: The terminology of DoS/DDoS attacks are not a newborn concept, but they pose a real security risk to the fixed access network function virtualization when executing various network services in parallel. DoS/DDoS attacks are a well-known technique to make a service incapable of responding to the client requests. The attackers may expose a target system to a large number of requests in order to overload the link capacity, resulting in a temporary halt response, in which the access network node can no longer serve other client requests.

– Compromising the management interfaces: legacy and virtual access nodes can coexist to share the fiber access network, common aggregation and service platforms. Particularly, the fixed access network nodes can be deployed into three different models: (i) pure legacy access networks, (ii) hybrid mode where the access node supports both legacy and virtualized access nodes and (iii) virtualized access nodes-based NFV solution. However, for both cases, they can be faced with management interface compromise [PÉK 13], as interfaces allow network operators to interact remotely with access network nodes that have been located in different locations. This can be done through management interfaces. Such interfaces let administrators and management systems connect to the device and allow them to access the resources. The lack of management interface, especially in design and implementation phases, can pose a backdoor and open up security vulnerabilities. Adversaries may take this benefit to gain privileged access to the access network nodes, operate illegal activities and perform harmful behaviors, such as shutdown, reboot and reconfigure traffic paths according to their desire.

– Not well-defined policy, SLAs, and isolation: virtualization provides additional benefits to support multiple tenancy, in which more than one organizational entity can be co-allocated in a dedicated partition of a virtual access node. For example, a single fibre-DSL node (FTTcab and FTTdp) can be deployed and dedicated to several organization entities in parallel. However, the term of service requirement, resource management and bandwidth allocation that is assigned for each particular entity could be involved with SLAs and policy enforcement. Thus, the lack of clearly defined SLAs and policy rules can pose security problems. The attackers could gain access to the virtualized access node and thus be able to control all operations running within its node such as accessing confidential data, re-changing configuration settings and re-routing the traffic paths.

– Hardware attacks: let us consider the hardware part of the access network device, where the existing access network devices can also pose security breaches. Generally, hardware design and manufacturing occur before or during software development; as a result, it is important to address on hardware security in the product lifecycle. If attackers compromise the hardware, then software security mechanisms that are running on the devices are useless. In [PAG 13], the author discusses about the common hardware attacks as the following:

- manufacturing backdoors for malware or other penetrative purposes;

- eavesdropping by gaining access to protected memory without opening other hardware;
- inducing faults by causing the interruption of normal behavior;
- hardware modification tampering with invasive operations through jailbroken software;
- backdoor creation for bypassing illegal access;
- and counterfeiting hardware assets that can produce extraordinary operations and to gain malicious access to the system.

In addition, the authors in [GED 12] also investigated hardware vulnerability and proposed security solutions to defend against cyber attacks. For example, to design automation tools to improve the trustworthiness or hardware that can support software to provide secure execution throughout a cyber physical system's lifetime. Also to provide a trusted base for computing if the hardware is trustworthy or secure, thus this can help to build a secure system from trusted hardware primitives.

2.5.3. *Security requirements*

Virtualization is a powerful technology for increasing the efficiency of computing services including fixed access network function virtualization. However, besides the advantages, it also raises a number of security issues as already discussed above. In this section, we emphasize on security requirements to countermeasure the security threats.

– Secure management and orchestration: When fixed access functions are moved to virtualization, secure management and orchestration can help to improve security analysis and mitigate security risks. If virtualized access nodes are well-defined and orchestrated, all operations have to fulfill security needs. For example, the way to define the bandwidth resources shared between multiple organizational entities without being compromised by each other depend on the management interfaces that should be implemented in a secure manner. Also, data flow through the virtualized access nodes and the data packets are securely transmitted.

– Establish trust relationship: For trusted NFV, ETSI NFV security [ETS 14b] defines network services that can be created, managed and communicated with other network services in a secure manner. The trust definition also encompasses a variety of assurance elements including identity, attribution, attestation and non-repudiation. As a result, any particular virtualized access node's deployment that relies on NFV implementation needs to be evaluated for the trust relationship, whether an entity (entity A) should trust another entity (entity B). Thus, the evaluation process can be performed based on the contracts, policy rules and guidelines. If one of the VNF services is not trusted, a trust relationship becomes unworkable. Additionally, the trust relationship can be built, maintained and revoked by using a Certificate Authority (CA), which is considered as a key service in NFV contexts. Clearly, CA is applied to certify VNF components across various vendors, certify hardware components and identify management and orchestration of various NFV components. Moreover, the ETSI NFV security has divided the trust relationship into three levels: (i) intra-VNF trust, the trust within VNFs, (ii) inter-VNF trust, the trust between VNFs and (iii) extra-VNF trust, the trust with external VNFs.

– Policy and isolation: More than one organizational entities are associated to one virtualized access node, so that each network service may require multi-tenancy. Therefore, control policies of the virtualized access network should be implemented and maintained in an appropriate manner, for providing the same level of security that each legacy access network would have. Thus, preventing suspicious activity that could lead to security risks and protecting the underlying physical infrastructure from any unforeseen attacks initiated by workloads from virtualized access networks are carried out.

– Separation of roles: When legacy-fixed access network functions are moved to the virtualization environment, the entire network services with layer 2 and control plane functionality are controlled and managed directly by the administrators at the central office. In case the administrators are malicious parties, they can take complete control over network services. Therefore, it is essential to identify the administrative roles based on their functionality, duties and access rights. For example, a storage administrator should not get (by default) an access to network functions, firewalls or monitoring services. On the other hand, multi-factor authentication and Role-based Access Control (RBAC) should also be considered to reduce the risk from a malicious supervisor.

– Securing the network, end-to-end security and authentication: Virtualized access nodes can be faced with several kind of network attacks (eavesdropping, spoofing and man-in-the-middle attacks), as similar to other virtual network services. The effective way to protect against these attacks is by using appropriate security mechanisms. Some security solutions are as follows:

- using IPSec and SSL/TLS mechanisms – to protect the links between two communication entities;

- using the VLAN mechanism – to mitigate the security risks by disallowing virtual guest tagging and disallowing the attacker to plug or get access to its communication channel;

- and performing cross checking and authentication of Address Resolution Protocol (ARP) – to verify authorized access.

Also, these mechanisms can be deployed to protect the new threats, introduced by NFV scenarios.

– Adequate logging and monitoring: The logging and monitoring of all activities in a deployed virtual environment are highly recommended. Logs and monitoring should be assigned directly for every specific physical-fixed access network's nodes (OLT, ONT, ONU, MDU, DPU and DSLAM). The benefit of this function is to contribute to identify and analyze the data breaches coming from either, any compromised behaviors that affect the integrity of communication channels, or event logs from security controls and segmentation operations. Meanwhile, the information gathered from the log can be used for further forensics analysis.

– Disable unused interfaces: Unused physical interfaces should be disabled in order to control the attack surface and limit the cause of damage. These interfaces of virtualized access nodes should be restricted in terms of control, as it can simultaneously provide access to the legacy access nodes.

2.6. Concluding remarks

In this chapter, we consider five NFV use cases to comparatively study their objectives and architectures. For example, use case 1 targets at Network Functions Virtualization Infrastructure as a Service (NFVIaaS), which provides underlying resources (e.g. processing, storage, networks and other fundamental computing resources) to support VNF instances; use case 2 is about Virtual Network Platform as a Service (VNPaaS), which provides toolkits and pre-configuration to users for convenient development, deployment and management of VNF instances. The capability of the VNPaaS allows users to arbitrarily modify and reconfigure their own network services based on their particular business needs. The purpose of studying these use cases is to understand the fundamental impact of the NFV on traditional networks in terms of both advantages and shortcomings. We conclude that all the studied use cases illustrate the NFV advantages in terms of rapid service innovation through a software-centric approach, reduced hardware cost, improved operational efficiency, shortened development lifecycle of network service and elastic scalable network functions. The latest developments of NFV technology in both industry and academia are thoroughly investigated as well.

Driven by the use cases, an in-depth layer specific threat analysis is conducted for identifying the novel vulnerabilities of each NFV scenario. For example, a large set of vulnerabilities, especially the ones in the NFV infrastructure and VM hypervisors, are commonly shared by more than one use cases. We therefore conclude that the security threats in the NFV infrastructure, as those identified in use case 1 and use case 2, deserve more attention and careful studies than the ones in upper layers. In other words, the lower the layer of the security vulnerabilities, the higher is the threat they may pose to NFV-based network services. Hopefully, our use case-driven threat analysis can help to establish a comprehensive threat taxonomy, laying down a basis for NFV service providers and users to further analyze the potential security threats of specific scenarios.

As a result of threat analysis, we identify the fundamental security requirements for each use case. As such, potential countermeasures for attack prevention, detection, mitigation and reaction can be holistically studied. Although a majority of existing security mechanisms have been proposed, their actual implementations and deployment remain unclear. In the next chapter, we specifically discuss this point. In particular, it is worth mentioning that one of the interesting findings is that NFV offers an opportunity to adopt security or privacy by using the design approach.

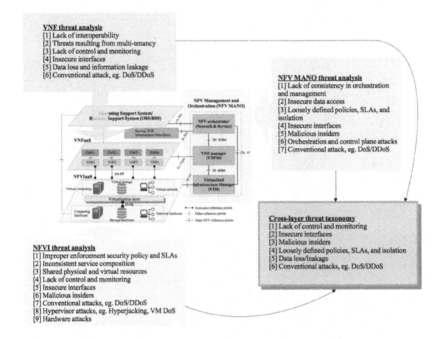

Figure 2.11. *NFV-layer specific threat taxonomy based on the ETSI NFV architecture. For a color version of this figure, see www.iste.co.uk/zhang/networks.zip*

The five use cases-driven threat analyses discussed in the previous section can finally allow us to establish a comprehensive threat taxonomy, ultimately laying down a foundation to design NFV-based effective security mechanisms. For better illustration, we refer to the

ETSI NFV reference architecture and further conduct a layer-specific threat taxonomy as shown in Figure 2.11. For each NFV layer, we also identify the corresponding security requirements, with the purpose to mitigate and protect the novel security threats and vulnerabilities introduced by NFV.

3

NFV-based Security Management

Today's network infrastructure is being significantly changed by the emerging networking technologies like SDN and NFV. The industry has especially attempted to put NFV to practical use in order to accelerate the transition to a new era for cloud computing networks. In addition to the advantages of changing the entire landscape of the market, such as improving product capabilities and shortening and simplifying the service chain and application provisioning processes to meet new user requirements, NFV has the potential to enhance the security of a wide spectrum of networking services. For example, the dedicated hardware-based security appliances, such as deep packet inspection (DPI), firewall, IPS and IDS, can be shifted to the virtual appliances that interface directly with hypervisor and NFV orchestration platforms. In particular, the platforms can significantly simplify security management and increase the network security posture for both service providers and users thanks to the dynamic nature of NFV infrastructure, which offers easy and flexible manners to create and manage security functions over virtualized infrastructure. For example, a network administrator can automate the placement of virtualized firewalls, create dedicated software-based firewalls on demand to protect specific network domains, and remotely update security rules of deployed firewalls.

The rest of this book is devoted to the discussion of security functions for NFV, covering NFV-based security management (this chapter) and the implementations of several basic security mechanisms such as identity and access management (IAM) (in Chapter 4), IDS/IPS (in Chapter 5), network isolation (in Chapter 6) and data protection (in Chapter 7).

In this chapter, we investigate NFV-based security management. First, we address the need to have built-in security mechanisms for NFV-based infrastructure and platforms. We then exemplify the deployment and management of middleboxes, which are essential for network security management, in the context of NFV, and discuss the feasibility of security services orchestration. Finally, a number of existing NFV platforms are discussed and compared in terms of their capabilities of hosting security management.

3.1. Essential security requirements

Basically, one of the fundamental requirements of using virtualized network functions is that the desirable features of the original networks should remain intact. More importantly, the essential security properties must be preserved. However, virtualized network functions (VNFs) may run in datacenters that are either owned by network operators or outsourced to third parties, potentially leading to a broader attack surface and introducing new security threats along with the benefits. In particular, as pointed out in [ETS 14b], the dynamic nature of NFV requires that security policies, mechanisms, functions, processes and practices must be embedded in the genetic fabric of NFV. To meet these requirements, we exemplify three major security use cases and identify the challenges. One of the major motivations is that by seamlessly integrating security properties into NFV service architecture, the complexity and load of security management can be significantly reduced.

– Security external to VNFs (Extra-NFVSec): Extra-NFVSec deeply relies on the security of physical infrastructure, executing environment, and external services. The following characteristics identify key issues that directly impact VNF and VNFC (virtual network function component) security.

- Regulatory impacts on NFV deployment: first of all, the service providers need to take into account high-level security requirements, including lawful interception, auditing and SLAs. In particular, as future NFV deployment will increasingly take place across borders, multiple sets of requirements will be placed on the operators. Each of these requirements supposes well-identified trust and security settings to ensure that every process is performed appropriately under security guidelines.

- Authentication, authorization and accounting for NFV: as a matter of fact, the deployment of NFV is a very complex process. One VNF component can be operated by multiple administrative domains, cooperating among each other between NFV infrastructure (e.g. network, hypervisor, compute, storage) SDN, service network, VNF manager, and orchestration module for serving desired service-level expectations to users. This clearly indicates that authentication, authorization and accounting are essential requirements to preserve the security of VNFs.

– Security between virtual network functions (Infra-VNFSec): the VNFs that communicate directly with each other have special security needs, as generally network-level security requirements are not automatically inherited from security on communication path. In general, the essential characteristics of infra-VNFSec must include the following:

- secure orchestration between VNF domains;
- flows generally go through firewalls or other network policy enforcement points;
- service chaining capabilities need to be enforced, if available;
- strong VNF-VNF security measures and individual VNF resiliency to attacks.

– Security within virtual network functions (Intra-VNFSec): within VNFs, security measures and processes are required for VNF and VNFC operations, as well as secure interfaces to interact with external assets and services. Some general security characteristics of intra-VNFSec can be discussed as follows:

- Sensitive authentication data in workloads[1]: data in workloads should be protected during its whole lifecycle. Thus, trusted lifecycles should be carefully considered in order to maintain confidentiality at a sufficient level, ranging from VNF instantiation, operation, to retirement.

- VNF instantiation: when a VNF instance is initiated, secure boot is required to ensure that the system boots using only software that is trusted and signed by its provider. In the NFV context, secure boot of one VNFC instance is controlled by VNF manager (VNFM), which is responsible for maintaining the boot integrity and assuring that the VNFC has been operated in a secure way. In addition, security process of VNF instantiation may require other assurance processes, such as attestation, authentication and authorization mechanisms, to improve the security level of VNF instances.

- VNF operation: during the VNF operational phase, appropriate security control for each VNFC should be well-defined, for example by using role-based access control (RBAC) or attribute-based access control (ABAC) to control access. Only an authorized entity is granted access to the requested services/resources. According to NFV, the authorization process may be controlled by an entity in the chain of trust like an AAA (Authentication, Authorization, Access) server.

- VNF retirement: when VNF and associated VNFCs are decommissioned or removed, there are two processes that have to be performed: one is license retirement by unregistering all the relevant certificates and licenses from retired VNF/VNFCs, another is to erase the data that is relevant to VNF/VNFCs in memory and storage, including RAM on the hypervisor, local and remote storage.

– Function and capability authorization control for VNFs: as a huge set of networking functions and capabilities can be enabled by VNF, the inter-dependency makes it impossible to always provide appropriate authentication for an entity to access these functions. Also, the authorization for using these functions and capabilities can be implemented by a number of different techniques. As a

---

1 The workload here refers to the amount of processes/works handled by a set of VNF components to serve/deliver/complete one service.

result, it is necessary to consider security requirements separately in different operations, such as: VNFC creation, VNFC deletion, VNFC configuration and package management, VNFC migration, VNFC operational state changes, VNFC topology changes, VNFC scale up/down and scale in/out.

Moreover, some deployment cases also require an external operational environment. The following guidelines have been documented for such cases:

– External physical security guidance: refers to the standards for physical security requirements, including facility, specialized hardware, and other considerations that are served in confidentiality, integrity, availability and audit for NFV.

– External hardware guidance: focuses on trusted computing base (TCB) which acts as a set of hardware, software and functional components to provide the system with a secure environment by enforcing appropriate security policies.

– External service guidance: relies on external services for further enhancing security in the system, such as:

- Domain Name Service (DNS): ensures the ability to update images with relevant DNS information.

- IP addressing, Dynamic Host Configuration Protocol (DHCP), and routing: ensures the ability to update images relevant to IP addressing, so that a VNF instance acting as a router or DHCP must be validated before routes.

- Time services and Network Time Protocol (NTP): ensures the ability to update images with current time zone information.

- Geolocation: ensures the ability to update images with relevant geolocation information.

- Security visibility and testing: ensures security outside the NFV such as security monitoring, vulnerability scanning, penetration testing and event log reporting.

- Certificate authority: allows a trust relationship between different VNF components within any given NFV context so that it can certify VNF components across various domains.

- Identity and access management (IAM): manages user's credential assets when new VNF is instantiated, suspended or retired.

– External policies, processes, and practices guidance: involves unique aspects of policies, processes and practices that should exist in the external environment for supporting and maintaining NFV security.

- Regulatory compliance: ensures that every process complies with the relevant laws and regulations.

- Forensic consideration: ensures that all the forensic investigation activities are executed according to the law enforcement standards.

- Lawful interception and SLAs: ensures that all the effective lawful interception and SLA requirements are satisfied.

3.2. Middleboxes

The past years have witnessed a sharp increase in Internet services, making network management and configuration extremely complicated, especially due to a wide spectrum of additional appliances. Thus, multiple functional middleboxes are introduced to the networking infrastructure to improve its manageability. Several examples of middleboxes are given as follows:

– Improved security, such as firewalls and IDS which are used to secure network from intruders.

– Improved performance, such as a load balancing proxy server installed in a network to distribute network flows into the target server.

– Reduced bandwidth costs, such as WAN optimizers to maximize the efficiency of data flow across a wide area network.

However, non-trivial infrastructure and management costs are incurred due to their sophisticated and specialized processing, various management tools for different devices and vendors, as well as the need to consider policy specification and interactions between these appliances and network infrastructures.

3.2.1. *Issues with the current middleboxes*

Let's give an example scenario, in which a company network needs to cover several departments that have different objectives and security requirements. Usually the pre-installed security service in a certain department cannot be applied to others. Cloud datacenter networks are another interesting example showing the complexities of network management because a large set of diverse security requirements covering multiple tenants and sub-cloud networks should be specified. Then, each tenant may require for different security functions to achieve their demands. One of the great challenges of current management is to make flexible and efficient security resource utilization.

Large capital expenditure. To improve security and performance of modern enterprise networks, middlebox processing services are almost ubiquitously deployed. Unfortunately, as the authors pointed out in [SHE 12], today's middlebox infrastructure is expensive, complex to manage, and creates the pain points of network administrators in terms of difficulty. The failures may also occur when middleboxes interact with each other. The study shows that the middleboxes impose significant infrastructure change and management overhead across a spectrum of enterprise networks. Even though the number of middleboxes are not very large, their deployment can be costly and require high upfront investment in hardware. For example, a very large network with more than 100k hosts can cost more than million dollars on middlebox hardware, while the median networks with 1k–10k hosts may cost 50K to 500K dollars.

High management complexity and operational expenses. Clearly, handling a large set of heterogeneous devices requires broad expertise and consequently a large management team. As reported in [SHE 12], even a small network composing of only tens of middleboxes may require a management team of 6–25 people. Also, most administrators have to spend one to five hours per week dealing with middleboxes failures, 9% spent between six to 10 hours per week. It has been recognized that the top three most common issues with middlebox deployment are misconfiguration, overload and physical/electrical failure, and a major cause of failure is misconfiguration. Also, as stated in [QAZ 13], ensuring the traffic to be directed through the desired sequence of middleboxes requires significant manual effort and operator expertise. This complexity stems from the need to carefully plan the network topology, manually set up rules to route the traffic through the desired middleboxes, and implement safeguards to guarantee correct operations in the presence of any failures and overload.

Non-optimal deployment of security middleboxes. Considering the aforementioned issues, it is important to specify on which location the middleboxes have to be installed in order to achieve the expected security, while minimizing the overall costs. In fact, most middleboxes provide specific security functions. For example, we usually apply firewalls to control network access, NIDS to monitor malicious attacks in network payloads, and network behavior anomaly detection (NBAD) to detect DDoS attacks. Nevertheless, the network operators have to choose reasonable security functions and middleboxes while deploying them into appropriate locations in order to achieve the best protection coverage. In practice, as the authors argued in [SHI 15], it is difficult to place security middleboxes with unpredictable threats coming from different network's tenants, and it is a tough task for network operators to configure middleboxes without any errors. Especially for multi-tenancy environments, these installed security functions may not lie in the optimal location to offer the best security service.

Lack of fine-grained control. As the analysis given in [GEM 13] describes, today's middleboxes have very limited configuration policies and narrow range in parameter manipulation. Also, the internal algorithms and operational states are completely inaccessible and unmodifiable. Apparently, it lacks fine-grained control and offers no way to understand the behavior of middleboxes, such as how middleboxes examine and modify network traffic. As a result, many negative consequences may occur, such as lack of the capability to re-route traffic flows across middleboxes, lack of scalability to meet cost performance, and lack of reliability in case of middleboxes failures.

Lack of efficiency. As the authors pointed out in [SEK 12], today's middlebox infrastructure has been developed in a largely uncoordinated manner. A new form of middleboxes typically emerges as a one-off solution to meet specific needs, then it is patched into the infrastructure through *ad hoc* and manual techniques. This leads to serious inefficiency on two aspects:

1) Inefficiency in the use of infrastructure hardware resources: middlebox applications are typically resource intensive and each one is usually deployed as a stand-alone device and independently provisioned for peak load. This makes these resources hard to be amortized across applications even though their workloads offer natural opportunities to do so.

2) Inefficient in management: each type of today's middlebox applications has its own custom configuration interfaces, without hooks or tools that offer network administrators a unified view to manage middleboxes across the network.

Clearly, these inefficiencies in terms of management resource utilization are increasingly critical issues for network deployment, considering the fact that the deployment of middleboxes continues to grow in both scale and variety.

3.2.2. *Improvements through NFV*

In the previous section, we discussed the middlebox issues by taking advantage of SDN and NFV. Some improvements are discussed in the rest of this section.

Reducing deployment and management complexity. In [QAZ 13], the authors show that SDN can simplify the policy enforcement at middleboxes, thanks to the logically centralized management and the separation between data plane and control plane. Also, SDN provides programmability for configuring traffic forwarding rules [CAS 07]. In particular, the network operators are allowed to specify logical middlebox routing policies, which are automatically translated into forwarding rules by taking into account the physical topology, switch capacities, and middlebox resource constraints. In general, SDN-enabled middleboxes can achieve the following functions:

– Composition: network policies typically require packets to go through a sequence of middleboxes, e.g. firewall, IDS, IPS, proxy, while SDN can eliminate the need to manually plan the middleboxes' placement or pre-configure the routes to enforce such policies.

– Load balancing: a key factor of middlebox deployment is to balance the processing load to avoid overloading that results from packet processing complexity in the middleboxes. SDN provides the flexibility to implement load balancing algorithms in the network and avoids the need for network operators to manually install traffic splitting rules.

– Packet modifications: as middleboxes are able to modify packet headers (e.g. NATs) and even change session level behaviors (e.g. WAN optimizers, proxies), the network operators have to place middleboxes carefully. For example:

- Placing an IDS after the proxy to ensure that all traffic traverses to all the middleboxes.

- Carefully identifying the appropriate network devices to deal with specific threats.

- Manually performing configuration on each network device.

From a network wide view, SDN can address these concerns by taking into account dynamic packet transformations.

Improving controllability of middleboxes. In [GEM 13], a software-defined middleboxes networking (SDMBN) framework was proposed to control the behavior of middleboxes, with an objective to improve the flexibility and efficiency of middleboxes, while reducing management overhead. In particular, the framework aims to solve the problems such as how to make the middleboxes examine and modify the network traffic, how to configure policies, and how to preserve the correctness and fidelity of middlebox operations. By doing so, it offers useful abstractions for fine-grained, software-driven control of the middlebox's internals without wresting too much control away from the middleboxes themselves. Therefore, it simplifies management of complex middlebox deployments and leads to a variety of rich dynamic middlebox control scenarios.

Improving efficiency of middleboxes. As mentioned previously, today's middleboxes are developed in a largely uncoordinated manner, where it seems difficult to properly operate a large number of middleboxes to meet the user requirements. Thus, consolidating middleboxes (CoMb) architecture was presented in [SEK 12] to tackle the problem of management inefficiencies in today's middlebox deployment, as they are built and managed as stand-alone devices and independently provisioned. Specifically, the architecture takes a top-down design approach, consolidating and systematically constructing middlebox infrastructure at two levels, as follows:

– Individual middleboxes: CoMb decouples the hardware and software, enabling software-based implementations of middlebox applications to run on a consolidated hardware platform.

– Managing a group of middleboxes: CoMb consolidates the management of different middleboxes' applications/devices into a single (logically) centralized controller. This controller takes a unified and network-wide view configuration, accounting for the policy requirements across all network traffic, applications, and network locations. There is a fundamental difference from today's middlebox deployments, where each middlebox application and networking device is managed independently.

In general, CoMb architecture presents an opportunity to systematically explore the potential of NFV and SDN for consolidating middlebox applications provided by different vendors, allowing them to run on a shared hardware platform, and managed in a logically centralized manner. In fact, the use of centralization to simplify network management has already been introduced in [MCK 08, GRE 05, CAE 05].

Improving manageability and security as a whole. As we previously analyzed, today's enterprise networks are often large, run a wide variety of applications and protocols, and typically operate under strict reliability and security constraints. Also, substantial manual configuration by trained operators is usually required in order to achieve even moderate security. To address these issues, a novel network architecture called Ethane was proposed in [CAS 07], which achieves three fundamental design principles:

– The network is governed by policy declaration at a high level: networks are more easily managed in terms of entities such as users, hosts, and access points, than using low-level identifiers. For example, it is more convenient to declare what services can be used by which users and who is allowed to connect to which machines.

– Policy determines the path that packets go through: there are several reasons for policy to specify the paths. First, policy might require packets to pass through an intermediated middlebox. For example, a guest user might be required to communicate via a proxy, or the user of an unpatched operating system might be required to communicate through an IDS. Second, traffic can be handled with better quality if its path is controlled. For example, directing real time communications over lightly loaded paths, critical communications over redundant paths, and private communications over paths inside a trusted boundary would all lead to better services. These allow network administrators to determine the paths via high-level policy, which is specified using high-level names, finally leading to finer level control and greater visibility than the current design of middleboxes.

– The network should enforce a strong binding between a packet and its origin: today it is difficult to reliably determine the origin of packets due to dynamic change of addresses, and they are easily spoofed. The loose binding between users and their traffic is a constant target for attacks in enterprise networks. If the network is governed by a policy declaration with high-level names (e.g. users, hosts), then the packet should be accurately identified as coming from a particular physical entity. This requires a strong binding between users, the machine they are using, and the addresses generated in the packets. It is necessary to keep consistent binding all the time by tracking users and machines when they move.

Optimal deployment of security middlebox. In order to achieve best security and network performance, the middleboxes should be placed in the most appropriate locations. In [SHI 15], the authors propose a number of routing algorithms to redirect suspicious or malicious traffic to the dedicated security middleboxes, in which security functions are dynamically virtualized. It is a fact that today's DDoS defense mechanisms mainly rely on expensive and proprietary hardware appliances deployed at fixed locations. By using new networking paradigms SDN and NFV, a flexible and elastic DDoS defense system called Bohatei is proposed in [FAY 15] for addressing the key DDoS defense challenges with respect to scalability, responsiveness and adversary-resilience. In particular, two dynamic optimization algorithms are developed to redirect the DDoS traffic to the ISP datacenters, then further datacenter servers. DDoS countermeasure functions are then dynamically created and loaded into VM instances of datacenter servers, eventually mitigating DDoS traffic according to their particular patterns.

3.3. Security service orchestration

Although the feasibility of implementing security functions for NFV has been validated, it is still unclear how the basic security functions can be dynamically and optimally orchestrated for particular NFV use cases. This section starts with a general framework, as shown in Figure 3.1, and focuses on discussing the orchestration module that bridges the needs of users and basic security functions.

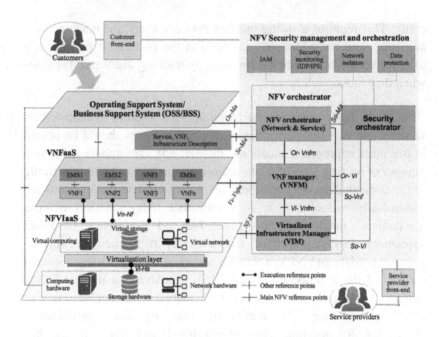

Figure 3.1. *Conceptual architecture of NFV security management and orchestration. For a color version of this figure, see www.iste.co.uk/zhang/networks.zip*

3.3.1. *High-level features*

In general, as discussed in [DUT 14, LEM 14], the advantages of an orchestration framework can be summarized as follows.

1) Lower cost of ownership: as NFV can reduce CAPEX/OPEX by migrating network functions from expensive proprietary hardware to lower cost commodity hardware, and from dedicated devices to virtual machines, the same advantages will apply to the security functions. NFV itself enables advanced security functions, such as security zoning, Deep Packet Inspection (DPI), automated security assessment and remediation. So, moving security functions from dedicated hardware devices to software-based environments will allow security administrators to achieve high-level agility and efficient service deployment.

2) Simplifying service architecture and reducing management complexity: as hardware-based network functions can be implemented via software, the number of hardware devices can be reduced, naturally improving physical security, since there are fewer devices and fewer datacenters for taking control. Also, attack surface can be potentially reduced, due to the separation of hypervisor software from hardware. As a matter of fact, the complexity of hypervisor software is limited; therefore, the attack surface resulting from the hypervisor is bounded.

3) Improving scalability for massive attack defense: by using NFV, network operators are able to specify bandwidth threshold and flow information for each virtual router. The metadata associated with a particular flow can be used to detect DDoS attacks [FAY 15]. Also, by monitoring on virtual routers whether there is any large amount of traffic or huge number of service requests to the target nodes that exceed the threshold value, DDoS attacks can be detected. In general, NFV can help improve DDoS mitigation, thanks to the dynamically provision-based software, intelligent configuration in the system and well-defined optimization detection.

4) Interoperability: it is widely acknowledged that the use of NFV infrastructure, the development of virtualized interfaces, and common protocols will allow us to integrate multiple virtual appliances from various vendors with different hardware and hypervisors. As such, a large set of security functions is allowed to be virtualized and provided as agile security services by different service providers. More importantly, NFV-based multi-vendor solution can reduce the number of physical appliances and power consumption, thereby allowing NFV service providers to offer fast disaster recovery and powerful forensic analysis capabilities for creating cheaper intrusion detection tools. Also, NFV allows the control of fine-grained access to resources, maintaining a certain visibility of the information flows, and making it easier to isolate unstable or compromised element from other appliances.

5) Automation and central management: NFV security service orchestration facilitates consistent policy configuration and easier regulatory compliance, thanks to the automation and central management of security functions. In particular, centralized security management allows security functions to be configured according to

common policies, rather than a collection of per-network function security procedures that may not be consistent and up to date. For example, patch management and incident response can be implemented in an automated and centralized manner, significantly reducing operational complexity and cost. More specifically, automated incident response can enable rapid and flexible reconfiguration of virtual resources. Then if one network function component is compromised, a cleaned version can be instantiated automatically to replace them, while the compromised version can be revoked and used for further forensic analysis.

6) Streamlined security operations: NFV enables flexible network configuration, potentially achieving easier patch management, quicker incident response, and more effective traffic management. Empowered by automation and central management, a set of diverse security functions can be encapsulated as on-demand security services, and further be holistically integrated or orchestrated, achieving dynamic and flexible multi-layered defense mechanisms.

3.3.2. *Typical frameworks for service orchestration*

In general, an orchestration framework needs to provide reliable and scalable network functions, easy management of VNF lifecycle processes, and automate the highly dynamic delivery of VNFs upon user demands.

EXAMPLE 3.1 (Orchestration software).– It is well known that the diversity of applications make deployment and management in cloud computing complex. To improve service reliability, the authors of [DUD 15] proposed an orchestration software based on Monasca, a monitoring software for OpenStack [MON 14]. Specifically, the framework contains three major components:

– Service manager: each user requests a service deployment through the service manager, which then deploys a service orchestrator for each new deployment upon user request.

– Service orchestrator: managed by service manager and contains all the logic necessary to implement and manage the services, such as service descriptions, configuration information.

– Cloud controller: supports the lifecycle of service orchestrator and service instances, e.g. deployment, provisioning, runtime and disposal. The service manager and service orchestrator contact with cloud controller to interact with the underlying infrastructure.

EXAMPLE 3.2 (VNF orchestration).– In [RIG 15], a programmable network fabric architecture (PNFV) called *Scylla* was proposed for enterprise WLANs which supports basic VNF lifecycle management functionalities, e.g. instantiation, monitoring and migration, making network services more flexible and scalable when a new feature or service is deployed. Specifically, as illustrated in Figure 3.2, the architecture contains a set of packet processing nodes and a controller node.

– Packet processor node: includes an OpenVSwitch instance, one or more VNFs and one packet processor agent. In particular, the packet processor agent is used to monitor the status of each VNF, as well as to handle CRUD (create, read, update, delete) requests coming from the programmable network fabric controller (PNFC).

– Programmable Network Fabric Controller (PNFC): which acts as an orchestrator to decide whether a particular VNF request can be accepted or refused. If the request is accepted, then the PNFC maps the request onto the substrate network, where network resources are allocated and configured for that particular VNF request.

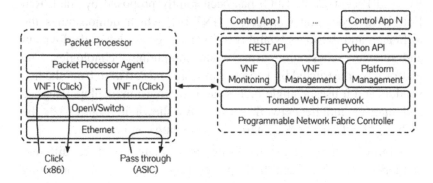

Figure 3.2. *VNF orchestration with Scylla [RIG 15]*

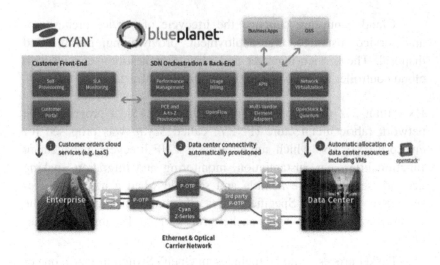

Figure 3.3. *Virtualizing WAN and datacenter resources for end-to-end service orchestration [INT 14]. For a color version of this figure, see www.iste.co.uk/zhang/networks.zip*

EXAMPLE 3.3 (End-to-end service orchestration).– With the proliferation of VNF applications, the level of automation in provisioning and service delivery becomes increasingly complicated, thereby requiring sophisticated orchestration software to handle it. To that end, an end-to-end service orchestration platform for a virtual Evolved Packet Core (EPC) has been jointly proposed by Intel, Red Hat, Dell, Cyan and Connectem [INT 14], which demonstrates the technical and business viability of carrier grade NFV deployment and service orchestration using cloud computing technologies. The platform is constructed by various hardware and software from the five vendors and it uses a single orchestrator to provision, deploy, integrate and manage mobile network service. As shown in Figure 3.3, the orchestration framework contains the following components.

– Infrastructure: at the hardware level, there are three different vendors who offer such high power processing, secure operating environment, and efficient resource sharing.

- Intel [INT 15] provides Intel Xeon processors and 10 gigabit Intel Ethernet technology with extreme power processing and virtualization capabilities to support SDN and NFV applications. Thus, developers can leverage the Intel Data Plane Development Kit (Intel DPDK) to optimize vSwitch and improve NFV performance.

- Red Hat [HAT 15] provides the secure and reliable operating environment to support VNF applications by utilizing Red Hat Enterprise Linux OpenStack Platform to deliver an integrated foundation to create, deploy and scale a secure and reliable OpenStack in cloud.

- Dell [INT 15] Dell uses Dell PowerEdge C6220 servers to establish shared infrastructure and to help build the scale-out cloud environment.

– Management and orchestration: Cyan's Blue Planet [PLA 15] is responsible for the management and orchestration of all the resources of the cloud datacenter, including computing, networking, storage and VMs. It provides management and orchestration (MANO) guidelines to manage and automate the VNF lifecycle and intelligently orchestrate NFV infrastructure resources across multiple datacenters.

– VNF applications (e.g. vEPC) [INT 15, CON 15]: Connectem provides vEPC software solution to serve higher network performance during peak usage periods, where millions of users could access a mobile network via smart phones or tablets. It helps reduce the time deployment when new service is created.

EXAMPLE 3.4 (NFVOps orchestration).– This framework is proposed by Calsoft Labs [LAB 15], with an objective to help users easily deploy, manage and orchestrate VNFs and roll out new services, thereby significantly simplifying network operations. In particular, it enables automated service provisioning, service fulfillment and end-to-end service quality assurance on virtual clouds. Based on ETSI NFV ISG specification, NFVOps allows service providers to create virtual private multi-tenant clouds deployable on any cloud platform.

3.4. NFV-based security management platforms

This section presents the analysis of several existing platforms for NFV orchestration, with particular focus on NFV's vendor contribution, motivation and architecture. The ultimate objective is to understand how the NFV platform can run in a secure manner, and whether or not they can serve for security management. In particular, we study (1) the ways that VNFs are deployed, automated, orchestrated and managed, and (2) what kind of security solutions NFV vendors propose to improve the security of their orchestration platforms. As a result, Table 3.1 shows the comparison analysis of NFV orchestration implementation with respect to security management from both academic and industrial perspectives.

Sectors	Project Lists	Motivations	Architecture
Industry	1) CloudNFV project [CLO 17]	1) Build on existing standards proposed by ETSI ISG NFV and add more robust management and orchestration capabilities 2) NFV integration into existing OSS/BSS and management systems in the existing operator environments 3) Establish a model for NFV called "Three pillars": network functions, function virtualization, and operationalization 4) Test the integration of cloud computing, SDN, NFV and the Tele Management Forum (TMF) in an open, real world way	1) CloudNFV is designed to follow ETSI ISG NFV, with a mixture of VNFs, cloud application components, real network devices and services, and multi-operator federated services 2) It supports interfaces specified by the ETSI ISG NFV, but also provides open access to services, composition, deployment and management features outside the NFV scope 3) The architecture is based on management and the orchestration is based on an agile data/process model called *Active Virtualization*, which provides *Active Contract* and *Active Resources* 5) Active contract consists of standardized service templates for particular VNFs 6) Active resources use policy rules to designate the best hardware and infrastructure to be used for these VNFs

| | 2) Telco cloud [NET 15] | 1) With the advent of NFV, many network functions and network elements are implemented as cloud-based solutions, leading to security risks for IP-based communication networks and cloud infrastructure
2) Define future security as a built-in feature of an orchestrated network, to design and deploy a secure cloud
3) To provide an overall synchronized management of security functions and orchestration in telecom cloud, with VNF lifecycle and global resource management
4) To offer management and orchestration tools that automatically deploy, configure, optimize and repair a set of VNFs with fully automated network lifecycle management
5) To describe a concept of an end-to-end automated security resilience, update, and transparency system to help operators for security regulation in threats and increase user expectations
6) To build and deliver secure networks of clouds by applying security mechanisms such as security zoning, traffic separation, mutual authentication, encryption and access control | 1) Cloud-based telco networks introduce virtual security appliances to achieve a grade of security comparable to physical networks
2) There are two different approaches for virtual security appliances: the VM-based approach, and the hypervisor-based approach (e.g. a virtual firewall to protect telco applications)
3) It stores VM images and databases as encrypted objects and with encrypted communications to ensure data protection and privacy
4) The architecture involves security management entities including security orchestrator, VNF manager, OSS/BSS, element management systems (EMS), and the virtual and physical security functions, to achieve flexibility in order to automation and lifecycle management of the telco cloud security
5) Figure 3.4 shows the end-to-end telco cloud security components that keep pace of automation, orchestration and security management as specified by ETSI NFV architecture |

	3) CloudBand [NOK 17]	1) CloudBand is the first to market a carrier grade NFV management and orchestration (MANO) platform, built for service providers from proof of concept (PoC) to production 2) Build a fully automated and highly distributed cloud infrastructure with centralized MANO platform that optimizes services deployment between network and cloud environment 3) Offer high availability service deployment and assurance capabilities, such as automated orchestration, service assurance, and a pre-integrated solution 4) Provide VNF lifecycle management that automates deployment, scaling, healing and maintaining of VNFs 5) To provide rapid launching, flexible service scaling, and to simplify network operations with automated operating model, fault isolation, complexity reduction and cost efficiency 6) Ensure service provider's infrastructure is protected against unsolicited access	1) CloudBand comprises two main modules: *CloudBand management system* and *CloudBand Node* 2) The CloudBand management system manages, orchestrates and optimizes an aggregate view of distributed sets of CloudBand nodes (NFV orchestration functions), and supports NFV application layer management including VNF lifecycle management (VNF manager function) 3) The CloudBand node is a pre-designed, pre-integrated software stacks and architectural blueprint designed to manage, automate and monitor the compute, storage and network resources for large-scale NFV deployment 4) The CloudBand node can be partitioned into security zones to isolate and protect VNF applications 5) The CloudBand node uses VLAN traffic separation and a web application firewall to filter inbound requests, identify access management to guarantee confidentiality, and data tracking and monitoring to detect abnormal behavior

| Academic | 1) SECURED project (SECURity at the network EDge) [SEC 16, MON 15] | 1) As users deal with many terminals (e.g. smart phones, tablets, notebooks) with very different security level and policy requirements, it's extremely difficult to achieve the same level of protection while inducing management complexity of security control
2) Design and create prototype of trusted and secure environment for multiple applications with support of hierarchical and multi-source policies
3) To propose a model to unify and homogenize the protection and security policies for each user
4) Create virtualized infrastructure on network edge devices, guarantee on independent security applications and protect network traffic based on policy rules
5) Create the lightweight sensors for fast inspection of potential security issues (e.g. normal, suspect or compromised VNFs)
Remark:
- SECURED consortium consists of five relevant European research institutes and two major companies whereas Politecnico di Torino University acts as the main coordinator | 1) SECURED is a paradigm shifting from device-centric protection to a user-centric model based on Trusted Virtual Domain (TVD)
2) The TVD can be instantiated either on the user's side (e.g. on the home gateway) or the provider's side (e.g. on the broadband access server dealing with user's connections)
3) The TVD is a logical container that is instantiated per user and must be trusted; appropriate techniques (e.g. remote attestation, contractual agreement) must be put in place to guarantee the trust level based on security needs for specific users
4) SECURED model is composed of three policy abstraction layers: (i) High-Level Security Policy Language (HSPL), (ii) subject-verb-object-attribute authorization language, and (iii) low-level policy abstraction stack, and two translation services
5) The main components of SECURED include: *security module, authentication system, network edge device (NED) control and management, orchestration system, security policy manager, personal security applications (PSA) repositories*, and *SECURED app*
5) The generic deployment is shown in Figure 3.5 |

| 2) T-NOVA project [TNO 14, XIL 14] | 1) Introduce a novel enabling framework, allowing operators to deploy VNFs for their own needs, but also to offer value-added service (NFaaS) (e.g. security functions such as firewall, proxies can be provided on-demand as a service) 2) Design and implement a management and orchestration platform for automated provision, configuration, monitoring and optimization of NFaaS over virtualization infrastructure 3) To leverage and enhance cloud management architectures for elastic provision and re-allocation of IT resources by exploiting SDN platforms for efficient management *Remark:* - T-NOVA was an integrated project co-funded by the European Commission | 1) T-NOVA architecture can be hierarchically organized into four layers: - *NFVI layer:* includes physical and virtual nodes - *NFVI management layer:* comprises infrastructure management entities (virtualized infrastructure management (VIM), transport network management (TNM)) - *Orchestration layer:* deals with resource orchestration, network service orchestration, and VNF management - *Marketplace layer:* facilitates multi-actor involvement and implements business-related functionalities 2) The management and orchestration layer in the T-NOVA architecture orchestrates network and IT assets, manages virtual network setup, traffic steering, VNF instantiation and placement, and controls the provisioned services 3) There are mainly four security functions that have been integrated in the T-NOVA platform: - *Virtual security appliance (vSA):* diverse security technologies (e.g. firewall, IPS, DPI, IPS) used to protect computer networks from suspicious traffic; it can be deployed at the edges of the network, close to user premises, or at other convenient locations within the virtual network |

			- *Virtualized session border controller (vSBC):* works as a gateway between two different IP networks, to provide important roles including interconnecting of private and public IP networks, topology abstraction, and other security services (e.g. NAT) - *Virtualized DPI (vDPI):* to monitor network traffic, gather statistical information, and prevent malicious activities based on policy enforcement - *Virtualized home gateways (vHG):* used to connect a LAN to Internet, to provide cost-effective, QoE-driven solution for content delivery
3) NETSECTOR [SHI 15]	1) Current network security management suffers from a lack of flexibility, it is complicated to manage network security devices, and security resource utilization is not sufficient 2) NETSECTOR prototype presents a new concept of "Network Security Virtualization (NSV)", which virtualizes security resources/functions via dynamic service monitoring 3) To design a prototype system to foster tenants to easily use security services, by utilizing existing pre-installed (fixed-location) security devices and leverage SDN/NFV to virtualized network security functions	1) NETSECTOR contains i) a simple script language to register security services and policies; ii) a set of routing algorithms to determine optimal routing paths for different security policies; and iii) a set of security response functions/strategies to handle security incidents 2) NETSECTOR architecture consists of five main modules - *Device and policy manager* - *Routing rule generator* - *Flow rule enforcer* - *Response manager* - *Data manager*	

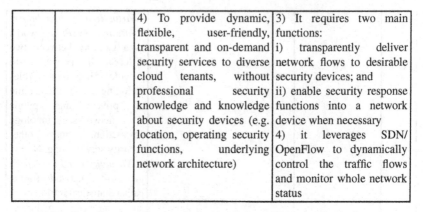

| | | | 4) To provide dynamic, flexible, user-friendly, transparent and on-demand security services to diverse cloud tenants, without professional security knowledge and knowledge about security devices (e.g. location, operating security functions, underlying network architecture) | 3) It requires two main functions: i) transparently deliver network flows to desirable security devices; and ii) enable security response functions into a network device when necessary 4) it leverages SDN/OpenFlow to dynamically control the traffic flows and monitor whole network status |

Table 3.1. *Comparative analysis of existing NFV frameworks from academic and industry point of view*

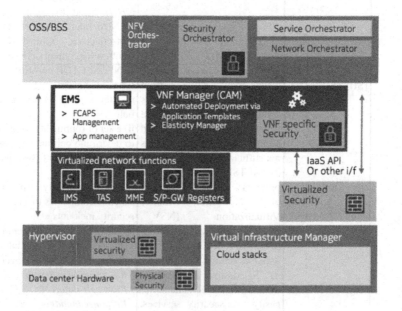

Figure 3.4. *Secure telco cloud architecture [NET 15]*

In conclusion, NFV orchestration presents a fresh look at the operator's network, showing that the infrastructure landscape of both telecom and cloud service providers has massively changed. In particular, it brings cloud computing and IT technologies into the networking domain to help service providers reduce network equipment and operational costs, power consumption and time to market when deploying new services and functionalities. As NFV is based on a software-driven approach, service providers can achieve a higher degree of automated network operations, independent generic hardware layer, agile application development and deployment model. Thanks to NFV technology, operational processes such as service deployment, on-demand resource allocation, failure detection, on-time recovery and software upgrades can be programmed and executed with minimal or no human intervention (zero-touch). All of these benefits provide an opportunity to reduce time processing for configuration and maintenance.

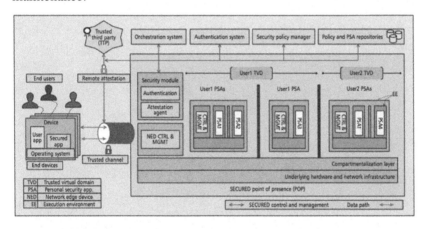

Figure 3.5. *The "basic SECURED" architecture showing a multi-tenant scheme on a point of presence (POP) [MON 15]. For a color version of this figure, see www.iste.co.uk/zhang/networks.zip*

More importantly, NFV brings advanced capabilities of security management for VNF applications on the shared network infrastructure. In particular, one of the major advantages is to potentially automate security management for the entire network elements, so that complex security solutions are easier to perform. It also enables seamless automation and orchestration across multiple cloud platforms, unleashes potential network security functions to improve the security level of VNF applications, and allows dynamic scaling (up and down) as required by the network load to serve multi-tenancy demands. As shown, all the current and future network security functions, such as access control, IDS/IPS, network isolation, data protection, can be automated with virtualized placement and implemented with high performance and robustness. More details of NFV-based security functions are discussed in the following sections.

4

Identity and Access Management in NFV

IAM (Identity and Access Management) is widely accepted as the first defense line of today's ICT infrastructures and services. Some of the major functions include authentication, authorization, accounting and access control. In this chapter, we first present the basic functions and basic implementations of IAM and then discuss their NFV-based implementations. We finally provide a comprative analysis between these two variants.

IAM is a very broad topic that covers both technical and non-technical areas, involving business processes, technologies, and policies for managing digital identities, monitoring network access and controlling access to company assets. In other words, IAM is about how to enable the right individuals to access the right resources at the right time for the right reasons. Technically speaking, IAM is used to initiate, capture, record and manage user identities and their related access permissions to information assets in an automated way. As a result, access privileges are granted to the users according to the interpretation of policy rules, which are then enforced by a sequence of authentication, authorization and auditing functions.

The implication of IAM has two independent elements: *identity management* and *access management*. Identity management describes the process of authentication, authorization and user privileges across system boundaries, whereas access management is more focused on the access control to verify whether users are granted privileges to access particular services or resources. The decision result is evaluated based on policy rules, user's roles and other elements that are predefined by the administrators.

4.1. Major functions

More specifically, the IAM framework is composed of the following functions [IDE 12], which are briefly explained as follows:

– Authentication: a process of determining whether the user credentials are authentic. Authentication is activated only when the users intend to access information in the system. Then, the users are required to prove their right and identity, basically through the username and password or biometric identities. The system verifies user identity by matching the provided credentials with a specific abstract user object that is stored in the system. Once the two objects match, the access is authenticated. To date, there are several types of authentication that have been widely used in the current ICT context such as tokens, public keys, certificates and biometric authentication [CLO 12, HAV 07].

– Authorization: a process of allowing users to perform an action with the resource that they are granted, i.e. preventing users from accessing the resources that they are not allowed to access [HAV 07]. For example, if a user tries to write a file with only read permission, then the authorization fails and the requested operation for writing could be rejected. Furthermore, the users can be authenticated using a certain identity but they can be authorized to access a specific resource under a different identity. Many authorization functions are built upon the four following methods:

- Discretionary Access Control (DAC): which allows users or administrators to define an access control list (ACL) in regards to specific resources, such as which users can access the resource and what privileges they are granted. An example of DAC was proposed by [WAN 11] to mitigate user privacy and data leakage problems in collaboration clouds.

- Mandatory access control (MAC): which is defined by the administrator to manage the access control based on policy and cannot be modified or changed by users. The policy specifies the access rules for the requested services/resources. Some examples of MAC are used for end-to-end access control in Web applications [HIC 10] and in commodity OS to support intrusion detection [SHA 11].

- Role-base-access control (RBAC): which is based on defining a list of business roles and permissions and privileges are then granted to each role. Some concrete examples related to RBAC were discussed in [KER 03, KER 05].

- Attribute-based access control (ABAC): which uses attributes as the policy building blocks to define access control rules and describe access requests. Authorization-based ABAC typically relies on the evaluation of attributes (users), targeted resources, desired action (read, write), and access control/policy rules to verify whether access right are granted. The ABAC is widely used in various domains such as authorization services [LEE 08], Web services [CAP 14] and data protection services [IRW 05, IRW 09].

– Auditing: it is a process of recording security events related to the accounting and traceability process. It can provide historic information about when and how a user accessed the assets, and whether there were any attempts to violate authentication policies. The historic information of user status is stored in the log files for further analysis.

– User management: the area of user management in the IAM context is not only related to user management but also covers password management, role management and user provisioning. User management is one of the authentication features that provides administrators with the ability to identify and control the state of users when logged into the system. It encompasses a set of administrative functions such as identity creation, propagation, and maintenance of user identity and privileges. This enables the administrator to have better granularity to control the user authentication and manage the lifespan of user accounts through user lifecycle management, thus ranging from the initial stage of authentication to the final stage when the user logs out of the system. The flexibility provided by user management allows administrators to implement IAM efficiently with a closer match to the security policy.

In addition, user management incorporates the *central user repository*, providing storage for user data and data delivery to other services when it is required. The aggregation of data is kept and maintained in the repository. The user repository can be located either in a distribution network composed of multiple databases/files or a local area directly accessible by the user without having to travel across the network. An example of a central user repository is the lightweight directory access protocol (LDAP) [YEO 95] that is an industry standard application protocol for accessing and maintaining distributed directory information over the IP network. The concept of LDAP is based on a hierarchical information structure (a simple tree hierarchy) in order to deal with several kinds of information stored in the directories. Starting from the root directory (the source of the tree), it branches out to, for example but not limited to, countries, organizations, organizational units (e.g. divisions and department) and individuals (e.g. users, files and shared resources).

4.2. Case studies

We exemplify the applications of IAM in several typical scenarios, illustrating their implementation, deployment and management, so that NFV-based implementations can be compared.

IT scenario. In [RAN 07], the authors reported the problems that were experienced by the South African Social Security Agency (SASSA), which is responsible for distributing grants to underprivileged citizens. It has been estimated that approximately 187.5 million dollars are lost annually due to fraud.

According to the social grant distribution in the South Africa, the organization consists of four main components: (1) South African Department of Home Affairs (SADHA), which is responsible for issuing to South African citizens; (2) South African Social Security Agency (SASSA), which is formed by the Ministry of Social Development to distribute grants; (3) distribution companies, which are responsible for the actual payment of the social grants to the eligible recipients; and (4) social grant recipient. In particular, there are two types of processes related to the social grant recipient: the registration process and authentication process. In the registration process, all the recipients must be registered with a payment system. Four good fingerprints from the recipient and the recipient's information (e.g. recipient's photograph, biometric data, type of grant they are eligible to receive and history of payment) are stored in the databases. This personnel information is also replicated and encoded onto the smart card before issuing the smart card to the recipients. Once enrollment into the company's database is complete, the recipient can be paid the grant. The authentication process is activated when receiving grants, the smart card is swiped and the beneficiary places their fingers onto a biometric reader. The fingerprints are verified with the fingerprint's information stored in the database and those encoded in the smart card. If the authentication is successful, the recipients can receive the financial grant.

4.2.1. *Telco scenarios: mobile devices and networks*

In [ARD 06], location-based access control policies were proposed for telco scenarios by considering both users' location and their credentials. Compared with the conventional access control systems, more parties are involved: requesters, the access control engine (ACE) and the location service, as shown in Figure 4.1:

– Requesters: whose access request to a service must be authorized by a location-based access control (LBAC) system.

– Access control engine (ACE): if the evaluation result of access requests is matched to LBAC policies, then the ACE enforces access control to the available services.

– Location service: which provides the location information to ACE, by measuring position as well as the environmental condition of requester.

Technically, ACE receives access requests, evaluates policies and returns answers. It communicates with the location service to acquire the location information of the requester. To describe how the access control has been operated, the authors define an access control rule with 4-tuples of request form (*user_id, SIM, action, object_id*), where: *User_id* is an optional identifier of the requester who makes the request; *SIM* is the optional SIM card number; *action* is an action being requested; *object_id* is the identifier of the object on which the user wishes to perform the action. Thus, access is granted if the subject expression evaluates to 'true' for every applicable rule.

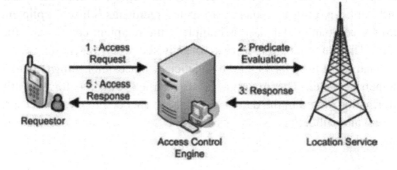

Figure 4.1. *Location-based conditions in access control policies [ARD 06]*

However, user privacy in location-based services remains an important issue [CHO 09]. With an untrustworthy location service provider, the revealed private location information of the requester could be abused by adversaries. Therefore, location privacy-based anonymity solutions for the purpose of blinding user's requests/queries were proposed by [TEE 10], allowing requesters to send requests or queries to the LBS servers without revealing their personal information.

The proposed framework is classified into two major parts: authentication and querying processes; both the processes are done via *anonymity (trusted third party)* as described in [MAL 08].

– Authentication process: during the authentication process, a one-way hash function technique has been applied to provide better privacy authentication. In addition, location blurring (or *K-anonymity*) is used to hide the actual location when the requester needs to interact with an untrusted service provider.

– Querying process: in the querying processes, time fuzzy logic is used to examine the degree of confidence about whether the requester is requesting the service under the right privileges.

4.2.2. *Public clouds*

Due to the fact that cloud service providers may have different users, access control and user identity privacy protection is extremely complicated in the multi-tenant environment. Therefore, in [XIO 13], the authors proposed an approach called *privacy preserving access management (PRAM)* to address identity privacy and access control concerns in cloud services by: (1) using both blind signature and hash chains which are used to protect identity privacy and secure authentication; (2) integrating on-demand access control with a service level agreement (SLA) to provide flexible fine-grained access management. As shown in Figure 4.2, the PRAM consists of five components: users, cloud service provider, registration servers, authentication and policy decision point (PDP).

– Users: the first time, a user U must register at a registration server RS, which issues authorized credential SID to U. This SID will be used for further authentication with the PDP when a user attempts to access a cloud service.

– Cloud service provider (CSP): which is in charge of providing the cloud service data to authorized users.

– Registration server (RS): which is responsible for the registration of all the users and all the kinds of cloud services.

– Authentication: which refers to the process of determining whether U is who they claim to be. In order to evaluate the access control decision, PRAM adopts the attribute-based access control mechanism [JIN 12] and the access control policies stored in the policy repository of PDP. If the authentication is successful, PDP allows U to access the requested service and relays this decision message back to PEP.

– Policy decision point (PDP): which is connected with the access control policy repository and policy enforcement point (PEP). In particular, the PEP is responsible for receiving message requests from U, forwarding this message to PDP for taking decision, and finally returning the decision result back to U. When PDP receives the requested message from U, it then first authenticates U to access the requested service in the cloud. The evaluation is done based on the description of the user's attributes and SLA. The PDP finally issues the decision result to PEP, which then uses it to inform U (access or reject).

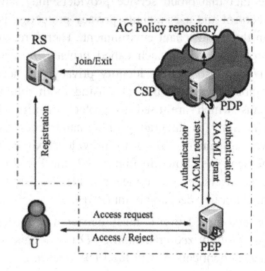

Figure 4.2. *The PRAM architecture [XIO 13]*

Although a lot of IAM schemes for public clouds [IRW 09, XIO 13, GHA 13] have been designed, there are no standards available. Basically, the designs need to meet the following requirements, as suggested by the authors of [YAN 14]:

– Strong and flexible authentication: one-time password (OTP) and multi-factor authentication should be available as alternative options.

– Data loss prevention: it should be able to monitor, protect and verify the security of data during processing as well as stored in the cloud.

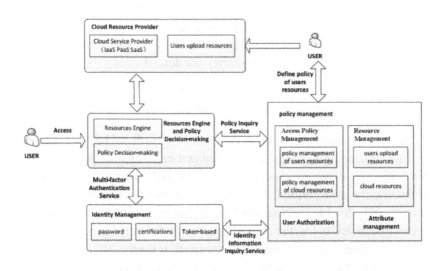

Figure 4.3. *Identity and access management architecture [YAN 14]*

To meet the requirements, the authors proposed an IAM architecture, as shown in Figure 4.3, which consists of four components: cloud resource provider, identity management (IdM), policy management (PM) and resource engine and policy decision-making (REPD). Their specific roles are explained as follows:

– Cloud resource provider is responsible for providing access to resources based on a user's asserted identity and privilege.

– Identity management (IdM) is used to manage users and their identities, issue credentials, and authenticate and assert the user's identity.

– Policy management (PM) enforces access rules that associates users with resources. In particular, it ensures that provisioning requests conform to the policies that are defined through four functions: attribute management, user authorization, resource management and access policy management.

– Resource engine and policy decision-making (REPD), which has two functions: (i) determining whether to allow users to access the requested resources and (ii) finding resources that meet user request. After REPD receives user requests, the REPD submits the authentication request to the IdM. If authenticated, the REPD then submits a query to PM. Once authorized, the user can gain access to the requested resources, otherwise they are denied.

4.2.3. *Collaborative network scenarios*

Several organizations have recognized the benefits of being involved in inter-organization, multi-disciplinary and collaborative projects that may require diverse resources to be shared among participants. However, the conventional IAM solution is not sufficient to support robust and flexible access control in such collaborative network scenarios. In [RUB 15], the authors proposed a federated and distributed access management to support automated resource sharing in the collaborative network environment, allowing each entity to possibly implement their own security domain and their own dedicated federated access management infrastructure. In particular, resource providers are required to guarantee that the information and resources have been released only to trusted collaborators within the community. To do that, various types of security policies are specified to ensure the degrees of assurance. Figure 4.4(a) presents its framework and Figure 4.4(b) illustrates the process of federated access management by defining three main components: actor, targets and context.

– Actor: refers to end users (e.g. human agents) or subjects (e.g. computer processes) acting on behalf of users. When users request access to the resources/services, it involves access control entities. The access control entities then contact local attributes (if the request exists in the same security domain) or federate attributes (if across collaborative network environments) to check whether users have the right privilege to access the requested resources. However, local attributes are related to federated attributes through *attribute derivation rules (AD-rules)*, which define how local attributes are ultimately related to federated ones. The AD-rules can be organized into a graph-like structure, known as an *attribute derivation graph (AD-graph)*, which presents how attributes are related to permission.

– Targets: targets are the protected resources within a security domain.

– Context: context is the running environment, e.g. operating system and supporting platform, where a given request is issued.

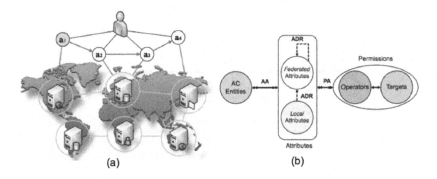

(a)   (b)

Figure 4.4. *(a) A federated access management framework and (b) a model for federated access management [RUB 15]*

4.3. NFV-based implementations

To date, we have seen some efforts on virtualizing IAM mechanisms through the use of virtualization technology to support a large number of VNFs running in a NFV environment. For example, in [JAC 14], access control virtualized network function (AC-VNF) is proposed to control a large number of VNF appliances and authenticate the end users. The objective of AC-VNF is the provisioning of security services and providing more concrete access control to the services and policy enforcement. In particular, the authentication and authorization mechanisms are required to verify the VNF appliances whether they are eligible to access the requested resources or not. Furthermore, the service providers who own network infrastructures and share resources can define arbitrary security policies based on their needs, so each VNF appliance can be controlled independently according to those pre-defined policy rules.

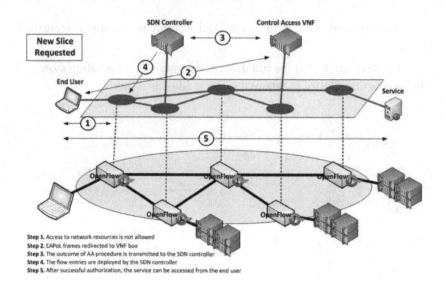

Figure 4.5. *An access control VNF procedure [JAC 14]*

The AC-VNF is implemented based on the IEEE 802.1X standard (IEEE standard for port-based network access control (PNAC)) and a modified version of the standard to implement the access control per service (instead of per port). Figure 4.5 shows the AC-VNF architecture interacting between four different domains: (1) *End user*, who requests for the services and the request can be initiated both in a VM from another virtual server or a physical PC. The machine running the user's request is directly connected to one of the physical ports of any OpenFlow switches; (2) *SDN controller*, which is a software application maintaining the state of user traffic. It enforces the flow entries by enabling or disabling them to access the requested resources/services. In addition, it performs two tasks: redirect user's request to access control VNF box for further authentication and redirect end user to requested services after the user has been successfully authenticated; (3) *Access control VNF*, which is built on a VM with a Linux distribution and uses the modified versions of HostAP [HOS 12] and WPA supplicant [WPA 12]. It acts as software authenticator and implements the IEEE 802.1X-based authentication and authorization (AA) mechanism. Once the AA procedure succeeds, the access control VNF box then transmits the evaluation result to the

SDN/NFV controller; (4) *Service*, which is a specific type of resource provided by CSPs. The owner of resources can control them independently, using different security procedures.

To summarize regarding the automated deployment of an access control VNF, in which it is possible to activate or deactivate the access control VNF without disrupting other services: network operators can easily reconfigure the access control VNF by using the provided tools. This approach is particularly well adapted to a stateless SDN/NFV infrastructure, as the access control VNF is able to store the data needed for the AA procedure. However, when considering the design, it needs to be carefully addressed in terms of the configuration, not only for the VMs (supporting deployed access control VNF), but also the underlying infrastructure for maintaining the proper isolation.

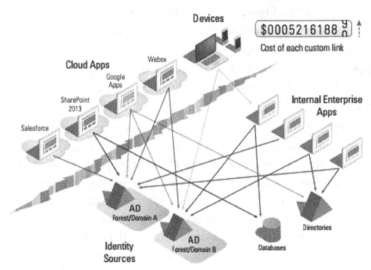

Figure 4.6. *N-squared problem with traditional identity infrastructure [LOG 14]. For a color version of this figure, see www.iste.co.uk/zhang/networks.zip*

Radiant Logic Inc. [LOG 14] pointed out that identity infrastructures face the traditional challenges of multiple links to multiple sources and targets, which create an unmanageable "n-squared" problem, as shown in Figure 4.6. The problem implies that there are many custom links, each one is extremely expensive to manage and deploy, inflexible to maintain, and complex in terms of hard-coded point-to-point connection. To solve the problem, the authors proposed a virtualized IAM solution based on the federated identity system, which provides flexible management, increases security, flexibility and end user experience with seamless single sign-on. In particular, a large number of heterogeneous and distributed identity modules (e.g. active directory, LDAP directories, databases and APIs) can be presented as a global view of identity and attributed over the federation access layer. The federated identity can be operated on the fly for further user evaluation. It adopts federation standards such as SAML 2.0 (security assertion markup language) [SAM 08], OpenID Connect [CON 14] and OAuth 2.0 [HAR 12], which are designed to better manage security and address complexity. Figure 4.7 shows the concept of a federated identity system based on virtualization and the architecture involves two parties:

– Service provider (SP), which provides the functionality of the application and controls the access to the resources. It delegates authentication and attribution management to a trusted external identity source.

– Identity provider (IdP), which manages user's identities, their profiles, and provides users with access to the new applications. In particular, the IdP adopts a common authentication method (based on standard-based tokens) for verifying user identity and an identity hub is leveraged to support the IdP for easier and more efficient routing. The identity hub has a central repository (e.g. virtual meta-directories) for integrating and synchronizing all the identity directories from heterogeneous systems via an abstraction layer.

Another example design is reported in [WRA 10], which proposes content-aware identity and access management solution to protect user information in a virtualization environment by controlling identities, access and information usage. The major advantages include: (1) privileged user management; (2) fine-grained access controls on virtual hosts and guests; (3) enhanced user activity and compliance reporting; (4) sensitive data discovery and information protection on virtualized systems; (5) extension of identity and access management capabilities to virtual system and applications. The architecture is shown in Figure 4.8, which contains three major parts:

– Role and access policy management: it is prespecified and defines different roles for accessing the VMs.

– System and application access: these applications will be running on the VMs and monitored by security apps.

– Virtual system and applications: which consist of three main modules: (1) *privileged user management*, which controls privilege users (e.g. role-based) along with fine-grained access control; (2) *compliance reporting*, which collects users' activities from all the event logs; (3) *information protection*, which facilitates the management of sensitive data.

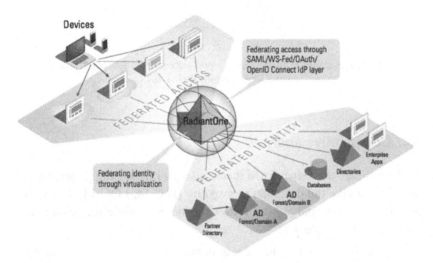

Figure 4.7. *Federated identity system through virtualization [LOG 14].*
For a color version of this figure, see www.iste.co.uk/zhang/networks.zip

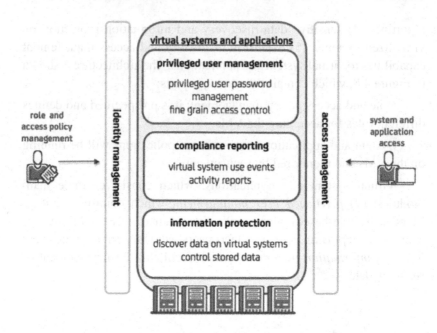

Figure 4.8. *A content-aware identity and access management through virtual environment [WRA 10]*

4.4. Comparative analysis

To compare the legacy IAM mechanisms with their implementations in NFV, we take the designs proposed by [JAC 14, LOG 14, WRA 10] as reference and analyze the following metrics, while the results are summarized in Table 4.1:

– Specific functions: the access control VNF box is implemented based on virtualization technology to provide security services and ensure that access privileges are granted to the right resources according to the policy rules. These policy decisions are centralized in a single point to assure the coherence in the definition. In [JAC 14], the AC-VNF is implemented based on FlowNAC [MAT 14], inspired by the IEEE 802.1X standard of the port-based network access control (PNAC), which is a basic NAC solution for enforcing the access control at the port level (e.g. the physical port of the network node). It is designed to maintain the whole authentication and authorization (AA) process in the data plane to further avoid overload on the control plane. When end users are requested to access the services/resources, this associated traffic coming from the end users will be redirected to the access control VNF box, which then identifies the end users (e.g. authentication) and applies a policy (e.g. authorization) as a result of a decision made at the policy decision point (PDP). The outcome of AA procedure is then transmitted to the SDN/NFV controller. Once the end users are authorized, the flow-based port entries are generated, thus the end users are allowed to access the requested services.

More specifically, the access control service relies on a virtualized infrastructure, implemented based on layer 2 (MAC address). Thus, one physical port is shared by multiple users through the use of virtual port (each virtual port is identified by the MAC address of the user) so that the users are isolated virtually. Although it is acceptable in terms of flexibility, cost and physical layer independence, there are limitations on capacity, security and overhead. It is worth noting that VLANs can possibly create 4094 different VLANs for the same network, and each VLAN is assigned a unique ID between 0 and 4093 [CIS 12]. Thus, if a network spans more than one geographical location, the traffic needs to go through the third parties. This exposes the traffic to potential sniffing and man-in-the-middle attacks, which are hard to deal with, unless higher layers offer additional security mechanisms. Additionally, if the VLANs rely on port-based or MAC-based configuration, it requires lots of effort and time to manage the network.

An alternative solution to improve the VLAN limitation is VXLAN [MAH 14], which can be implemented to support flexible and large-scale virtualized multi-tenant environment over a shared common physical infrastructure like a cloud.

– Cost: it is well recognized that NFV can reduce the total cost of hardware acquisition and capital investment through the use of commodity standard hardware platforms. For example, HP reports that the cost for a small-scale NFV deployment can be reduced from $34,015 to $27,828 (about 18%), whereas for a large-scale deployment cost can be reduced from $18,935 to $14,435 (about 24%) [HP 14a]. It is worth mentioning, however, that although the cost for hardware investment, installation, configuration and power consumption is decreased, the software cost could increase.

The example design reported in [LOG 14] clearly illustrates the advantages of NFV-based IMA implementation for solving "n-squared" problems, as shown in Figure 4.6. In particular, using IAM based on virtualization can significantly reduce the costs from hardware investment and management complexity, while access policy rules are allowed to be redefined and reconfigured remotely in real time.

– Complexity of lifecycle management: instead of deploying network equipment at customer sites and using them to provide a set of pre-defined services, NFV makes it possible to deploy hardware at provider sites and provision services dynamically using centralized management tools. Therefore, both cost and complexity resulting from service deployment and configuration can be reduced. Thus, security functions like virtual IAM can be quickly deployed and easily managed through a centralized management platform. As shown in the given examples [JAC 14, LOG 14, WRA 10], with IAM based on virtualization, administrators can flexibly deploy access control boxes, define security policies, assign specific actions according to user's attributes and role-based access control on the fly. NFV-based IAM especially allows security administrators to keep better control over the upcoming users' requests and offer efficient fine-grained policy enforcement.

– Effectiveness: if there is a large number of independent VNF appliances deployed in the NFV infrastructure, the effectiveness of management and communication overhead will become an important concern. A question arises regarding the location where an access control VNF box should be installed and the number that has to be deployed in order to achieve the best performance. Let us revisit Figure 4.5: if the end users are located closely to the requesting service's server, while the access control VNF box is deployed on a VM which is distant, then the SDN/NFV controller redirects the network traffic to the access control VNF box, regardless of the physical location of the end users. As such, a very large volume of traffic over virtual network switches and routers would be created, consuming lots of bandwidth.

This clearly indicates that it is necessary to take into account the trade-off between security objectives and performance efficiency during the deployment of access control VNF box.

– Availability (single point of failure of a centralized controller): in the example designed in [JAC 14], a controller is deployed to redirect all the traffic to an access control VNF box. While the centralized management can get a global view of the network, the platform or controller itself could be overloaded, failed or possibly attacked. As a result, the overall network latency will be heavily degraded. To share the processing load, a distributed control scheme was proposed in virtualized networks [ZUC 15]. In particular, multiple controller instances are created and organized in *clusters*, while the benefits of centralized network control remains. As such, the network control workload can be distributed across the cluster by deploying each instance of SND/NFV controller on dedicated VMs. Thus, a better trade-off between scalability and centralization can be achieved.

– Scalability: theoretically, NFV can make network services agile, cost-effective and scalable, allowing network operators to dial up/down network capacity as demand changes and providing elastic scale in/out of network resources assigned to VNFs depending on the dynamic traffic load and resource management. For example, in [JAC 14], a NFV-based scalable service deployment is proposed, where an access control VNF box can be activated or deactivated in real time without disrupting other services. Furthermore, the authors of [WRA 10] proposed a scalable access management to help network operators to manage the risk of data loss, allowing all the user requests and resources to be controlled efficiently, and policy rules to be dynamically inserted into existing VNF IAM box. Since the virtualized IAM box usually contains a large number of databases and directories, which are used to store user identities, attributes and policy roles, a scalable virtual directory is presented in [LOG 14], which aims to reduce the complexity of meta-directories when they are deployed or upgraded. The identities across heterogeneous sources can be easily integrated, providing a logical view, no matter where or how they are stored.

Example design of IAM	Easy deployment (no specific function required)	Cost saving	Complexity reduction of lifecycle management	Effectiveness	Availability (e.g. single point of failure)	Scalability
IAM for social grants in South Africa [RAN 07]	/	X	X	/	X	X
Location-based access control policies [ARD 06]	X	X	X	X	X	X
Access control-based anonymous location [TEE 10]	/	X	X	/	X	X
PRAM: privacy preserving access Management for cloud [XIO 13]	/	X	X	/	X	/
IAM solution for cloud [XIO 13]	/	/	X	/	X	/
Federated access management for collaborative network [RUB 15]	X	X	X	X	X	/
Agent-based framework for access control and trust management [SHA 05]	X	/	X	/	X	/

Access control virtualized network function (AC-VNF) [JAC 14]	X	/	/	X	X	/
Virtualized IAM solution based on federated identity service [LOG 14]	X	/	/	/	X	/
Content-aware identity and access management [WRA 10]	-	/	/	/	X	/

Notations: "/" and "X" denote that NFV characteristics are satisfied and not satisfied, respectively; "-" means data sources are insufficient.

Table 4.1. *Gap analysis between conventional and virtualized IAM*

5

Intrusion Prevention
and Detection in NFV

This chapter is focused on Intrusion Detection Systems (IDS) and Intrusion Prevention Systems (IPS), which are designed to monitor and detect malicious or unwanted behaviors that attempt to access, manipulate or disable computer systems, so as to prevent or terminate them in real time. We start with a brief introduction of the design principle of IDS/IPS and their typical implementations and then specifically discuss NFV-based implementations.

5.1. Case studies

Essentially, IDS/IPS are designed to protect critical assets against cyber threats, by examining system events or network traffic flow of interest. In particular, IDS is designed to *detect* vulnerability exploited against a target application or service. To do so, it is necessary to monitor all the inbound and outbound network activities and identify suspicious or anomalous patterns, if any. IDSs can be classified into anomaly-based ones and misuse-based ones in terms of design models. They can be either host-based or network-based, depending on the particular deployment and operating scenarios. Unlike IDS, IPS is also used to monitor network traffic and identify anomalous activities, often sitting directly behind the firewall and provides a complementary layer of analysis. In general, IPS is considered as an in-line security component that is able to actively prevent attacks from happening, whereas IDS is considered more of a passive monitoring, as its main function is to warn administrators of suspicious activities taking place rather than taking immediate actions to prevent any malicious activities.

Despite the similar design principles, the design architectures of IPS/IDS vary significantly with the operating scenarios. In the following, we exemplify the design of IPS/IDS in three typical scenarios: IT, wireless mobile networks and public cloud scenarios.

5.1.1. *IT scenario*

By design, IDSs usually employ dedicated network processors and memory, inevitably leading to computational overhead and limited flexibility. Also, most of them can hardly achieve high throughput, despite modern hardware that supports multiple hardware queues. To handle those issues, a highly scalable software IDS architecture, called *Kargus*, was proposed in [JAM 12], which can quickly detect malicious attack patterns. In particular, *Kargus* uses modern hardware innovation (e.g. multiple CPU cores), Non Uniform Memory Access (NUMA) architecture [MAN 10], multi-queue 10 Gbps Network Interface Cards (NICs) and heterogeneous processors like Graphic Processing Units (GPUs). Then, *batch processing* is used for packet reception, flow management and pattern matching. Meanwhile, parallel execution-based load balancing is implemented in order to balance the load of flow processing and pattern matching across multiple CPU and GPU cores: when CPU is faced with heavy computation stress or the workload exceeds the CPU capacity, the load-balancing algorithm will be used to dynamically adjust the consumption of resources.

In terms of architecture, *Kargus* contains three parts: *preprocessing*, *multi-string pattern matching* and *rule options evaluation*, as shown in Figure 5.1. These parts are described as follows:

– Preprocessing: *Kargus* reads incoming packets using a packet capture library (e.g. pcap [GAR 15] and ipfirewall [FRE 15]) and then re-assembles IP packet fragments, verifies the checksum of a TCP packet and manages the flow content for each TCP connection. Then, it identifies the application protocol that each packet belongs to and finally extracts the pattern rules to match against the packet payload.

– Multi-string pattern matching: once flow re-assembly and content normalization are completed, each packet is forwarded to the signature detection engine, which performs two-phase pattern matching by first scanning the entire payload to match simple attack strings from the signature database of the IDS.

– Rule option evaluation: if the signature is matched, the packets are further evaluated against a full-attack signature relevant to the matched string rule and finally produce the evaluation output.

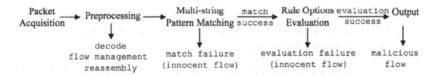

Figure 5.1. *Functional components of IDS [JAM 12]*

Another long-standing issue in the IPS/IDS domain is to run the systems over encrypted traffic like HTTPS. To enable middlebox processing, a Deep Packet Inspection (DPI) middlebox, called *BlindBox*, is proposed in [SHE 15], which can perform packet inspection directly on the encrypted payload without decrypting it. In particular, *BlindBox* contains three major components: *DPIEnc* and *BlindBox Detect, Obfuscated Rule Encryption* and *Probable Cause Decryption*. More specifically, (i) *DPIEnc* and *BlindBox Detect* use searchable encryption scheme [SON 00] and fast detection protocol to inspect encrypted traffic for certain keywords; (ii) *Obfuscated Rule Encryption* relies on the techniques proposed in [YAO 86, RAB 05] to enable the middleboxes to obtain encrypted rules based on the rules from middleboxes and the endpoints private key, while neither the endpoint nor the middlebox can learn the rules or the private key and (iii) *Probable Cause Decryption* allows flow decryption when a suspicious keyword is observed in the flow.

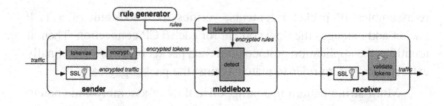

Figure 5.2. *System architecture of BlindBox [JAM 12]*

Figure 5.2 illustrates the operational process of *BlindBox*, where four parties are involved: sender (S), receiver (R), middlebox (MD) and rule generator (RG):

– RG generates attack rules to be used by MD to detect attacks.

– When MD receives the HTTPS traffic and the encrypted tokens from S, the detect module, BlindBox Detect, will search for matching between the encrypted rules and the encrypted tokens.

– If attack rules generated by RG match the traffic between R and S, regular actions such as dropping the packets, terminating the connection and notifying an alarm to administrator will be performed.

– Otherwise, MD should not learn the contents of the traffic that do not match RG's attack rules.

5.1.2. *Telco scenarios: mobile devices and networks*

Mobile ad hoc networks (MANETs) represent a large class of telecommunication networks, in which the nodes share the same physical medium. Network topology is dynamic and centralized monitoring and management points are not available. These characteristics result in a broad attack surface, ranging from passive eavesdropping to active signal interfering. An intrusion detection and response system was proposed in [ZHA 03], in which individual IDS agents are placed on each node to monitor malicious activities, as shown in Figure 5.3, and they cooperatively participate in global intrusion detection actions. In particular, each IDS agent contains six modules: *local data collection, local detection engine, cooperative detection engine, local response, global response* and *secure communications.*

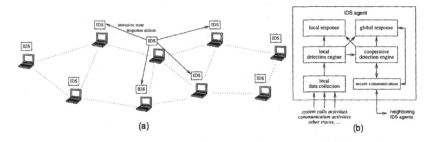

(a)   (b)

Figure 5.3. *(a) IDS architecture for wireless ad hoc network. (b) A conceptual model for an IDS agent on each mobile node [ZHA 03]*

Although the IDS architecture does not provide a detailed design of cooperation detection algorithms, the authors of [MOR 12] proposed a new distributed IDS to exchange events and for cooperation between the nodes. In particular, an IDS tool runs on each node in order to passively monitor the traffic and detect attacks in collaboration with the neighbors. On the basis of a cooperative consensus mechanism coordinated among the neighboring nodes, each node is able to detect malicious traffic with the help of its neighbors in real time. The proposed system is based on a popular IDS tool, *Bro* [PAX 99], to monitor traffic, and contains two layers:

– An event engine layer, which transforms a stream of filtered packets into a stream of higher-level network events. A *routing protocol analyzer* located inside this layer for capturing and analyzing data packets.

– A policy script interpreter layer, which executes security policy scripts and specifies even handlers. It consists of two components: *distributed intrusion detection mechanism* that provides misbehaving metrics to routing protocol analyzer, and *cooperative consensus mechanism*, which coordinates among the neighboring nodes for exchanging routing events of distributed attack detection.

5.1.3. *Public clouds*

With the rapid development and deployment of cloud computing, security service vendors are migrating their services like McAfee to public clouds, thus making them on-demand service. Some advantages of cloud-based IPS/IDS, as pointed out in [OBE 08], are better detection of malicious software, enhanced forensics capabilities, retrospective detection and improved deployability and management. The design principle is illustrated in Figure 5.4.

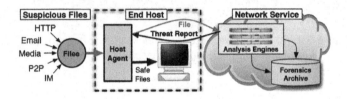

Figure 5.4. *CloudAV: N-Version Antivirus in the Network Cloud [OBE 08]. For a color version of this figure, see www.iste.co.uk/zhang/networks.zip*

In [MOD 12], the authors proposed a framework which integrates open-source NIDS *Snort* [ROE 13] and Decision Tree (DT) classifier [HAN 00] module for detecting network attacks. Specifically, Snort is employed to detect known attacks based on policy rules specified in the knowledge base. DT classifier builds a decision tree using behavior base and predicts class label of preprocessed packets. The NIDS module is installed on every processing servers as well as all VMs in the cloud, and the architecture consists of four main components: *packet processing, intrusion detection, storage* and *alert system*. In particular, the *storage* component contains three databases: *knowledge base*, which stores known attack signatures; *behavior base*, which stores network behavior having both malicious and normal packet and *central log database*, which is used to record malicious event's log reported by Snort or DT classifier.

Despite the widespread application of Snort [ROE 13] and Bro [PAX 99], their technical limitations always remain in the typical application scenarios. For example, setting up a small-scale Snort instance is a well-documented activity, but it quickly becomes a significant engineering challenge when network size is enlarged. Systems like Bro may provide flexibility, customization and analysis capabilities but are significantly complex in setup and require domain experts.

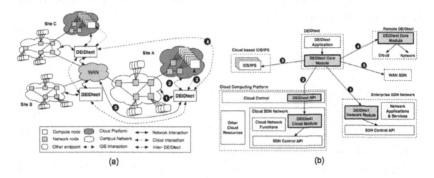

(a)   (b)

Figure 5.5. *(a) DEIDtect architecture. (b) Components within DEIDtec system [SHA 14]*

To tackle these problems, the authors of [SHA 14] proposed a distributed elastic intrusion detection architecture, called *DEIDtect*, to provide a distributed framework for cross-site intrusion detection. In particular, the DEIDtect exploits cloud computing technologies to consolidate compute resources to handle the computing needs by IDS/IPS tools. It applies SDN technology to allow administrators to monitor network traffics at any point in the network (e.g. at the access edge, distribution, core or Internet border) and feed back the monitored traffic streams to security collectors for further anomaly detection. The high-level view of DEIDtect architecture is shown in Figure 5.5, which is composed of the following components:

– enterprise SDN network, which creates tap points in the network, to deliver monitored traffic to the cloud;

– cloud computing platform, which instantiates cloud-based IDS/IPS instances and routes traffic from the network to the appropriate IDS/IPS instances;

– instantiated IDS/IPS instances, which implement intrusion detection and prevention;

– remote DEIDtect systems, which enable distributed security functions;

– WAN SDN network, which allows delivery of monitored network traffic between distributed locations.

5.2. NFV-based implementations

It is well recognized that one of the major attack targets in the cloud is related to cloud virtual infrastructure, including hypervisor, virtual switch (vSwitch) and hosted VMs. For example, a monitoring appliance called *CloudSec* is proposed in [IBR 11] to provide active, transparent and real-time security monitoring. Thanks to the Virtual Machine Introspection (VMI) technique that facilitates fine-grained inspection of VM's physical memory, multiple VMs hosted on a cloud platform can be concurrently monitored without installing any monitoring code inside the hosted VMs. The architecture of CloudSec is shown in Figure 5.6, where the VMI layer serves as the core of CloudSec architecture and contains two components: *back end component* and *front end component*. Specifically, the *back end component* enables the hypervisor to gain control over the hosted VMs to suspend any access to physical memory and CPU. It performs necessary security checks and alerts the front end when malicious attacks occurred. The *front end component* is a set of APIs that retrieve information about the monitored VM's and control accesses to physical memory and CPU registers. The front end makes CloudSec an external extension of the hypervisor that enables transparent access to physical memory without installing any additional security code.

In [YAO 14], the authors propose an encrypted VMI system, called *CryptVMI*, to provide users a complete status of their virtual instances while keeping confidentiality of user's data from attackers by using encryption technique. Figure 5.7 shows a high-level view of CryptVMI architecture, which consists of three main components: *User*, *Query handler* and *Introspection application*:

– User sends request to query handler for anomaly detection. Once a query is accepted, the user will assign a unique ID and a random symmetric key s. Thus, all the communication between the user and query handler will be encrypted with this key s.

– Query handler: When the query handler receives user request, it firstly checks whether the user is associated with any VMs. If so, the query handler then uses the cloud service API to locate the IP address of the compute node that holds those VMs.

– Introspection application inspects malicious attacks using VMI tools built on the top of the VMI library.

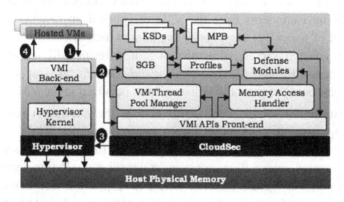

Figure 5.6. *High-level architecture [IBR 11] of CloudSec*

In [ZHA 15], the authors attempt to address the same security issue about resource sharing, as the scheme previously discussed. In particular, a flexible architecture, called *CloudMonatt*, was developed to monitor the security status of the user's VMs. It provides a flexible distributed cloud architecture that can detect and monitor the security health of the user's VM on the basis of a rich set of security properties for VM attestation. The CloudMonatt is built upon the property-based attestation model and provides several novel features, such as monitoring different aspects of security health, mapping actual measurement, to be easily exploited by users, and taking countermeasures on the basis of the monitored results. Specifically, the architecture consists of the following four components, as shown in Figure 5.8:

– Cloud customer: The "customers" or users are the initiator and end-verifier in the system. CloudMonatt gives the users two modes of operations: (1) *One-time attestation*, which allows users to request the attestations at any time; (2) *Periodic attestation*, which allows users to request for periodic attestations with a specified constant or random period.

– Cloud controller: It acts as the cloud manager that is responsible for taking VM requests and serving them for each user. It contains three modules: (1) *Policy validation module*, which collects the monitored security measurements from the VMs of concern, in response to the requests of users; (2) *Deployment module*, which allocates each VM on the selected server, while the measured result will report back to the controller and (3) *Response module*, which takes appropriate countermeasures if potential vulnerabilities occurred in the VMs.

– Attestation server: This server acts as the attestation requester and appraiser. It consists of two essential modules: (1) *Property interpretation module*, which is responsible for validating security measurements, interpreting properties and making attestation decisions; (2) *Property certificate module*, which is responsible for issuing an attestation certificate for the monitored properties. In addition, the attestation server is used to monitor malicious attacks on user's VMs, while the cloud controller is responsible for management.

– Cloud server, which is the computer that runs multiple VMs. In CloudMonatt, a cloud server has two modules: (1) *Monitor module*, which contains different types of monitors to provide comprehensive and rich security measurement; (2) *Trust module*, which is responsible for server authentication.

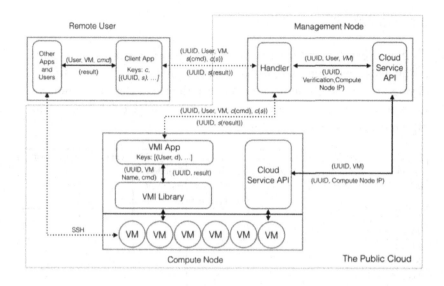

Figure 5.7. *High-level view of CryptVMI architecture: dotted lines represent secure connections between the encrypted components [YAO 14]*

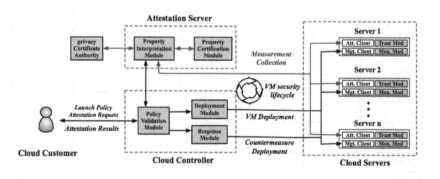

Figure 5.8. *Architectural overview of CloudMonatt [ZHA 15]*

5.3. Comparative analysis

It is clear that NFV-based IDS/IPS implementations have some advantages over the traditional implementations. This section is devoted to a careful comparison between the two cases. To summarize the specific discussions in terms of several selected criteria, some highlights are presented in Table 5.1.

Example design of IAM	Flexible deployment	Centralized control and management	Complexity reduction of life cycle management	No specific function required	Scalability	Cost saving
Kargus [JAM 12]	X	X	X	X	/	X
BlindBox [SHE 15]	X	X	X	X	X	X
IDS for wobile network [ZHA 03]	/	X	X	X	/	X
Distributed IDS for wobile network [MOR 12]	X	X	X	X	/	X
NIDS for cloud [MOD 12]	X	X	X	X	/	/
DEIDtect [SHA 14]	/	/	/	/	/	/
CloudSec [IBR 11]	/	/	X	X	/	/
CryptVMI [YAO 14]	/	/	X	X	/	/
CloudMonatt [ZHA 15]	/	/	/	/	/	/

Notations: "/" and "X" denote that NFV characteristics are satisfied and not satisfied, respectively, "-" means data source is insufficient.

Table 5.1. *Comparative analysis between conventional and virtualization-based IDS/IPS*

– Specific functions: The traditional concept of IDS/IPS is often placed directly behind the firewall to provide a complementary layer of analysis by monitoring malicious events, known as in-line deployment. Having an IDS/IPS in-line means that all data coming into or leaving a corporation network will be captured by this device. However, their capabilities are limited to support monitoring inside the host itself, especially for VMs in the cloud environment. Moreover, the nature of virtualization makes cloud environments complex; it is therefore difficult to monitor malicious processes/activities. These facts lead to the development of Virtual Machine Introspection (VMI) techniques [GAR 03]. Nevertheless, embedding VMI into their systems requires customized settings that fit into specific environments, making VMI more difficult to integrate with the existing security monitoring system, such as Bro network security monitor [PAX 99]. Also, applying the VMI technique might also break the boundaries of the segregation between multiple tenants, leading to the exposure or leakage of data privacy. Although the authors in [YAO 14] proposed an encrypted Virtual Machine Introspection system, *CryptVMI*, to maintain user confidentiality, it incurs the costs of encryption and computation on encrypted data.

– Flexible deployment: Many high-performance IDSs/IPSs rely on dedicated network processor and RAM, apparently increasing the cost and limiting operation flexibility. In contrast, NFV-based implementations can consolidate security network functions onto industry-standard servers, switches and storage hardware located in the distribution center, thereby reducing the cost and operational complexity, mainly thanks to automation and orchestration. It also aims to increase compatibility with existing deployment, facilitate operations and maintain procedure. For example, the CloudSec monitoring application [IBR 11] is used to inspect security threats on virtual infrastructure. The basic idea of CloudSec is to utilize VMI technique to provide monitoring capability without installing any security code inside the VMs. It is worth noting that most recent VMI researches are developed on the basis of installing code inside the hosted VMs to achieve real-time and active monitoring.

– Centralized control and management: Traditionally, network operators need to set up and configure IDS/IPS boxes directly at the location according to the business requirements. This makes the configuration and management process very complicated and time consuming. The given examples illustrate that NFV has the potential to reduce the complexities based on software-centric approaches. Another example is CloudMonatt proposed in [ZHA 15], in which a controller module acts as a manager for malicious detection and VM attestation: when the controller accepts the request from users to monitor security health of their VMs, it will assign attestation server to inspect user's VMs whether any potential vulnerabilities have occurred. Then, results are sent back to the user after verification is succeeded. The controller carries out appropriate re-mediation response once vulnerabilities are found.

– Complexity of lifecycle management: If we consider the current IPS/IDS deployment, this native function is allocated and operated directly behind the firewall to provide a complementary layer of analysis for detecting dangerous contents. The IDS/IPS is placed in-line (in the direct communication path between source and destination), actively analyzing and taking automated actions on all internal traffic flows. They are configured and controlled by network administrators. When transitioning to virtual IDS/IPS appliances, service providers who provide underlying infrastructure and security services have to deal with a lot of complexity. The challenges include navigating a myriad of business processes and operational complexities ranging from management, installation, administration and maintenance. Additionally, the complexity of network management of independent security monitoring could make it more complicated to handle and potentially produce communication overhead, thereby bringing negative impacts on system performance. For example:

- operational complexity: in [IBR 11], as CloudSec utilizes VMI technique to monitor volatile memory for further detecting user or kernel rootkits. The challenges of CloudSec implementation is the mapping of the introspected low-level raw bytes of memory into high-level OS data structure instances. For this, the authors construct two components in the VMI layer: VMI back end and VMI APIs front end. The VMI back-end enables the hypervisor to gain control over the hosted VMs. The VMI APIs front end is an external extension of the hypervisor that controls access to physical memory and CPU registers, if threats are detected. The operational complexity is that every time when a hosted VM is powered on, the VMI back end sends notification message to VMI APIs front end. Then, the VMI APIs front end interacts with VM-Threated Pool Manager to create a separate thread for each newly activated VM, checks the control registers of VM's CPU to know memory layout of VM's hardware and queries the kernel version using Kernel Structure Definition (KSD). Next, Semantic Gap Builder (SGB) read specific physical memory pages and map physical memory bytes to obtain high-level OS view. This view (including running processes table, system table and interrupt table) will be analyzed by Defense Module to detect security threats. The sequential steps can be found in Figure 5.6. However, these overall operations incur complexity, especially communication overhead and process synchronization;

    - management complexity: in [YAO 14], every communication between users and management node needs to be encrypted using a random symmetric key provided by its management node. This symmetric key is consequently encrypted with user's public key. Consecutively, each user needs to establish a Secure Socket Layer (SSL) connection to communicate with their VMs. Each time the query handler module (in management node) receives user request, it first checks whether there is any associated VMs belonging to this user. If the condition is true, the query handler uses cloud service API to locate the IP address of the compute node that holds the designated VM, and sends inspection request to *introspection application module* to monitor malicious events. If a large number of users are concurrently requesting to the service, the management node could be faced with management complexity and communication overhead, leading to a potential single point of failure. While NFV is initially intended to bring simplicity and ease of use in virtual network service for those cloud tenants, the lack of flexibility for VMI integration with existing security monitoring system and the possibility of preserving confidential information in VMs make deployment of virtual security monitoring difficult.

– Dynamic and elastic scaling of services: NFV brings significant advantages that allow service providers to scale up and scale down network services on demand. This dynamic scalability improves service request response times significantly, with a faster reaction, in the presence of service configuration updates, such as re-configure forwarding paths and resetting policy rules. This characteristic of NFV facilitates the design of security monitoring and attestation of VMs like CloudMonatt [ZHA 15], which can (1) dynamically add or remove new cloud servers; (2) arbitrarily integrate desirable security properties with security policy rule sets in real time, avoiding effects on the system performance.

– Cost: If an enterprise network becomes larger and continues growing, hardware investment will increase, and non-trivial efforts need to be paid to configure IDS/IPS device. Thus, using NFV-based IDS/IPS solution such as the one reported in [ZHA 15], the cost and management complexity can be significantly reduced. The users can leverage a centralized monitoring, which is introduced in the cloud system, to perform checking process and inspect suspicious events at the end-node without incurring additional capital expenditure and installation cost.

6

Network Isolation

Virtual datacenters in cloud environment become increasingly popular and widely used for many types of business service. In particular, it leverages standardization and consolidation of commodity hardware to allow effective and safe sharing of pooled resources. Through a hypervisor-based mechanism, it is able to isolate the compute resources between the tenants that are co-located on the same end host. However, resource sharing brings new challenges and security issues, mainly due to the fact that the tenants do not have full control over both underlying infrastructure and physical, virtual network resources. Thus, malicious attackers are given opportunities to get the information of the tenants of interest by intentionally or unintentionally consuming a large part of the network, intrusively trapping their data and further performing illegal operations through side-channel attacks or DoS attacks. One of the important solutions is network isolation, which has been taken as an essential building block for improving security level as well as ensuring security control in resource sharing and data communication.

This chapter surveys the basic functions of network isolation in different scenarios. Then, NFV-based implementations are exemplified and further identified. The differences and similarities between the two cases are compared.

6.1. Case studies

Generally, there are two main types of network isolation [ORA 12]: *network traffic isolation* and *network security isolation*. The first solution is to physically or logically segment networks to provide secure communication and offer higher bandwidth for specific users. In particular, in physical network isolation, NICs are normally dedicated to specific network services, so the segmentation is provided between the networks. The logical network isolation uses software to isolate physical network resources such as VLANs. Thus, network traffic from multiple users shares the same physical interfaces, while each application can only use its pre-allocated resource. The second solution of network traffic isolation is resource control or QoS management. This relies on efficient traffic monitoring and management, ensuring that users consume only their share of network bandwidth. Moreover, additional mechanisms are required to improve network traffic isolation, such as (1) establishment of SLAs to meet network QoS, (2) bottleneck identification to prevent network congestion and (3) security information gathering to prevent attacks. Several technical approaches include:

1) using network firewalls to filter potential security threats coming from untrusted sources, whereby the incoming data packets are blocked if they match the policy rules;

2) applying VLAN tagging to provide extra layers of security and bandwidth control and ensure that packets sent by one user cannot be observed by others;

3) adopting role-based security or role-based access control to employ fine-grained authorization to resource objects.

In the following discussion, we will exemplify the applications of network isolation in several typical scenarios.

6.1.1. *IT scenario*

In [JUB 14], the authors point out the security issues when network devices (e.g., computer and network printer) are connected to the network. These devices can be potentially compromised if they are not equipped with appropriate security mechanisms. Therefore, the authors proposed a system, *POSTER*, for keeping an intra-LAN in a secure state by isolating those network information devices. It is designed for (1) limiting the communication between devices in the LAN based on security control policy, (2) monitoring the communication in the LAN using an IDS system and therefore isolating network information devices which perform an illegal communication and (3) maintaining a secure state in the LAN.

The proposed system consists of three components: *IDS*, *OpenFlow switch*, and *OpenFlow controller*. The IDS first performs monitoring for all communications inside the LAN in order to detect attacks or preliminary attacks from LAN and then sends detected information to the OpenFlow controller. The OpenFlow controller analyzes the detected information to analyze the current LAN situation and to detect the device which illegal communication comes from. It then applies flow control to this device using the OpenFlow switch.

In [SUZ 05], the author pointed out the problem with network separation. Nowadays, network sites are often secured by a firewall to filter bogus traffic from outside at the border of the network site. This kind of defense model, however, obstructs the deployment of IPv6 application and services. Therefore, the author proposed a *quarantine model*, in which network nodes are accommodated to separate network segments according to their security level and different security policies are implemented on each network segment. According to this model, there is a quarantine server, which acts as a monitoring server to monitor the security level of the node, and a policy enforcer to accommodate the node to a network segment on the basis of its security level. The quarantine model consists of two features: security level measurement and dynamic network separation.

– Security level measurement: to measure security level, the authors utilize the tool from [MIC 05, NAR 98].

– Dynamic network separation: this relies on four corresponding separation methods:

- Layer 2 separation: by relying on separating network traffic using IEEE 802.1Q for VLAN and IEEE 802.1X for PNAC (Port-based Network Access Control).

- Layer 3 separation: this method of network separation relies on changing the IP address of a node through the use of DHCPv6 [DRO 03] and IPv6 address auto-configuration [THO 15].

- Tunnel-based separation: a node communicates with the assigned tunnel server for creating the tunnel, e.g. IPsec-VPN, SSL-VPN.

- Policy based separation: this is a high-level network separation. A node needs to periodically obtain the policy from the policy server, so that network administrators can take control over the node from outside. This network separation depends on a policy description defined by network administrators.

6.1.2. *Telco scenarios: mobile devices and networks*

To improve the use of physical infrastructure comprising a mobile wireless network as a platform for supporting *mobility as a service*, a Virtual Private Mobile Network (*VPMN*), is proposed in [BAL 11]. Specifically, the VPMN is able to leverage virtualization benefits to dynamically create a private, resource isolated, customizable, and end-to-end mobile network on a shared physical mobile network. Thus, the VPMN framework can be optimized over Long Term Evolution (LTE) and Evolved Packet Core (EPC) mobile technology.

Traditionally, when User Equipment (UE), e.g. mobile devices, intends to contact a server on the Internet, the UE first sends a request via radio link to Radio Access Network (RAN), e.g. eNodeB, and then forwards user packets to an appropriated Serving Gateway (S-GW). This S-GW will establish a service session context with a P-GW, which acts as a gateway to the Internet. To achieve isolated traffics of one UE from other UEs, the eNodeB uses a logical point-to-point link to the S-GW by encapsulating all data packets from the UE using GTP (GPRS Tunneling Protocol), and the S-GW similarly uses another GTP tunnel to the P-GW. However, traffic flows would be gained with convoluted data paths which depend on the application request.

Otherwise it might be infeasible for the enterprise that uses cloud computing resources.

A VPMN framework can help reduce complexity and dynamically create an isolated end-to-end mobile network. It consists of a *VPMN controller* responsible for accepting UEs' requests and creating and manipulating infrastructure for the UEs. With virtualization and partition mechanisms, each UE will have its own mobility elements (e.g. virtual instances for eNodeB, S-GW and P-GW) rather than sharing network elements like a traditional model. The advance of virtualization, S-GW and P-GW in LTE can be realized through software implementation.

In [KOW 09], the authors identified security issues over Fourth Generation (4G) technologies like Worldwide Interoperability for Microwave Access (WiMAX), Long Term Evolution (LTE) and Ultra Mobile Broadband (UMB). The challenges of securing 4G networks are not fundamentally different from those of 3G networks in terms of confidentiality, authentication, network separation and network planning consideration. Therefore, the authors proposed network separation and IPsec CA certificate-based security management for 4G networks. Its contribution is to isolate various traffic paths among different Network Elements (NEs), restrict the operation and maintain packets to a specific network zone and prevent NEs from accessing unauthorized network zones. The proposed method mainly contains the following three parts:

– Setting up SSH connection: in order to set up the IPsec connectivity between various NEs, a certificate needs to be transferred across the network. That is, to avoid insecure transfer of IPsec certificates, an SSH connection must be established.

– Establishing secure communication channel-based IPsec: once the SSH connection has been established, two NEs need to run the Internet Key Exchange (IKE) protocol. IKE will perform peer-to-peer authentication by exchanging X.509 certificates among the two peers. After authentication is successful, the Management Element Security Agent (MESA) pulls the public certificate from NE securely through the use of SSH connection, which has already been established. Then, the

MESA securely transfers the signed NE certificate and root certificate to the NE for further establishing a secure communication channel.

– Network separation using VLAN: VLAN techniques achieve better security and isolate various traffic paths into a specific zone.

In addition, the Android OS has suffered various attacks recently due to the lack of effective isolation mechanism. For example, the authors of [BUG 11] proposed a practical and lightweight domain isolation on Android, called *TrustDroid* framework, which aims to mitigate unauthorized data access and provide secure communication among applications with different trust levels. The concept of *TrustDroid* is to group applications in isolated domains, so the applications that belong to different domains are prevented from communicating with each other. The isolation is provided at different layers of the Android software stack:

– At the middleware layer: prevents inter-domain application communication and data access. For example, TrustDroid enforces data filtering on standard databases so that applications can only have access to the data subset of their respective domains. The middleware layer is extended with four components: *policy manager, firewall manager and kernel Mandatory Access Control (MAC) manager, additional MAC for Inter Component Communication (ICC)* and *package manager*.

- Policy manager: the policy manager is responsible for the determination of the isolation domain for each different application and issue of the corresponding policies to enforce isolation.

- Firewall manager and the kernel-level MAC manager are instructed by the policy manager to apply the corresponding rules to enforce the isolation on the network layer and the kernel layer.

- Additional MAC for Inter Component Communication (ICC): with domain isolation, applications in different domains are prevented from communication with each other via ICC.

- Package manager: the package manager is responsible for installation of new applications.

– At the kernel layer: enforces mandatory access control on the file system and on Inter Process Communications (IPC) channels. For example, TrustDroid applies policies to enforce domain isolation at the file-system level.

– At the network layer: mediates network traffic regarding policy settings.

6.1.3. *Public clouds*

In [BRA 10], the author pointed out that the isolation capabilities provided by conventional enterprise datacenter technology are inadequate to support multiple tenants in a cloud environment. Isolation failure in a shared resource system is often characterized in terms of its impact on the performances, privacy and security of one or more tenants. Thus, the authors proposed to explore the strategic use of heterogeneous physical network hardware to isolate multiple tenants in the clouds. By introducing the use of Coarse Wavelength Division Multiplexing (CWDM) optical network technology, it leverages hardware-level support to ensure domain boundary integrity by:

– reducing the incidence of incorrect physical network configurations;

– eliminating the possibility of misconfiguration in inter-domain communication settings;

– facilitating visually verifiable domain isolation.

In fact, the main idea of CWDM is to multiplex multiple independent communication channels on a single optical fiber using passive optical devices. As such, one single fiber carries multiple sub-channels, which are segregated using wavelength and associated color-coding, as shown in Table 6.1.

1470 nm: Gray	1490 nm: Violet
1510 nm: Blue	1530 nm: Green
1550 nm: Yellow	1570 nm: Orange
1590 nm: Red	1610 nm: Brown

Table 6.1. *A set of wavelengths and associated case color-coding commonly used for 1 GBPS CWDM system [BRA 10]*

In [CIS 14b, CIS 15c], Cisco pointed out the problem in traditional network segmentation provided by VLANs due to the inefficient use of available network links, rigid requirement on device placements in datacenter networks and the limited scalability to a maximum 4094 VLANs. Using such VLANs becomes a limited factor in a cloud network. Therefore, Cisco, in partnership with other leading vendors, proposed the *Virtual Extensible LAN (VXLAN)* solution to provide elastic workload placement, higher scalability of layer 2 segmentation and large-scale flexibility to support multi-tenant clouds over a shared common physical infrastructure. The nature of VXLAN is designed to provide the same Ethernet layer 2 network services as VLAN does, but with greater extensibility and flexibility. Some examples of VXLAN products are the Cisco Nexus 1000V series [CIS 15a], Cisco Nexus 9000V series [CIS 15c] and QFX5100 Ethernet Switch [JUN 15]. The process of VXLAN can be discussed as follows.

– Sender site: when a VM needs to communicate with another VM on a different host, it first sends an Ethernet frame to its tunnel endpoint, called *VXLAN Tunnel End Point (VTEP)*. The VTEP on the physical host looks up the VXLAN ID associated with this VM and determines whether the designation MAC address is on the same subnet. If true, the VTEP inserts an outer header (e.g. consists of outer MAC address, outer IP address and VXLAN header) in front of the original MAC address of the original Ethernet frame. The final packet is transmitted to the destination VTEP as a unicast transmission to the IP address of the remote VTEP connecting to the destination VM.

– Receiver site: upon reception the remote VTEP verifies whether the VXLAN ID is valid and associated with the destination VM. If so, the VTEP strips its outer header and passes the original Ethernet frame to the destination VM. Thus, the destination VM never knows information about the VXLAN ID or VXLAN encapsulation process.

In [VMW 16], industry-leading virtualization software companies like VMware pointed out the endpoint security issue caused by the traditional client/server model. It increases the complexity and affects the overall performance while operating in a virtualization environment. For example, in endpoint security-based client/server models, all the VMs need to install client software that stores machine detail, signature and so on, resulting in a significant burden on CPU and RAM, as well as causing additional storage.

Therefore, VMware proposed vShield solution to have a more efficient security model. Specifically, it provides customers with different trust levels through the use of complete network isolation (e.g. firewall and VPN), so all the application deployments are enforced to the proper segmentation and trust zones. Also, it provides granular control over network traffic by using VPN services to ensure confidentiality and integrity of communication between tenants.

Additionally, vShield solutions provide the following key services:

– vShield App: creates application boundary-based policy enforcement.

– vShield Edge: enables secure multi-tenancy with firewall, VPN, DHCP, NAT, load balancing and port group isolation services.

– vShield Endpoint: provides on-host anti-virus and malware protection. This concept eliminates the need to maintain individual security software in each VM.

– vShield Manager: provides a central point of control for managing, deploying, reporting, logging and integrating third-party security services.

– vShield Zones: provides basic protection in virtual networks, such as firewall protection and traffic analysis.

The lack of visibility and the limitation of control over resources and underlying infrastructure mean cloud computing can be exposed to some security threats, potentially leading malicious tenants to mount attacks (e.g. DoS) against another. In order to tackle these risks, a cloud hosting infrastructure was proposed in [MUN 11] to provide a strong guarantee for resources and network isolation. In particular, the authors proposed *SilverLine*, a system that enables cloud providers to offer *security as a service* to protect tenant data in cloud environments. *SilverLine* relies on the cloud provider's virtual machine manager (e.g. XenServer or VMware ESXi) to perform data and network isolation between various cloud tenants and combines this isolation with modifications to the guest OS for additional data isolation. These mechanisms prevent data leaks due to compromise, misconfiguration or side-channel attacks from co-resident cloud tenants. The design of SilverLine implements two types of isolation: *data isolation* and *network isolation*.

– Data isolation: to enforce data isolation, the authors use a transparent OS-level information-flow tracking layer to allow tenants to label their data with a security level. It is assisted by an enforcement layer in the cloud provider's virtual machine monitor (e.g. Xen and VMware), to ensure that data from one tenant is not propagated to an untrusted server which belongs to other tenants. Figure 6.1 shows SilverLine installed by the cloud service provider in the privileged guest OS (ex. Dom0 in Xen). The design of SilverLine has three parts:

- Two software modules in the privileged guest OS (dom0), data isolation and network isolation.

- A labeling service attached to the cloud provider's storage services (e.g. a database service).

- An OS-level information-flow tracking component, called *Pedigree*, installed on VM instances. Pedigree uses a labels service to track information flow between all the files and processes associated with the VM's instances. If the data of tenants accidentally travels to another tenant's VM or to a machine outside the cloud provider's network, the *enforcer* component in dom0 will stop the flow and indicate potential data breaches.

– Network isolation: hence, a malicious cloud tenant can use side-channel attacks, either network-based or cache-based, to gain co-residence on a victim tenant's VM. In order to isolate these victim's VMs, the authors applied the OpenFlow/NOX platform [GUD 08, NOX 08] to perform network isolation and co-resident checks.

- Isolation using pseudo-IP address: each VM is assigned a randomly allocated pseudo-IP address to communicate with other VMs. The mapping between pseudo-IP address and the actual VM IP address is maintained by a single centralized service, known as a local NOX controller.

- Co-residence checks: used to defend against co-residence attacks by running a trace route to determine hop count to the victim. If hop count is zero or one, then the attacker is likely co-resident on the victim's VM. To defend this attack, for traffic between VMs within a physical machine, SilverLine drops packets with low Time To Live (TTV) values.

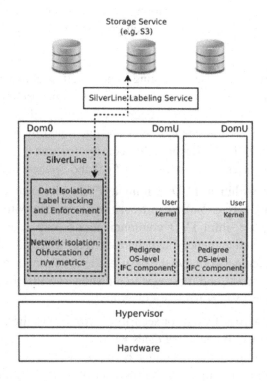

Figure 6.1. *SilverLine architecture, which is installed in the privileged guest OS [MUN 11]*

6.1.4. *Trusted environment*

In [CAB 07], the authors point out the problem in virtualization, as VM can use a virtual network card to connect to the actual physical network card of a physical machine. The potential security issue is that all VMs can see other VM's traffic passing around them because there is neither isolation nor other security guarantees. Therefore, the authors proposed the abstraction of Trusted Virtual Domains (TVDs) to enhance secure network virtualization frameworks. The framework allows groups of related VMs running on separate physical machines to be connected together as they were on their own separate network fabric. At the same time, it also helps to enforce cross-group security requirements such as isolation, confidentiality, integrity and information flow control, so that each group of VMs contains the same security protection.

The framework uses existing and well-established network virtualization technologies, such as Ethernet encapsulation, VLAN tagging and VPNs to enhance security of virtualized network zones. However, these existing technologies are integrated by a management framework. In TVD architecture, the security flow can be classified into two main categories: *security within a TVD* and *security across TVDs*.

– Security within a TVD: within a TVD, all Virtual Processing Elements (VPEs) (e.g. VMs) can freely communicate with each other. For this purpose, intra-TVD communications may take place only over authenticated and encrypted channels (e.g. IPSec) or alternatively through a trusted network. On the basis of the isolation, dishonest VPEs in one TVD cannot send messages to a dishonest VPE of other TVDs, unless the inter-TVD policies are identified.

– Security across TVDs: for security across TVDs, there is an Inter-TVD management module that deals with:

   - fabric information exchange between the TVDs;

   - enforcing the inter-TVD flow control policies among external zones. These policies specify conditions under which VLANs (belonging to different TVDs) are allowed to exchange information;

   - approving admission requests such as when a new VM requests to join the TVD;

   - associating the VM with the appropriate TVD master

Physically, each TVD is implemented on the basis of at least two VLANs: *external VLAN* and *internal VLAN*. The external VLAN serves as a backbone to send/receive information to/from other TVDs. The internal VLAN connects all machines that are part of a TVD. The benefit of having separate VLANs between internal and external communication help facilitate unrestricted communication within a TVD. It also provides a complete isolation of one TVD from other TVDs, if the inter-TVD policies identify that no information flow between TVDs is allowed.

6.2. NFV-based implementations

A large variety of isolation techniques exist. However, when a network size becomes larger due to the expansion of cloud computing technology, virtualized network isolation based on NFV implementation becomes essential. In this section, we investigate some example schemes about virtualized network isolation that supports a large number of VNFs.

In [NUN 13], the authors discussed efficient resource utilization in the cloud environment. Each tenant's resource needs to be isolated, which requires two major requirements. First, it is necessary to guarantee that services of one tenant are not affected by others, either accidentally or maliciously. Second, it is essential to make the model economically viable. Therefore, the authors proposed *DCPortals* as a virtual network abstraction, to provide traffic isolation in a virtualized datacenter environment based on an SDN solution. This, by offering logical isolation among multiple tenants that share the same infrastructure, without requiring any additional hardware. Each tenant sees its VMs as connected to a single virtual switch, apart from all others, for which VMs connected to the same network can communicate freely.

Figure 6.2 shows the DCPortals architecture implemented as a network hypervisor module built on the top of POX SDN controller [POX 08].

– DCPortals: in DCPortals, the virtual network abstraction provides a clear representation of the logic isolation among the multiple tenant networks that share the same infrastructure. It interacts with OpenStack for querying tenant's information and with Open vSwitch to identify network isolation.

– OpenStack: the OpenStack database contains all the tenant's information such as tenant's virtual networks, tenant identification, tenant's VMs and VMs' location. With these sets of information, Open vSwitches know how to handle packet flows to/from a given VM.

– Open vSwitch: Open vSwitches identify network isolation based on OpenStack's RSA access key. DCPortals assume that all VMs that share a given RSA key belong to the same isolated network. For example, to verify whether packets from VM A can reach VM B, the DCPortals query the OpenStack database and check if A's RSA key is the same as B's. If true, both VMs are in the same virtual network and traffic from one can reach the other. Otherwise, if A and B were found to be in separated networks, a packet from A to B will be dropped by the first Open vSwitch along its path to avoid extra processing in the network.

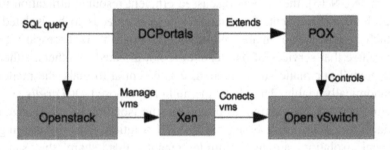

Figure 6.2. *DCPortals architecture and relations between each module [NUN 13]*

In [BER 08], the authors identified security attacks caused by sharing physical hardware platforms in cloud datacenters. Specifically, the authors proposed Trusted Virtual Datacenter (TVDc) for achieving strong resource isolation and integrity guarantee. In TVDc, a group of VMs and resources collaborate, called *Trusted Virtual Domains (TVDs)* [GRI 05, CAT 10]. In particular, TVDs provide a strong isolation between workloads by enforcing a Mandatory Access Control (MAC) policy throughout the datacenter. This policy defines which VMs can access which resources and moreover which VMs can communicate with each other. This ensures that resources allocated to one TVD cannot be accessible to VMs of another TVD. Additionally, it allows centralized management of the underlying isolation and integrity infrastructure. According to the design of TVDc, the isolation infrastructure can be divided into two parts: hypervisor-based isolation and network-based isolation.

– Hypervisor-based isolation: TVDc is implemented based on hypervisor security architecture, called *sHype* [SAI 05], to enforce information flow and control access to inter-VM communication and resources according to the active security policy. The sHype guards the assignment of resources to VMs and inter-VM communication by (1) implementing Mandatory Access Control (MAC), as a reference monitor, inside the Virtual Machine Monitor (VMM) and (2) leveraging access control policy to define the security contexts of policy enforcement for those VMs and resources and then determine whether requested communication is permitted or denied on the basis of access control policy rules.

Figure 6.3 (a) illustrates the architecture of sHype, which is embedded into a fully functional multiple platform research hypervisor (vHype).

– Network-based isolation: the basic concept of TVDc network isolation is based on VLANs. Such VLANs emulate separate physical LANs on a single physical LAN, by prepending to each Ethernet frame with appropriate VLAN ID. All VMs are restricted to connect only to those VLANs that have the same shared type. Therefore, VMs with the same type can communicate to other VMs through VLAN but cannot communicate with any other VMs that belong to different types.

Figure 6.3 (b) shows the concept of TVDc network isolation. Two Physical Machines (PM) are connected through a network switch. Each machine is running two VMs, one is labeled Market Analysis (MA) and the other is the Security Underwriting (SU). It consists of two different embodiments of VLANs, one embodiment is implemented in software by the VMM within each PM and the other is in hardware by a network switch external to PM. The VMM on each PM restricts each software VLAN to send/receive packets only to the appropriate hardware VLAN. The overall result is that MA VMs and SU VMs can communicate only with MA VMs and SU VMs, respectively.

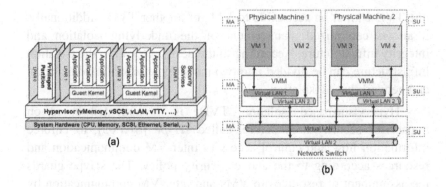

Figure 6.3. *(a) Hypervisor architecture with security services running on isolated partition [SAI 05], (b) TVDc network isolation [BER 08]*

In [CIS 09], the networking industry refers to the benefit of network virtualization, which can create logical isolated network partitions overlaid on top of a common enterprise physical network infrastructure. Each partition is logically isolated from others but provides the same services that are available in a traditional dedicated enterprise network, so that the end user is virtually connected to a dedicated network providing privacy, security, an independent set of policies, service level and even routing decision.

Therefore, the authors proposed a path isolation mechanism to achieve end-to-end isolated network virtualization, as shown in Figure 6.4 (a). Path isolation refers to the creation of independent logical traffic paths over a shared physical network infrastructure. It can be classified into two categories: *policy-based path isolation* and *control plane-based path isolation*.

– Policy-based path isolation: restricts the forwarding traffics into specific destinations based on a policy and additional information provided by the forwarding control plane. A classic example of policy-based path isolation used an Access Control List (ACL) to control network traffics. However, the use of policy-based path isolation could be faced with administrative burden, is error prone and has inconsistent policy updates, when policies need to be configured in a distributed way.

– Control plane-based path isolation: restricts the propagation of routing information, so that only nodes belonging to the same subnet can communicate among each other. To achieve control plane virtualization, a device must have multiple control/forwarding instances, one for each virtual network, and such by using Virtual Routing and Forwarding (VRF). The use of VRF allows the customers to virtualize a network device from a layer 3 standpoint, creating different virtual routers in the shared physical device, as shown in Figure 6.4 (b). In general, a VRF instance consists of an IP routing table, a derived forwarding table, a set of interfaces used for the forwarding table, a set of rules and routing protocols.

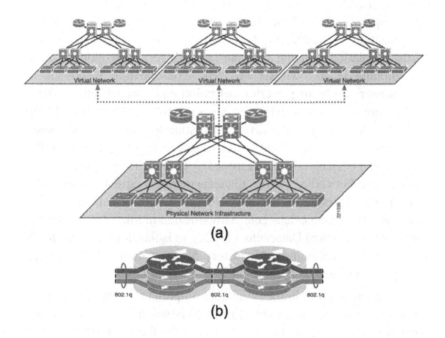

Figure 6.4. *(a) Path isolation design in network virtualization environment (b) VRF for virtualization in layer 3 network devices [CIS 09]. For a color version of this figure, see www.iste.co.uk/zhang/networks.zip*

6.3. Comparative analysis

In this section, we analyze the differences between virtualized network solutions and the classic implementations. In particular, we take the metric defined in [NUN 13, BER 08, CIS 09] as reference for discussions, while the conclusions are highlighted in Table 6.2.

– Cost and efficiency: traditional models of network services cause inefficient resource utilization, as specific hardware is assigned for a specific function and resource pools are customized per application usage. By using network virtualization solutions, capital and operational costs can be reduced as network services delivery are removed from a physical device to a virtual context, without the need to deploy specialized hardware for every network service instance. Also, virtualization can reduce the total cost of ownership by sharing each hardware platform among multiple network service workloads, each one running in its own set of VMs. Consolidating workloads in this manner results in powerful utilization and cost reduction. These benefits are consistent with the objectives identified in [BER 08, CIS 09, NUN 13]. In particular, the network isolation technique was proposed in [NUN 13] by using virtual switch to isolate tenant's network traffic from other. Path isolation was proposed by Cisco [CIS 09], using Virtual Routing and Forwading (VRF), to create different virtual routers in the same physical device, as shown in Figure 6.4 (b). Then, the authors of [BER 08] introduce datacenter virtualization in trusted environment, called Trusted Virtual Datacenter (TVDc), to isolate tenant's workloads form others by enforcing a Mandatory Access Control (MAC) policy throughout a virtual datacenter.

– Scalability: scalability is another important feature offered by NFV. For example, regarding scalability issues in NFV context, the authors [TAY 15] show that (1) it improves flexible deployment in real time to meet customer requirements and (2) it supports the growing demands, enabling new services to be quickly deployed, automated and managed, with minimal time consumption. The following examples illustrate how scalability and flexibility can be achieved through virtualized network isolation.

- Scalable service deployment [CIS 09]: administrators can quickly create independent logical traffic paths in a shared physical network infrastructure. By using policy-based path isolation, plus additional information provided by the control plane, one tenant's traffic is isolated and invisible to any other tenants that do not belong to the same group. However, if we consider the process of policy configuration, deployment of policy-based path isolation may encounter a problem when policy rules need to be configured across sites (i.e. at every edge device in the network). The configuration of distributed policies can be a significant administrative burden and error prone and the updates may cause a widespread impact.

- Scalable service management [BER 08]: as a simplified security management based on the abstraction of a Trusted Virtual Domain (TVD), it allows centralized management of underlying isolation and integrity infrastructure. In particular, each workload is isolated and enforced through the access control policy rules, allowing administrators to quickly and concisely express the policy rules to govern the sharing of resources among all the workloads in a virtualized datacenter. Therefore, administrators can simply create, deploy and update security policies at a central point in real time, without affecting the overall service performance.

– Effectiveness: in [BER 08], the authors propose using Trusted Virtual Datacenter (TVDc) for both hypervisor-based isolation and network-based isolation. Specifically, in hypervisor-based isolation, the TVDc group VMs contain common security requirements sorted into groups/workloads, called Trusted Virtual Domains. Then, each VM can only access resources that are granted privilege as pre-defined security policy. The VLANs technique is applied to isolate VMs' traffic in the network. That means that each VM is allowed to communicate only with other VMs that have the same shared type of VLAN (same VLAN ID). As a result, such strong isolation introduced by TVD can significantly enhance trust and security guarantees for the VMs that share physical hardware platforms.

– Centralized control and management: in traditional network isolation, there is no centralized control and management available. Therefore, administrators are usually required to take additional steps to configure network isolation, such as creating IP subnets and VLAN to match the local environment and configuring network interface and other parameters with respect to network isolation. It is clear that such operations may cause non-trivial administrative burdens and complexity regarding configuration and management. In contrast, NFV-based implementations provide centralized control and management to mitigate these complexities of device configuration, facilitating the update of policy rules in real time. For example, in [NUN 13], the authors proposed to use a centralized controller enabled by SDN/NFV to implement virtualized network isolation, which allows the administrators to deploy network service and define security policy quickly on end-to-end basis. In addition, it can reduce the human cost of carrying out network configuration tasks and create isolated virtual networks for each tenant in order to guarantee that one tenant's traffic will never reach the VMs of others.

– Complexity of lifecycle management: in many cases, the configuration of network isolation is simplified by assigning a dedicated (and possibly overlapping) IP address space and then segmenting it into the subnet associated with different user groups. However, this approach does not work well for large networks, such as a cloud environment, because of sophisticated routing management. The authors of [CIS 09, NUN 13, BER 08] use virtualization to simplify network isolation. The major idea is that each partition is logically isolated from others by a set of policies, which allow the administrators to easily create and modify the isolated virtual networks on the fly, supporting a large number of user groups and adapting to varying business requirements. In particular, because policies are centrally enforced, adding or removing users and services to/from isolated virtual networks does not require significant policy reconfiguration.

– Security: VLANs have been widely applied to create logical isolated network partitions over a shared physical network infrastructure [BER 08]. However, in [ROU 06], it is pointed out that although VLANs make it possible to isolate traffic on layer 2 that shares the same switch, the strong dependence on software configuration makes them easily attacked. Indeed, VLANs are mainly used to separate subnets and implement security zones. The possibility of sending packets across different zones would render such separations useless, as a compromised machine in a lower security zone could initiate DoS/DDoS attacks against machines in a higher-security zone. Another threat is the possibility of destroying virtual architecture by performing DoS/DDoS attacks against a whole-network architecture, which can significantly affect business operations and pose information disclosure.

Example designs	Cost and Efficiency	Scalability	Effectiveness	Centralized control and management	Lifecycle management Complexity	Security enhancement
POSTER [JUB 14]	/	/	X	/	/	-
Quarantine model [SUZ 05]	X	X	X	X	X	-
VPMN [BAL 11]	/	/	/	/	/	/
Network separation for 4G networks [KOW 09]	X	X	/	X	X	X
TrustDroid [BUG 11]	X	X	/	X	X	/
CWDM [BRA 10]	/	/	/	X	X	/
VXLAN [CIS 14b, CIS 15c]	/	/	/	X	X	/
vShield [VMW 16]	/	/	/	/	/	/
SilverLine [MUN 11]	/	/	/	X	X	/
Secure virtualized network [CAB 07]	/	/	/	/	/	X
DCPortals [NUN 13]	/	/	/	/	/	/
Managing security in TVDs [BER 08]	/	/	/	/	/	X
Path isolation [CIS 09]	/	/	/	/	/	/

Notations: "/" and "X" denote that NFV characteristics are satisfied and not satisfied, respectively, "-" means data sources are insufficient.

Table 6.2. *Gap analysis between conventional and virtualized network isolation*

7

Data Protection in NFV

Data protection is an important solution that is widely used to preserve the privacy and confidentiality of personal sensitive information, allowing users to take control over their information (e.g. how data are used, who can access data and for what purposes). This chapter first presents the basic concept of data protection, then exemplifies NFV-based implementation and finally provides comparative analysis between the classific implementations and NFV-based ones.

7.1. Case studies

In general, data protection involves data encryption, data isolation, data leakage prevention and key management, which are briefly introduced as follows:

– Data encryption: There are many cryptographic schemes available for data encryption, such as RSA and AES [STA 10]. Also, most of today's cryptographic protocols such as TLS and IPsec have data encryption functionality. However, using encryption alone is insufficient to secure data, especially considering the increasing novel applications and services. For example, to increase the level of security when decrypting data in cloud, there is often a need to specify a decryption policy in the ciphertext, and only individuals who satisfy the policy can decrypt it, or the cloud service provider may only allow access to a function depending on the decryptor's authorization. Additional mechanisms like authentication, authorization and policy enforcement together with encryption mechanism are required for achieving high-level security. Some examples related to data encryption are widely used in mobile networks [ZHO 08] and cloud environments [TAK 14, YAN 13].

– Key management: Encryption is often applied to protect information from unauthorized disclosure, detect unauthorized modification and authenticate user identities. This is essential when users need to send sensitive data via untrusted channels such as the Internet. The basic concept of encryption techniques requires the keys for encryption processes, in order to specify the particular transformation of plaintext into ciphertext or vice versa for decryption processes. These keys are managed and protected throughout their lifecycle by cryptographic key management. Therefore, key management plays an important role in cryptography systems that deal with key generation, distribution, storage and destruction. It is designed to reduce the complexity of managing cryptographic keys and provide a secure method for distributing the keys to authorized users. In practice, there are two modes of distributing the keys [MEN 96]: (1) point-to-point communication whereby two users communicate directly to share the keys and (2) centralized key management (using key distribution centers or key translation centers), which act as a trusted third party to distribute the keys between two users. Some examples of data protection-based key management have been widely discussed in IT scenarios [CHI 11], mobile scenarios [GHA 10] and cloud scenarios [DOD 12, SON 14].

– Data isolation: One of the top threats in the cloud is data loss and improper data isolation [CLO 10]. In particular, data isolation plays a significant role in protecting tenant's assets from unauthorized access, by ensuring the data of each tenant is isolated from others. Thus, any compromised data in one tenant will not affect other tenants. Some examples of data isolation can be used in file environments [JAI 08] and hardware-level environments [AZA 11].

– Data leakage prevention: Many enterprises have seen their sensitive internal data lost, stolen or leaked to the outside world, due to either malicious attacks or accidental system failures. This has negative consequences for the enterprises, resulting in tremendous harm to enterprise's reputation, customer trust, compliance, competitive advantage, finances and business partnerships. To prevent such data loss and data leaks, data leakage prevention was introduced to provide enterprises with better control of their sensitive information. It is designed to detect potential data breaches and protect them from malicious attacks when sensitive data are stored within the IT infrastructure (data at rest), are in transit across a network (data in motion) or are being accessed or used by a system at the end point (data in use). An example of data leakage prevention was discussed in [PRI 14], with the purpose of protecting data leakage between tenants in cloud environments.

In the following, we exemplify the applications related to data encryption, data isolation, data leakage prevention and key management schemes in different scenarios, such as IT scenarios, telco scenarios and public cloud scenarios.

7.1.1. *IT scenario*

The key exchange protocol is considered an important part of cryptographic mechanism to protect secure end-to-end communications. An example of key exchange protocol is the Diffie and Hellman key exchange [DIF 06, STA 10], which is known to be vulnerable to attacks. To deal with secure key exchange, a three-way key exchange and agreement protocol (*TW-KEAP*) was proposed by [CHI 11]. This protocol provides two communication parties with the same session key for establishing a secure communication. The concept of TW-KEAP is derived from the four-party key exchange protocol, whereby two clients are registered under the two distinct servers, and extended the benefit from its two predecessor protocols.

– Two four-party password authentication key exchange (PAKE) protocols [YEH 05]: one is four-party key transfer authentication protocol (KTAP), and the other is four-party key agreement authentication protocol (KAAP). However, there is a drawback related to this protocol, as it might be a vulnerable point to attack, while it cannot support lawful interception.

– A key agreement authentication protocol for IMS (IMSKAAP) was proposed by [CHE 08] to figure out the above problem. This IMSKAAP provides secure key exchange and allows servers to support lawful interception by integrating the advantages of the KTAP and KAAP protocols.

The proposed TW-KEAP architecture is shown in Figure 7.1(a), whereas the proposed TW-KEAP architecture could be applied in SIP-based network, which has a pair of SIP proxy servers responsible for handling and forwarding requests to other servers or other clients. According to the TW-KEAP design, it comprises the following elements:

– SIP proxy servers: These are involved in the key exchange procedure to derive the session key K, which ensures SIP proxy servers support lawful interception.

– Gateway: The gateway is used for forwarding the real-time transport protocol (RTP) stream, and helps the service provider to collect the monitored RTP stream for lawful interception.

– Client: Clients UE A and UE B are registered under the distinct SIP proxy servers (A and B, respectively). For session key exchange between UE A and UE B, the operation has been performed on the basis of the Diffe–Hellman key exchange protocol to provide perfect forward secrecy and ensure against key attacks. Figure 7.1 (b) illustrates the TW-KEAP procedure of key exchange between UE A and UE B.

Another issue of data protection may occur due to hardware resource sharing. Some research efforts are focused on the analysis and recovery of compromised systems. In order to deal with this security issue, there are two solutions for data protection: one is to isolate data at application level [JAI 08], and another one is to isolate data at hardware level [AZA 11].

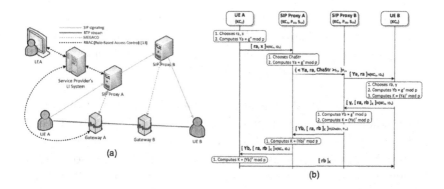

Figure 7.1. *(a) The TW-KEAP architecture. (b) The TW-KEAP procedure [CHI 11]. For a color version of this figure, see www.iste.co.uk/zhang/networks.zip*

For an application-level isolation and recovery system, *Solitude* [JAI 08] was proposed to limit the effects of attacks and simplify the post-intrusion recovery process. At its core, Solitude uses a file system-based isolation environment (Isolation File System: IFS) for running untrusted applications; it also uses an explicit file-sharing mechanism to limit attack propagation. If applications running in different isolation environments need to share data (e.g. a media file downloaded in a browser and used by a media player), then the Solitude allows explicit sharing of files between the isolation environment and the trusted base system, but it marks any such shared files as tainted. Any use of these tainted files is then logged and tracked. The design of Solitude essentially relies on the following two methods:

– Solitude leverages fine-grained access control for untrusted applications, when they are required to access trusted file systems, and uses isolation to separate each application into its own name space.

– Solitude restricts attack propagation in the file system by limiting system capabilities with the least privilege principle when untrusted applications request access to the files.

Solitude consists of three main components: (1) IFS isolation environments to provide a copy-on-write file system-based isolation;

(2) sharing policies, defined to support isolation environments, and consisting of three sharing modes for reading and writing and (3) the taint propagation and recovery to track whether there is any modification to the base file system.

For hardware-level isolation, Strongly Isolated Computing Environment (*SICE*) was proposed in [AZA 11], which is a framework that provides a hardware-level isolated execution environment for x86 hardware platforms. It aims to provide a feasible solution to sharing hardware resources with an isolated execution environment. SICE does not rely on any software component in the host environment (OS, hypervisor), instead the security of the isolated environment relies on Trusted Computing Base (TCB) (only includes the hardware, the BIOS and the System Management Mode (SMM)). According to the SICE design, it utilizes the hardware protection feature provided by the commodity x86 processor to create isolated execution environments, for example, using System Management RAM (SMRAM) for memory isolation. After the SMRAM is initialized by the BIOS, it can be locked, so that no software can access its content except the SMM code. Inside the SMRAM are the following two modules:

– SMI handler: it is responsible for two main tasks, maintaining the memory isolation of the isolated environments and securing at initialization the isolated environments while attesting to their integrity.

– Isolated environment: this contains two internal components:

- Isolated workload: represented by application programs or VMs that run in the isolated environment;

- Security manager: a thin software layer, which is mainly responsible for confining the isolated workload. SICE uses the security manager to prevent the isolated workload from accessing the memory of the legacy host. If a malicious workload in one isolated environment compromises its own security manager and consequently the legacy host, it will not be able to compromise any other isolated environment running on the same platform.

7.1.2. Telco scenarios: mobile devices and networks

Mobile networks are often deployed in environments where network nodes are unattended and have less security protection against attacks, making network nodes easy to compromise. Several approaches have been proposed to protect user privacy and their data confidentiality over mobile networks. For example, a distributed k-anonymity protocol for location privacy was proposed in [ZHO 08] to tackle the problem of user privacy in mobile location-based services (LBS) from revealing their location or credential to the untrusted party (service providers). The distributed k-anonymity protocol is based on homomorphic encryption and k-anonymity techniques [SWE 02]. The concept of k-anonymity is used to cloak the actual user's location when users need to request the service from untrusted service provider. This allows users to remain anonymous within the set of k users under a coverage area. To split the coverage area, it can be divided into a well-defined grid of equal size or square cells (e.g. one cell may have a width of 100 m). Figure 7.2(a) shows the system model of location privacy based on a k-anonymity technique that consists of four components: *Location brokers, Users, Secure comparison server* and *Directory server.*

– Location brokers: A location broker keeps track of the user's current location in the coverage area. In mobile networks, there are multiple location brokers, each one keeping track of a different subset of users' locations.

– Users: Users carry mobile devices for locating their current location. The goal of the user is to learn whether there are at least k registered users (including himself) in the user's query area, where k refers to a number of registered users within the same query area of user's current location. To learn whether there are at least k users in his/her query area, the user interacts with the relevant location brokers and a secure comparison server using public key cryptography - *additive homomorphic*, as shown in Figure 7.2(b). The sequential steps of a location-based query are described as follows.

1) User sends request to ask a particular broker for a total number of users who registered to the same query area.

2) After receiving user request, the contacted broker j chooses a secure comparison server l among the set of secure comparison server lists provided by the directory server. Then, the broker j calculates registered users v_j in the query area, encrypts v_j with public key C_l, as published by the directory server and sends $E_{C_l}(v_j)$ to the user.

3) The user calculates $E_{C_l}(r + \Sigma_i v_i)$ using the additive homomorphic property of the encryption scheme and sends it together with $E_{C_l}(r + k)$ to secure comparison server l, where r is a random number generated by the user to keep the total number of users hidden from the secure comparison server l.

4) The secure comparison server decrypts both values received from the user and makes a comparison. Finally, it informs the user of the compared result.

– Secure comparison server: This interacts with users to let them learn whether there are at least k users who are registered to the same coverage area.

– Directory server: This publishes contact information for the location brokers and for the secure comparison servers in the coverage area.

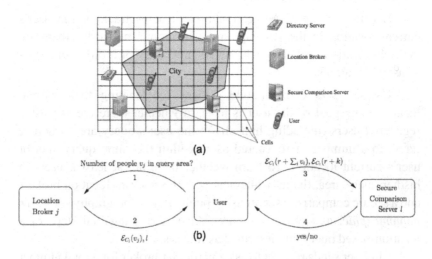

Figure 7.2. *(a) A system model of location privacy based on k-anonymity techniques. (b) Distributed k-anonymity protocol based on homomorphic encryption [ZHO 08]*

Another challenging issue of key management in mobile networks is that network nodes are moving dynamically. The key management has to deal with dynamic changes in members' locations, such as when a member leaves the old subnet and joins the new subnet. Therefore, a decentralized architecture for group key management was proposed [GHA 10] to support secure communication among members in mobile networks. With a new key management protocol, it provides generation and dynamic updating of keys (when the member is a moving, joining and leaving group member), and distribution of cryptographic key to group members. The major idea of this key management protocol, the multicast traffic, is encrypted by the source and decrypted by a valid receiver using the *Traffic Encryption Key (TEK)*. This TEK is updated when a new member joins the group or when an existing member leaves the group. The proposed group key management protocol is organized into multiple areas (or multicast hierarchy), as shown in Figure 7.3.

– Area Key Distributor (AKD): Each area is managed by an Area Key Distributor (AKD), while multiple areas that belong to the same cluster are controlled by one Domain Key Distributor (DKD). The role of the AKD is to ensure key management processes inside its area. Each AKD shares a *Key Encryption Key (KEK)* with its area members.

– Domain Key Distributor (DKD): This is responsible for creating a new TEK (when a joining or leaving event occurs) and distributing this TEK to all members within its cluster.

For example, when messages from one member pass across a cluster to another member, message decryption and re-encryption are performed, because different TEKs are used in each cluster. Therefore, upon receiving messages from one cluster, the DKD performs decryption using the relevant TEK and re-encryption using the TEK of another cluster, before forwarding this encrypted messages downward to its area member. If the member moves to a new area, the KEK key of that area will be received. With this process, member's mobility does not compromise group secrecy and does not require any re-keying operations.

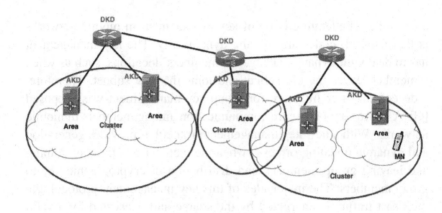

Figure 7.3. *Group key management protocol based on decentralized architecture that contains subgroup key managers [GHA 10]*

7.1.3. *Public clouds*

The limit of data protection in cloud environments poses security challenges. First, users have limited control over underlying infrastructure. Second, users may not completely trust the cloud service providers (CSPs), so they have to ensure that the CSPs do not violate confidentiality of their data. To tackle those challenges, several solutions have been proposed to protect data confidentiality and user privacy when operating in clouds. For example, a privacy aware access control system was proposed [TAK 14] to support secure data sharing over cloud environments. It provides two levels of data protection when the user's data are stored on a cloud service provider (CSP): at the first level, by using CSP to protect user's data from unauthorized access through the use of access control mechanism; and at the second level, by relying on a trusted third-party service provider to prevent CSP colluding through the use of multiple layers of commutative encryption [DAI 10]. As a result, there is no need for users to trust either the CSP or the third-party service provider. Thus, the data owners can protect their resources from untrusted CSP using encryption and from unauthorized users using fine-grained access control policies. Its architecture consists of four main components: *Data owner, Data consumer, CSP* and *Policy Management Service (PMS)*.

– Data owner: The data owner creates and stores the data on the cloud in an encrypted format and determines who can access the data, on the basis of access control policies. In addition, the data owner enables defining policies at various granularity levels, such as role-based, attribute-based or group-based access control policies.

– Data consumer: The data consumer is an authorized user who needs to access the protected data.

– Cloud service provider (CSP): The CSP is responsible for storing encrypted data and determining access control policies regarding whether the requested consumers are allowed to access these encrypted data.

– Policy Management Service (PMS): The PMS assists in encryption and decryption of users' data.

Let us assume Alice is the data owner who wants to share her encrypted data stored in CSP with Bob. Alice first encrypts the data using a symmetric key k and stores the ciphertext on the CSP. This key k, which was used for data encryption, is then encrypted using multiple layers of commutative encryption and stored on the PMS. When Bob wants to access Alice's data, and if Bob is granted access according to the access control policies, then the encrypted data are pulled from the CSP to Bob. Next, Bob needs to get access to the owner's key k to be able to decrypt these data. The associated key, which was used for the encryption of those data, is pulled from the PMS. Now, Bob can decrypt the encrypted data using the derived key.

Another approach of data protection was proposed in [YAN 13], by adapting Ciphertext-Policy Attribute-based Encryption (CP-ABE) [BET 07, WAT 11] to achieve fine-grained access control. In this framework, the access policy is defined and enforced by data owner rather than by cloud service provider. To achieve attribute-based fine-grained access control, the owner first splits the data into several components and then encrypts each data component with different content keys by symmetric key encryption. Consequently, the owner applies the CP-ABE method to encrypt each content key, such that only the user whose attributes satisfy the access structure in the ciphertext can decrypt the content keys. The CP-ABE architecture consists of four entities: *Authority, Data owners, Cloud server* and *Data consumers (users)*, as shown in Figure 7.4.

– Authority: The authority is responsible for revoking and granting the attributes of users according to their roles or identities. There are two tasks for authority associated with owners and users.

    - First, the authority generates public parameters PP, and for each attribute x the authority generates public attribute keys PK_x. These PP and PK_x will be published to the owners.

    - When the user joins the system, the authority generates secret keys SK for this user and sends SK to the user via a secure channel.

– Owners: The owners determine the access policies and encrypt their data under the policy rules before hosting them on the cloud. In practice, the data are divided into several data components as $M = m_1, ..., m_n$. Then, each data component m_i is encrypted with different content keys k_i on the basis of symmetric key encryption, where $i = 1, ..., n$. The content key $K = k_1, ..., k_n$ is consequently encrypted by using the CP-ABE method.

– Cloud server: It stores the owner's data in ciphertext format and provides data access service to users, so that ciphertext can be accessed by all the legal users in the system, but only users who get eligible attributes that satisfy the access control policies can decrypt this ciphertext.

– Users: Each user is entitled to a set of attributes according to its roles and identity. The user's attribute set may change dynamically due to the role which can also change. For example, when a user role changes from the manager to the normal user, some of its attributes should be revoked. The users can decrypt the ciphertext only when they have sufficient attributes satisfying the access control policies associated with that ciphertext. In order to decrypt the data, user takes ciphertext CT and secret key SK as inputs into the decryption operation on the basis of CP-ABE to obtain a content key K. This key K is consequently used to decrypt encrypted messages on the basis of symmetric key encryption. Finally, the user obtains the clear message.

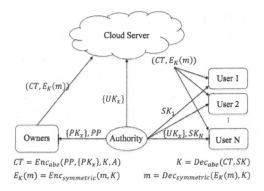

Figure 7.4. *System model of CP-ABE in cloud storage. Data are encrypted with a content key using symmetric key encryption based on CP-ABE [YAN 13]*

7.2. NFV-based implementations

Several types of data protection mechanisms have been proposed to improve secure communication across different scenarios (e.g. IT, telco and public cloud environments), as discussed in the previous section. In this section, we explore how to enable data protection in NFV environments. In [PRI 14], a monitoring data leakage system is proposed to examine the data flow of tenant applications in a cloud platform, especially in Platform as a Service (PaaS), and whether any data leakage occurred. It adds security tags to a subset of all tenant HTTP request fields and uses socket-level tag monitoring to observe the propagation of tags. The design of CloudSafetyNet shown in Figure 7.5 consists of three modules: *Client-side data tagging, Socket-level tag monitoring* and *Inter-tenant data leakage detection*.

– Client-side data tagging: The main idea behind the CloudSafetyNet is that each tenant must include *Security tags* in a subset of form fields in HTTP requests, in order to capture the propagation of tenant's network flows that have been tagged.

– Socket-level monitoring: This intercepts network flows between processes of a distributed Web application on the PaaS platform. Each monitor has been recorded in a tag log, which is periodically retrieved by tenants. Recording of foreign tags belonging to other tenants in the tag log indicates the occurrence of inter-tenant data leakage.

– Inter-tenant data leakage detection: This is used to detect foreign tags in their tag logs. Tenants try to decrypt the tags with their keys. Failure of the decryption indicates that the tag belongs to another tenant. This means, there is a breach in group isolation observed by a monitor. In addition, the tenants may cooperate with other tenants to confirm the source of the data leakage.

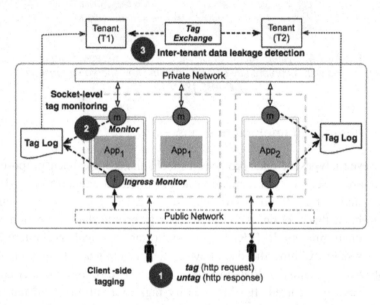

Figure 7.5. *Design of the ClougSafetyNet monitoring system [PRI 14]*

In [YAU 10], the authors attempt to address the same security issue of protecting data confidentiality when they are stored and processed in the cloud environment. Because users are not able to control the underlying infrastructure provided by different service providers, it is likely that an untrusted service provider performs unauthorized disclosure of the data of legitimate users. The objective of their scheme is to preserve user privacy and ensure that service providers are not able to collect any users' sensitive data when they are at rest, at transit or in process. The scheme involves three techniques:

– Separating software service provider and infrastructure service provider, with an objective of ensuring that the software layer and infrastructure layer are not managed by the same service provider;

– Hiding information about the owner of data by adding additional function for identity anonymization;

– Performing data obfuscation.

The proposed architecture of data protection is shown in Figure 7.6, which consists of seven entities.

– Software cloud: This provides software as a service upon user requests. Only authenticated users with proper credentials [IWA 08] can request and acquire the service from the software cloud.

– Infrastructure cloud: This provides virtualized system resources and network resources.

– Software service broker: This is responsible for two functions. First, it helps users automatically discover and access available software services in the software cloud. Second, it helps users to hide their actual identities when interacting with the software cloud using identity anonymization service.

– Infrastructure service broker: This is responsible for two functions, similar to a software service broker. First, it helps users automatically discover and use available infrastructure services in the infrastructure cloud. Second, it provides identity anonymization service to prevent the system from revealing the user identities.

– Software Service Attestation Authority (SSAA): A third-party authority to verify whether a software service instance performs any malicious activity that leads to disclosing users' confidential data. SSAA checks whether this instance satisfies the Web Service Description Language (WSDL) specification [DON 06] and monitors all network traffic that this instance produces during its process. If the test is successful, SSAA issues and attaches a digital certificate to the user's software service instance notifying that it passed the SSAA's testing.

– Data obfuscator: A middleware that is deployed on a virtual machine in the infrastructure cloud to perform data obfuscation and ensure that users' data are not disclosed to infrastructure service providers. In obfuscation processes, the user creates an encryption key, which is used to encrypt the user's data.

– Data de-obfuscator: The reverse process of data obfuscation to obtain the user's data in plaintext format.

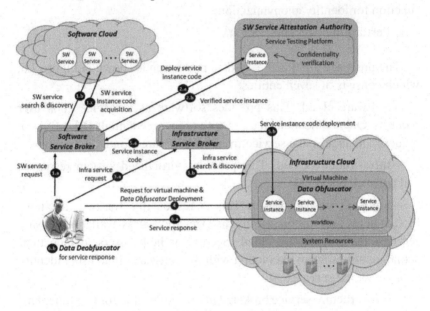

Figure 7.6. *Data confidentiality protection in a cloud-based environment [YAU 10]. For a color version of this figure, see www.iste.co.uk/zhang/networks.zip*

In [DOD 12], key-insulated symmetric key cryptography is proposed to tackle a problem of cryptographic key compromise. This protocol aims to mitigate the repeated exposures of secret keys, by updating the keys frequently. The scheme has been adapted from key-insulated public key cryptography [DOD 12] and integrated into Trusted Virtual Domains (TVD). Figure 7.7 (a) presents a concept of TVDs which allows customers to use multiple VMs running on top of multiple physical computers in the cloud. Only applications in the same TVD can be communicated and protected using a key-insulated schemes. Figure 7.7 (b) illustrates how key-insulated schemes can be integrated in TVDs. Suppose that two VMs running on the top of the same Virtual Machine Monitor (VMM) need to communicate. These two VMs need to establish a shared key using a key-insulated symmetric key cryptography method. Let each VM hold its master key, *Computer master key*, and VMM hold a set of master keys, *Device master keys*. For each time period, both VMs receive *Partial secret key*, as derived from its device master key, from the Device Key-Update module in VMM. After receiving the *Partial secret key*, the Computer-Key Update module in each VM generates a *Period secret key* by taking *Partial secret key* and the *Computer master key* as inputs in order to produce *Period secret key* as an output. This *Period secret key* will be used as a symmetric key for protecting the communication between the two VMs that belong to the same TVD.

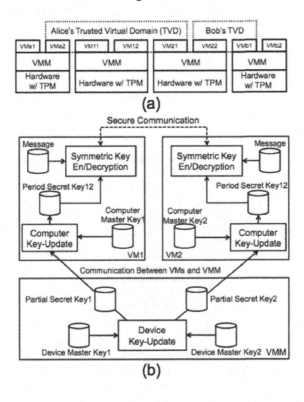

Figure 7.7. *(a) Trusted Virtual Domain in cloud-based environment. (b) Trusted Virtual Domain with key-insulated symmetric key encryption scheme [DOD 12]*

Another solution to handling and managing the secret keys in cloud in secure manner is proposed by [SON 14], called Encrypted Cloud, or *EnCloud*. The challenge of key management in clouds is the presence of a large number of keys that need to be properly managed to support multi-tenant requests. Different applications may require different keys for encryption. Thus, the total number of keys may increase and finally become unmanageable. An EnCloud system is designed to handle this issue by providing end-to-end encryption between multiple cloud applications. It aims to resolve the problem of insecure key creation, key management and key renewal, in which all encryption and decryption keys are located at the client side rather than the server side. This allows users to truly control the use of keys and manage their personal data.

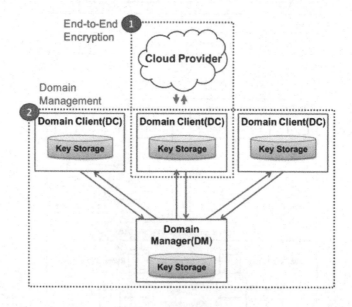

Figure 7.8. *"EnCloud" framework, with the Domain Manager (DM) responsible for managing its domain members (Domain Client or DC) and a DC responsible for data encryption/decryption [SON 14]*

EnCloud architecture comprises two functional components: Domain Manager (DM) and Domain Client (DC), as shown in Figure 7.8. User *U* installs a DM application on one of their devices and installs DC application on other devices. With this concept, users' data can be protected within their personal domain through end-to-end encryption and domain management.

– Domain Manager (DM): Responsible for managing its domain members (e.g. Domain Clients) by registering and revoking them. The DM application creates a domain key k and distributes this key k to all domain members for further encryption and decryption processes. The tasks of DM are associated with registering and removing device and updating domain key.

– Domain Client (DC): Responsible for encrypting users' data before exporting and being stored in the cloud, as well as decrypting the encrypted data after downloading from the cloud into the personal domain. Thus, the encryption and decryption processes can be illustrated as follows:

- Uploading data: When a user U needs to upload personal data d to the cloud server S, the cloud application interacts with DC_i and asks for the encryption key dek. The DC_i creates encryption key dek, then user U uses encryption key dek to encrypt data d. Consecutively, this encryption key dek is together encrypted with domain key k, which is provided by the DM at the beginning of the registration phase.

- Downloading data: When user U wants to download data d from the cloud server S, the cloud application returns $(E_{dek}(d), id_d)$ and $(E_k(dek), id_d)$. Then, the DC_i decrypts $E_k(dek)$ with the domain key k and decrypts $E_{dek}(d)$ with dek. After decryption of both objects, DC_i returns the plain data d to user U.

7.3. Comparative analysis

In this section, we emphasize the effect on the performance of data protection mechanisms when they are deployed and implemented in the NFV environment. In particular, we take the designs proposed by [PRI 14, YAU 10, DOD 12, SON 14] as an example and analyze the following metrics (the results are summarized in Table 7.1).

– Cost: Many enterprises usually need to invest in encryption and key management systems as well as data leakage prevention systems to protect their data from external threats. However, these types of equipment are quite expensive and complex to configure and manage. With NFV-based implementation, network services can be quickly deployed and managed through the use of software-based approaches. These advantages allow enterprises to earn additional revenue without the need for significant investment in hardware. In fact, the aforementioned schemes [PRI 14, YAU 10, DOD 12, SON 14] have clearly indicated that end-users and enterprises can dynamically deploy virtual appliances for data protection services on the fly, without too many concerns about costs in terms of hardware investment, configuration and maintenance.

– Communication overhead: In fact, conventional encryption may not be sufficient and no longer suitable to fulfill the mandatory need for security requirements. For example, users traditionally encrypt their data with a secret key and then deliver this key to the authorized user for decryption. This approach makes users a cumbersome process and creates a high risk of key attack. Although the authors in [DOD 12, SON 14] proposed a new model of encryption and key management to support cloud, in which end-users do not need to manage keys by themselves, there is still communication overhead in the key exchange stage. This is because the secret keys need to be updated frequently at the beginning of each time period, e.g. when time is expired, when the number of communicate users change [DOD 12] or when a device keeping the secret key is lost or stolen [SON 14]. These processes consume a lot of computational time, memory, bandwidth and other resources to achieve key sharing.

– Complexity of lifecycle management:

- Management complexity: The difficulty of data protection in the cloud environment is management complexity. Network administrators have to deal with setting complex configuration tasks. Unlike conventional data protection, simple encryption and key management are sufficient to protect data confidentiality. When data are moved and processed into the cloud, the users may lose control over their data, while service providers may also pose a risk to users by performing unauthorized disclosure of their sensitive data and violating their privacy. As a result, the complexity of data protection could be high, as it requires a complex level of data protection to ensure that every stage of data processing is not disclosed to any third party except the authorized ones. These goals are partially achieved by the designs reported in [DOD 12, SON 14].

Although these kinds of data protection make user's data more secure and make it difficult to attack the cryptographic keys, they could lead to management complexity when generating, managing and distributing the keys to communicating parties, especially when the network becomes larger and a large number of users are requesting the keys simultaneously. This makes key management more difficult and complex.

- Operational complexity: Although CloudSafetyNet [PRI 14] contributes to increasing the confidence of tenants for keeping data isolated, the procedure of CloudSafetyNet could increase data traffic in the network, producing operational overhead and processing delay. It can be observed that for each HTTP request packet that requires adding a security tag, an encryption with tenant's public key is consequently performed. Once socket level monitors the packet, the log will be recorded. The tenant can periodically check the data leakage from log information. We observe that the outcomes from these operations result in high operating costs, longer time to revenue and ongoing operational complexity.

In addition, a framework for protecting data confidentiality proposed by [YAU 10] also faces operational complexity. Although the concept of separation between software layer and infrastructure layer where the two layers are not managed by the same service provider can ensure data confidentiality, it introduces a lot of communication traffic and data processing between components.

– Specific designs: Traditional data protection mechanisms provide limited security support when data are operated in the cloud. Most of these mechanisms aim to prevent data leakage against outsider attacks, while it cannot prevent malicious attacks caused by untrusted cloud service providers. Therefore, data protection schemes for the cloud are quite different from the traditional approaches, as they need to consider the intrinsic characteristics as well as the fundamental security requirements of the cloud. For example, the authors of [YAU 10] propose seven entities for data protection and defined that service layer and infrastructure should not be managed by the same service provider. Also, the authors of [PRI 14] propose three parts for data leakage detection, whereby every HTTP request needs to add a security tag and use Socket-level tag monitoring to observe the propagation of tags.

– Effectiveness: In traditional models, a specific instrument can offer a specific task related to data protection. For example, enterprises generally use key management devices to generate secret keys as well as encryption devices to encrypt data with secret keys derived from the key management device. However, this approach may not be the most effective way to protect overall security posture. In particular, when data are stored in the cloud, it might face the problem of malicious service providers, and new designs are therefore necessary to meet the specific requirements. Some example designs can be found in [YAU 10, SON 14], in which users are not required to trust or rely on service providers.

– Scalability: NFV provides scalability by allowing service providers to quickly scale up and scale down network services according to the business goals. As discussed in [YAU 10], service providers can dynamically initiate and deploy software services upon user requests. Thus, service providers can rapidly interact with infrastructure layers in order to allocate virtualized resources and freely add or modify security policy and attestation rules in real time.

Despite the availability of a large variety of security mechanisms, it remains unclear whether or not and how they can be migrated and implemented in NFV-based networking scenarios. In fact, the analysis indicates that very limited research efforts have been made on this aspect, although both academia and industry admit that it deserves extremely careful study. However, we believe that in the short term, sharply increasing attention will be attained, considering the rapid advancement and widespread deployment of NFV and SDN technologies.

To balance the breadth and depth of the discussions, five basic security functions have been selected: IAM, IPS/IDS, network isolation, data protection and security management in general.

Example design	Cost saving	Less communication overhead	Reduced complexity of life cycle management	Easy deployment (no specific function required)	Effectiveness	Scalability
TW-KEAP [CHI 11]	X	X	X	X	/	X
Solitude [JAI 08]	X	/	X	X	/	X
SICE [AZA 11]	X	/	X	X	/	X
Homomorphic encryption for location privacy [ZHO 08]	X	X	X	X	/	/
Key management in dynamic group [GHA 10]	X	X	X	/	/	/
Secure data sharing in cloud [TAK 14]	/	X	X	/	/	/
CP-ABC [YAN 13]	X	X	X	/	/	/
CloudSafety Net [PRI 14]	/	X	X	X	/	/
Data confidentiality protection [YAU 10]	/	X	X	X	/	/
Key-insulated symmetric key cryptography [DOD 12]	/	X	X	/	/	/
EnCloud [SON 14]	/	X	X	/	/	/

Notations: "/" and "X" denote that NFV characteristics are satisfied and not satisfied, respectively, "-" means the data sources are insufficient.

Table 7.1. *Data protection: Comparative analysis between native functions and NFV-based implementations*

Conclusion

Challenges and Perspectives

NFV research activities in both industry and academia are more focused on the practical implementations with respect to management and orchestration, with the purpose of providing easy creation, configuration and deployment of network services in complex network scenarios. Another objective is to achieve flexibility and agility of service provision, while reducing capital and operational expenditures (CAPEX/OPEX). However, as previously discussed, NFV is still under development and deployment, many important issues remain and should be properly addressed before its large-scale deployment in the real world. In this chapter, we point out some research challenges and future directions, including security management and orchestration, NFV-based security functions, security as a service and quality of service (QoS).

Security management and orchestration

When network services are transitioned to an NFV environment, service providers of NFV infrastructure have to deal with the complexity. The challenges include a myriad of business processes and operational complexities, ranging from configuration and maintenance to management and orchestration. In particular, NFV MANO plays an important role in handling configuration and lifecycle management of VNFs and network services. Recent research challenges concern the level of intelligence that must be achieved in NFV MANO. For example, the orchestration should be accomplished at an acceptable level so as to ensure that all the required functions are instantiated in a coherent and on-demand way [MIJ 16, BRO 14, BER 16, LIU 16, CAR 15]. To achieve that, NFV MANO should be smart enough to support service dynamism, flexibility and scalability. Also, the configurations should be intelligently automated at a large scale, especially those of network services deployed in the runtime environment across heterogeneous cloud platforms.

More importantly, a basic set of security functions should be automatically orchestrated and intelligently deployed to the appropriate NFV infrastructure point of presence (NFVI-PoP) for protecting network assets based on the pre-specified policies. To do that, security management and orchestration should be presented as an additional function block, providing security countermeasures and offering security as a service for achieving both service quality and security guarantee. Meanwhile, it must be seamlessly operated with the NFV orchestrator to accomplish security tasks such as providing security assessments. One of the objectives is to authenticate user requests and validate whether network services/resources meet certain security properties based on the pre-defined security policies. Furthermore, the functions related to this security management and orchestration can be extended to provide a monitoring service that can keep track of malicious events in the whole lifecycle of network services and VNFs, so as to quickly deploy the appropriate security functions in the presence of attacks.

The corresponding concept of security management and orchestration has been recently addressed in [PAT 17], with an objective of empowering the current NFV orchestrators to manage security mechanisms. Therefore, the most appropriate security functions can be dynamically and optimally deployed. An alternative approach to security management and orchestration is shown in Figure 3.1. In particular, there are two possibilities to develop and implement this module in the existing cloud orchestration platforms. As for the processes of security management and orchestration, when

NFV orchestrator receives service requests from customers, it first decomposes the request and retrieves the necessary recipes (e.g. VNF descriptor, network service descriptor and virtual link descriptor) for execution. The NFV orchestrator may interact with various functional blocks such as the VNFM to instantiate VNF instances, the VIM to allocate virtual resources, and the security orchestrator to perform security operations. Specifically, this security orchestrator may use a set of security APIs to interact with a set of diverse security functions (e.g. IAM, IDS/IPS, network isolation and data protection) and then select and configure the most appropriate ones for handling the user request. Nevertheless, performance impact based on the proposed model of security management and orchestration is not yet evaluated, which would be one of the major challenges that needs further consideration and exploration.

NFV-based security functions

Security by design

NFV introduces a very large, comprehensive and dynamic attack surface. The security challenges with NFV are the number of new malwares (up to 30,000 per day), error prone processes from manual deployments and distributed policy configuration are significantly multiplied, and dynamic re-mediation and security service assessment are not sufficiently addressed [MCD 14]. Furthermore, the authors of [HAM 06] claim that manual configuration of network security technologies, such as firewall and IPsec, on the extended sets of devices are prone to configuration errors and intra- and inter-policy conflicts. This configuration complexity is one of the main reasons for generating serious vulnerabilities and threats in the network. Similarly, in [CIS 09], the authors point out that the challenge in distributed policy configuration over NFV environments can represent a significant administrative burden and is prone to error. For instance, any update in policies can potentially lead to widespread impact. Overall, current research activities do not sufficiently address and take into account these security challenges.

Therefore, the implementation and deployment of virtual network services should be initially started from *security by design*, complemented with *security as a service*, which is generally a more realistic solution to ensure confidentiality, control all access to the underlying infrastructure assets, and ultimately improve the security as a whole in NFV environments. The related discussion on security by design is outlined in [MCD 14]. The authors mentioned that the design process should start with enforcing a zero trust model by blocking all the network traffic until security policies are applied such as authenticating tenant requests, verifying certificates from VM deployment based on the requested services and applying policy according to the tenant requirements. In addition, in [MYE 14], the authors point out that there are four phases involved in security by design: (1) asset identification - by identifying users, service providers and hardware assets running in NFV environments; (2) identification of adversaries - identifies all the potential attacks; (3) layers of defense oriented approach, in order to provide security solutions that can be used to mitigate and defend against security threats and vulnerabilities; (4) review phase - all processes and procedures must be periodically and frequently rechecked to ensure they have sufficient security protection when user requirements are changed or when security services are out of date.

Security as a service

As a matter of fact, many users are seriously concerned with security, privacy and trust issues introduced by the cloud models such as NFV technology. The most common reasons are as follows. First, they are not able to monitor all the data transaction processing in the cloud environment, especially when the underlying infrastructure is owned by third party service providers. Second, they have no idea where the data is, who gets access to their data, how data is performed or even how the data is transferred over the network links. Third, they may not have a total trust in the cloud service providers. Hence, the sensitive user data can be presented in unencrypted form owned and operated by the third party service providers. The risks of unauthorized disclosure of their data performance by untrusted service providers could be high. The challenge is that users have to ensure that the service providers do not break down their privacy and confidential data. Despite the fact that ETSI has published the document related to NFV security [ETS 14b, ETS 15b], which aims at providing general guidelines on how to establish a secured baseline for NFV operations (e.g. security within VNFs, between VNFs, external to VNFs and secured interfaces), it does not cover prescriptive requirements or specific implementation details.

So far several solutions have been proposed, such as the ones reported in [TAK 14, YAN 13, DOD 12] which aim at protecting data confidentiality and user privacy when their data is operated in the cloud. However, the management complexity and communication overhead cannot be avoided. Practically, network operators have to deal with complex operational tasks, such as orchestrating, managing, configuring and maintaining the network services. Especially, when the network size gets larger, they must contain a diverse set of network services implemented by different NFV vendors and spanning across multiple platforms at different geographical locations. Therefore, it is important to obtain the optimal balance between network performance goals and essential security requirements. This is in fact a long-standing challenge for many ICT scenarios.

Quality of service (QoS)

The primary objective of NFV is to reduce management and operational complexity while maintaining the quality of network services. It is therefore of great importance to study QoS issues in different use cases and scenarios, especially when security is an essential requirement.

Network performance

Fundamentally, NFV consolidates multiple network equipment onto industry standard, high volume servers, switches and storage. The network functions are essentially implemented by using software-based approach and run on a range of commodity hardware platforms. Thus, they can be migrated or instantiated freely across various locations on demand, without the need to install new equipment. Despite the potential of NFV, there are challenging issues related to the network performance [HAN 15, BRO 14]. Some of these issues are: (1) how to offer the best security practices and guarantee network performance (e.g. latency, throughput, queuing capabilities and security) for particular virtual appliances; (2) how to design network equipment so as to provide programmability to efficiently enable network services; and (3) how virtual appliances running on industrial standard servers can achieve a performance comparable to those running on specialized hardware.

As a matter of fact, not all the network equipment can adapt and support virtualization environment. This means that some specific network equipment is difficult to virtualize without performance degradation. As previously addressed, mobile network devices like RAN nodes are naturally and physically implemented on purpose-built hardware, hence the baseband processing functions of RAN nodes cannot be efficiently implemented on software [MAC 13]. Theoretically, NFV allows service providers to provide infinite numbers of user requests with unpredictable demands of network services at a high throughput, while guaranteeing end-to-end service performance. In contrast, the practical implementation of NFV does not always achieve high network performance, especially in a short-term period. Due to the fact that most current commodity hardware platforms are not naturally designed to support multi-tenancy requirements, the performance bottleneck represents potential threats, at any time and at any places, such as in-between VNFs, between commodity and purpose-built networking hardware, or even across network fabric.

Service reliability

It is generally believed that NFV can provide reliability for network services by allowing service providers to deploy, configure and scale multiple VNF instances in real time. In contrast, as pointed out in [ZON 14], the use of VNFs may introduce additional challenges associated with the reliability of the provided network services. As a matter of fact, the deployment of network services and VNF instances rely on low cost commodity hardware, while using software to orchestrate and manage a diverse set of complex network services. Typically, these kinds of commodity hardware do not have built-in reliability mechanisms, therefore they are more susceptible to attacks than the proprietary hardware platforms. Furthermore, the current version of commodity hardware faces several factors of risks, making network services and VNF instances unreliable. The reasons could be: (1) hardware failure and hardware status changes such as server overload; (2) software failure at various levels including hypervisor, VM and VNF instances; and (3) performance degradation due to capacity overloading, such as CPU, memory, disk I/O, server consolidation, or other service requirement changes.

To deal with these issues, an alternative solution is to adopt a pooling mechanism [ZON 14], in which a number of VNF instances which provide the same functions are grouped as a pool. Thus, a set of VNF instances can be grouped into multiple VNF pools and each pool corresponds to a specific VNF instance, providing a specific function. For each particular pool, there is a pool manager who is responsible for managing the VNF instances in the VNF pool and interacting with the service control entity to provide network functions with the desired reliability level. However, the pooling mechanism may also pose some challenges and open issues. For example, when a live VNF instance fails, one or more backup VNF instances in the same VNF pool must be selected, but how to select such backup instances is a key issue. In addition, it is unclear who is responsible for replicating its service states and what kind of information needs to be exchanged between a pool manager and service control entity.

In conclusion, complexity is one of the main characteristics of NFV, which is composed of a large amount of components, links, and chains for creating end-to-end network services. Thus, QoS provisioning, performance improvement, service composition, cross-domain orchestrations, security and privacy are all open research issues which need to be addressed before the large-scale adoption and deployment of NFV.

Bibliography

[6WI 14] 6WIND, "Network functions virtualization – network function virtualization paves the way to improved cost efficiencies", available at: http://www.6wind.com/solutions/service-providers/network-functions-virtualization/, 2014.

[AMD 03] AMD, "AMD platform for trustworthy computing", available at: http://www.intel.com/technology/security, 2003.

[AMD 15] AMDOCS, "Amdocs Network Cloud Ecosystem", available at: http://www.amdocs.com/about/partners/nfv/pages/use-cases.aspx, 2015.

[ANA 14] ANALYSYS MASON, "Network Virtualization & SDN World 2014: CSPs confirm Analysys Mason's NFV and SDN Forecasts", available at: http://www.analysismason.com/About-Us/News/Insight/NFV-SDN-forecasts-June2014-RMA16/, June 2014.

[ARB 97] ARBAUGH W., FARBER D., SMITH J., "A secure and reliable bootstrap architecture", *Proceedings, 1997 IEEE Symposium on Security and Privacy, 1997*, pp. 65–71, May 1997.

[ARD 06] ARDAGNA C.A., CREMONINI M., DAMIANI E. *et al.*, "Supporting location-based conditions in access control policies", *Proceedings of the 2006 ACM Symposium on Information, Computer and Communications Security*, ASIACCS'06, ACM, New York, pp. 212–222, 2006.

[AZA 11] AZAB A.M., NING P., ZHANG X., "SICE: a hardware-level strongly isolated computing environment for x86 multi-core platforms", *Proceedings of the 18th ACM Conference on Computer and Communications Security*, CCS'11, ACM, New York, pp. 375–388, 2011.

[BAL 11] BALIGA A., CHEN X., COSKUN B. *et al.*, "VPMN: virtual private mobile network towards mobility-as-a-service", *Proceedings of the Second International Workshop on Mobile Cloud Computing and Services*, MCS'11, ACM, New York, pp. 7–12, 2011.

[BER 08] BERGER S., CÁCERES R., PENDARAKIS D. *et al.*, "TVDc: managing security in the trusted virtual datacenter", *SIGOPS Operating Systems Review*, vol. 42, no. 1, pp. 40–47, 2008.

[BER 16] BERNARDOS C., RAHMAN A., ZUNIGA J. *et al.*, "Network virtualization research challenges", available at: https://tools.ietf.org/pdf/draft-irtf-nfvrg-gaps-network-virtualization-03.pdf, 2016.

[BET 07] BETHENCOURT J., SAHAI A., WATERS B., "Ciphertext-policy attribute-based encryption", *Proceedings of the 2007 IEEE Symposium on Security and Privacy*, SP'07, IEEE Computer Society, Washington, DC, pp. 321–334, 2007.

[BRA 10] BRASSIL J., "Physical layer network isolation in multi-tenant clouds", *IEEE 30th International Conference on Distributed Computing Systems Workshops (ICDCSW)*, pp. 77–81, June 2010.

[BRO 14] BRONSTEIN Z., SHRAGA E., "NFV virtualisation of the home environment", *CCNC'14*, pp. 899–904, January 2014.

[BRO 15] BROWN G., Service chaining in carrier networks, White paper, available at: http://www.qosmos.com/wp-content/uploads/2015/02/Service-Chaining-in-Carrier-Networks_WP_Heavy-Reading_Qosmos_Feb2015.pdf, 2015.

[BUG 11] BUGIEL S., DAVI L., DMITRIENKO A. *et al.*, "Practical and lightweight domain isolation on android", *Proceedings of the 1st ACM Workshop on Security and Privacy in Smartphones and Mobile Devices*, SPSM'11, ACM, New York, pp. 51–62, 2011.

[CAB 07] CABUK S., DALTON C.I., RAMASAMY H. *et al.*, "Towards automated provisioning of secure virtualized networks", *Proceedings of the 14th ACM Conference on Computer and Communications Security*, CCS'07, ACM, New York, pp. 235–245, 2007.

[CAE 05] CAESAR M., CALDWELL D., FEAMSTER N. *et al.*, "Design and implementation of a routing control platform", *Proceedings of the 2nd Conference on Symposium on Networked Systems Design & Implementation – Volume 2*, NSDI'05, USENIX Association, Berkeley, pp. 15–28, 2005.

[CAN 15] CANDID WUEEST M.B.B., O'BRIEN L., "Mistakes in the IaaS cloud could put your data at risk", available at: http://www.symantec.com/ content/en/us/enterprise/media/security_response/whitepapers/mistakes-in-the-iaas-cloud-could-put-your-data-at-risk.pdf, 2015.

[CAP 14] CAPRIN E., ZHANG Y., "Negotiation based framework for attribute-based access control policy evaluation", *Proceedings of the 7th International Conference on Security of Information and Networks*, SIN'14, ACM, New York, pp. 122:122–122:127, 2014.

[CAR 15] CARROZZO G., SZABO R., PENTIKOUSIS K., "Network function virtualization: resource orchestration challenges", available at: https://tools.ietf.org/pdf/draft-caszpe-nfvrg-orchestration-challenges-00.pdf, 2015.

[CAS 07] CASADO M., FREEDMAN M.J., PETTIT J. *et al.*, "Ethane: taking control of the enterprise", *SIGCOMM Computer Communication Review*, vol. 37, no. 4, pp. 1–12, 2007.

[CAT 10] CATUOGNO L., DMITRIENKO A., ERIKSSON K. *et al.*, "Trusted virtual domains – design, implementation and lessons learned", *Proceedings of the First International Conference on Trusted Systems*, INTRUST'09, Springer-Verlag, Berlin, Heidelberg, pp. 156–179, 2010.

[CHE 08] CHEN C.-Y., WU T.-Y., HUANG Y.-M. *et al.*, "An efficient end-to-end security mechanism for IP multimedia subsystem", *Computer Communications*, vol. 31, no. 18, pp. 4259–4268, 2008.

[CHI 11] CHIANG W.-K., CHEN J.-H., "TW-KEAP: an efficient four-party key exchange protocol for end-to-end communications", *Proceedings of the 4th International Conference on Security of Information and Networks*, SIN'11, ACM, New York, pp. 167–174, 2011.

[CHO 09] CHOW C.-Y., MOKBEL M.F., "Privacy in location-based services: a system architecture perspective", *SIGSPATIAL Special*, vol. 1, no. 2, pp. 23–27, 2009.

[CIS 09] CISCO, "Network virtualization – path isolation design guide", available at: http://www.cisco.com/c/en/us/td/docs/solutions/Enterprise/ Network_Virtualization/PathIsol.pdf, 2009.

[CIS 12] CISCO, "Understanding and configuring VLANs", available at: http:// www.cisco.com/c/en/us/td/docs/switches/lan/catalyst4500/12-2/20ew/ configuration/guide/config/vlans.html, 2012.

[CIS 14a] CISCO, "Evolved Programmable Network (EPN)", available at: http://www.cisco.com/c/en/us/solutions/service-provider/network-infrastructure/index.html, 2014.

[CIS 14b] CISCO, Flexible Workload Mobility and Server Placement with VXLAN Routing on Cisco CSR 1000V and Cisco Nexus 1000V: White paper, available at: http://www.cisco.com/c/en/us/products/collateral/routers/cloud-services-router-1000v-series/white-paper-c11-732382.pdf, 2014.

[CIS 14c] CISCO, "Network automation – evolved services platform", available at: http://www.cisco.com/c/en/us/solutions/service-provider/evolved-services-platform/index.html, 2014.

[CIS 15a] CISCO, "Deploying the VXLAN Feature in Cisco Nexus 1000V Series Switches", available at: http://www.cisco.com/c/en/us/products/collateral/switches/nexus-1000v-switch-vmware-vsphere/guide_c07-702975.html, 2015.

[CIS 15b] CISCO, NFV management and orchestration: enabling rapid service innovation in the era of virtualization, White paper, available at: http://www.cisco.com/c/en/us/solutions/collateral/service-provider/network-functions-virtualization-nfv/white-paper-c11-732123.pdf, 2015.

[CIS 15c] CISCO, "VXLAN overview: Cisco Nexus 9000 Series Switches", available at: http://www.cisco.com/c/en/us/products/collateral/switches/nexus-9000-series-switches/white-paper-c11-729383.pdf, 2015.

[CLO 10] CLOUD-SECURITY-ALLIANCE, "Top Threats to Cloud Computing V1.0", available at: https://cloudsecurityalliance.org/topthreats/csathreats.v1.0.pdf, 2010.

[CLO 12] CLOUD-SECURITY-ALLIANCE, "SecaaS Implementation Guidance: Category 1 Identity and Access Management", available at: https://downloads.cloudsecurityalliance.org/initiatives/secaas/SecaaS_Cat_1_IAM_Implementation_Guidance.pdf, 2012.

[CLO 17] CLOUDNFV, "CloudNFV: Taking NFV to the Cloud", available at: http://www.cloudnfv.com/, 2017.

[CON 14] CONNECT O., "Welcome to OpenID Connect", available at: http://openid.net/connect/, 2014.

[CON 15] CONNECTEM, Project for providing vEPC to demonstrate the Worlds First Fully Virtualized LTE Core, Telekom Austria, 2015.

[DAI 10] DAI W., Commutative-like Encryption: A New Characterization of ElGamal, *CoRR*, vol. abs/1011.3718, 2010.

[DAW 10] DAWOUD W., TAKOUNA I., MEINEL C., "Infrastructure as a service security: challenges and solutions", *The 7th International Conference on Informatics and Systems (INFOS)*, pp. 1–8, March 2010.

[DIF 06] DIFFIE W., HELLMAN M., "New directions in cryptography", *IEEE Transactions on Information Theory*, vol. 22, no. 6, pp. 644–654, 2006.

[DOC 13] DOCKER, "Docker Containers", available at: https://www.docker.com/, 2013.

[DOD 12] DODIS Y., LUO W., XU S. *et al.*, "Key-insulated symmetric key cryptography and mitigating attacks against cryptographic Cloud software", *Proceedings of the 7th ACM Symposium on Information, Computer and Communications Security*, ASIACCS'12, New York, ACM, pp. 57–58, 2012.

[DON 06] DONG W.-L., YU H., "Web service testing method based on fault-coverage", *Enterprise Distributed Object Computing Conference Workshops, 2006, EDOCW'06, 10th IEEE International*, pp. 43–43, October 2006.

[DRO 03] DROMS R., BOUND J., VOLZ B. *et al.*, "Dynamic Host Configuration Protocol for IPv6 (DHCPv6)", available at: https://tools.ietf.org/ pdf/rfc3315.pdf, 2003.

[DUD 15] DUDOUET F., EDMONDS A., ERNE M., "Reliable Cloud-applications: an implementation through service orchestration", *Proceedings of the 1st International Workshop on Automated Incident Management in Cloud*, AIMC'15, New York, ACM, pp. 1–6, 2015.

[DUF 05] DUFLOS S., GAY V., KERVELLA B. *et al.*, *Improving the SLA-based Management of QoS for Secure Multimedia Services*, vol. 3754, Springer, Berlin, Heidelberg, pp. 204–215, 2005.

[DUT 14] DUTTA A., "NFV security – opportunities and challenges (slides for discussion in IEEE SRPSDVE Study Group)", available at: http://grouper.ieee.org/groups/srpsdv/meetings/2014%20October/ SRPSDVE_10292014_04_Ashutosh_NFV_Security_IEEE_Standards_ SRPSDVE_29O ct2014.pdf, 2014.

[ERI 14] ERICSSON, "Network functions virtualization and software management", available at: http://www.ericsson.com/res/docs/ whitepapers/network-functions-virtualization-and-software-management.pdf, 2014.

[ERI 15a] ERICSSON, "Ericsson review: OpenStack as the API framework for NFV: the benefits, and the extensions needed", available at: http://www.ericsson.com/res/thecompany/docs/publications/ericsson_review/ 2015/er-openstack-api-nfv.pdf, 2015.

[ERI 15b] ERICSSON, "Network functions virtualization (NFV)", available at: http://www.ericsson.com/spotlight/cloud/network-modernization/nfv, 2015.

[ETS 12] ETSI, "Network functions virtualization: an introduction, benefits, enablers, challenges & call for action", available at: http://portal.etsi.org/ NFV/NFV_White_Paper.pdf, 2012.

[ETS 13a] ETSI, "Network functions virtualization (NFV); architectural framework", available at: http://www.etsi.org/deliver/etsi_gs/NFV/001_ 099/002/01.01.01_60/gs_NFV002v010101p.pdf, 2013.

[ETS 13b] ETSI, "Network functions virtualization (NFV) use cases", available at: http://www.etsi.org/deliver/etsi_gs/nfv/001_099/001/01.01.01_ 60/gs_nfv001v010101p.pdf, 2013.

[ETS 14a] ETSI, "Network functions virtualization (NFV); management and orchestration", available at: http://www.etsi.org/deliver/etsi_gs/NFV-MAN/ 001_099/001/01.01.01_60/gs_nfv-man001v010101p.pdf, 2014.

[ETS 14b] ETSI, "Network functions virtualization (NFV); NFV security; security and trust guidance", available at: http://www.etsi.org/ deliver/etsi_gs/NFV-SEC/001_099/003/01.01.01_60/gs_NFV-SEC003v 010101p.pdf, 2014.

[ETS 14c] ETSI, "Network functions virtualization (NFV); virtual network functions architecture", available at: http://www.etsi.org/deliver/etsi_gs/ NFV-SWA/001_099/001/01.01.01_60/gs_nfv-swa001v010101p.pdf, 2014.

[ETS 15a] ETSI, "Network functions virtualization (NFV); management and orchestration; functional requirements specificiation", available at: https://docbox.etsi.org/ISG/NFV/Open/Drafts/IFA010_MANO_Functional_ Rqmts_Spec/, 2015.

[ETS 15b] ETSI, "Network functions virtualization (NFV); NFV security; privacy and regulation; report on lawful interception implications", available at: http://www.etsi.org/deliver/etsi_gs/NFV-SEC/001_099/004/ 01.01.01_60/gs_NFV-SEC004v010101p.pdf, 2015.

[FAY 15] FAYAZ S.K., TOBIOKA Y., SEKAR V. *et al.*, "Bohatei: flexible and elastic DDoS defense", *24th USENIX Security Symposium (USENIX Security 15)*, Washington, DC, USENIX Association, pp. 817–832, August 2015.

[FRE 15] FREEBSD, "IPFW", available at: https://www.freebsd.org/doc/handbook/firewalls-ipfw.html, 2015.

[GAR 03] GARFINKEL T., ROSENBLUM M., "A virtual machine introspection based architecture for intrusion detection", *Proceedings of Network and Distributed Systems Security Symposium*, pp. 191–206, 2003.

[GAR 15] GARCIA L.M., "Tcpdump & Libcap", available at: http://www.tcpdump.org/, 2015.

[GED 12] GEDARE BLOOM EUGEN LEONTIE B.N., SIMHA R., "Hardware and security: vulnerabilities and solutions", available at: http://www.seas.gwu.edu/simha/research/HWSecBookChapter12.pdf, 2012.

[GEM 13] GEMBER A., GRANDL R., KHALID J. *et al.*, "Design and implementation of a framework for software-defined middlebox networking", *SIGCOMM Computer Communication Reviw*, vol. 43, no. 4, pp. 467–468, ACM, August 2013.

[GHA 10] GHAROUT S., BOUABDALLAH A., KELLIL M. *et al.*, "Key management with host mobility in dynamic groups", *Proceedings of the 3rd International Conference on Security of Information and Networks*, SIN'10, ACM, New York, pp. 186–194, 2010.

[GHA 13] GHAFOOR A., IRUM M., QAISAR M., "User Centric Access control policy management framework for Cloud applications", *2nd National Conference on Information Assurance (NCIA), 2013*, pp. 135–140, December 2013.

[GIO 15] GIOTIS K., KRYFTIS Y., MAGLARIS V., "Policy-based orchestration of NFV services in software-defined networks", *1st IEEE Conference on Network Softwarization (NetSoft), 2015*, pp. 1–5, April 2015.

[GRE 05] GREENBERG A., HJALMTYSSON G., MALTZ D.A. *et al.*, "A clean slate 4D approach to network control and management", *SIGCOMM Computer Communication Review*, vol. 35, no. 5, pp. 41–54, ACM, October 2005.

[GRI 05] GRIFFIN J.L., JAEGER T., PEREZ R. *et al.*, "Trusted virtual domains: toward secure distributed services", *Proceedings of the First Workshop on Hot Topics in System Dependability (Hotdep05*, IEEE Press, 2005.

[GUD 08] GUDE N., KOPONEN T., PETTIT J. *et al.*, "NOX: towards an operating system for networks", *SIGCOMM Computer Communication Review*, vol. 38, no. 3, pp. 105–110, ACM, July 2008.

[HAM 06] HAMED H., AL-SHAER E., "Taxonomy of conflicts in network security policies", *IEEE Communications Magazine*, vol. 44, no. 3, pp. 134–141, March 2006.

[HAN 00] HAN J., KAMBER M., *Data Mining: Concepts and Techniques*, Morgan Kaufmann Publishers Inc., San Francisco, 2000.

[HAN 15] HAN B., GOPALAKRISHNAN V., JI L. *et al.*, "Network functions virtualization: challenges and opportunities for innovations", *IEEE Communications Magazine*, vol. 53, no. 2, pp. 90–97, February 2015.

[HAR 12] HARDT D., "The OAuth 2.0 authorization framework", available at: https://tools.ietf.org/html/rfc6749, 2012.

[HAT 15] HAT R., "Red Hat Enterprise Linux OpenStack Platform", available at: https://access.redhat.com/products/red-hat-enterprise-linux-openstack-platform, 2015.

[HAV 07] HAVIGHURST R., "User identification and authentication concepts", available at: http://www.infosectoday.com/Articles/AU5219_C01.pdf, 2007.

[HIC 10] HICKS B., RUEDA S., KING D. *et al.*, "An architecture for enforcing end-to-end access control over web applications", *Proceedings of the 15th ACM Symposium on Access Control Models and Technologies*, SACMAT'10, New York, ACM, pp. 163–172, 2010.

[HOS 12] HOSTAP, "Hostapd: IEEE 802.11 AP", IEEE 802.1X/WPA/WPA2/EAP/RADIUS authenticator, available at: http://w1.fi/hostapd/, 2012.

[HP 14a] HP, The reality of cost reduction, Business White paper, available at: http://www8.hp.com/h20195/V2/getpdf.aspx/4AA5-2160 ENW.pdf?ver=1.0, 2014.

[HP 14b] HP, Manage the future now – transforming operations for network functions virutualization, Business White paper, available at: http://www8.hp.com/h20195/v2/GetPDF.aspx/4AA5-6431ENW.pdf, 2014.

[HP 14c] HP, Network functions virtualization, Technical White paper, available at: http://www.hp.com/hpinfo/newsroom/press_kits/2014/MWC/White_Paper_NFV.pdf, 2014.

[HUA 12] HUANG Y.-L., CHEN B., SHIH M.-W. *et al.*, "Security impacts of virtualization on a network testbed", *SERE*, IEEE, pp. 71–77, 2012.

[HUA 14] HUAWEI, Huawei observation to NFV, White paper, available at: http://www.huawei.com/ilink/en/download/HW_399662, 2014.

[HUA 15] HUAWEI, "NFV/SDN Open Lab for OPNFV", available at: https://wiki.opnfv.org/lab4_huawei, 2015.

[HUS 13] HUSSAIN Z., GUMMADI A., "Vulnerabilities in cloud computing", available at: http://www.chinacloud.cn/upload/2013-05/13050613111874.pdf, 2013.

[IBR 11] IBRAHIM A., HAMLYN-HARRIS J., GRUNDY J. *et al.*, "CloudSec: a security monitoring appliance for virtual machines in the IaaS cloud model", *5th International Conference on Network and System Security (NSS)*, pp. 113–120, September 2011.

[IDE 12] IDENTITY AND ACCESS MANAGEMENT (IAM), Report, The Hong Kong PolyTechnic University, 2012.

[INF 14] INFONETICS RESEARCH, "Carrier SDN and NFV Hardware and Software market size and forecast", available at: http://www.infonetics.com/pr/2014/Carrier-SDN-NFV-Market-Highlights.asp, 2014.

[INO 15] INOVACAO P., "An NFV/SDN enabled service provider: a new generation of digital services", available at: http://www.ptinovacao.pt/content/WP-An-NFV-SDN-Enabled-Service-Provider.pdf, 2015.

[INT 13] INTEL, "Open, simplified networking based on SDN and network function virtualization", available at: http://www.intel.com/content/dam/www/public/us/en/documents/white-papers/sdn-part-1-secured.pdf, 2013.

[INT 14] INTEL, "End-to-End NFV – vEPC Service Orchestration", available at: https://networkbuilders.intel.com/docs/Network_Builders_RA_E2E_NFV.pdf, 2014.

[INT 15] INTEL, "End-to-end optimized network function virtualization deployment", available at: http://www.intel.com/content/www/us/en/communications/end-to-end-optimized-nfv-deployment-paper.html?wapkw=nfv+orchestration, 2015.

[IRW 05] IRWIN K., YU T., "Preventing attribute information leakage in automated trust negotiation", *Proceedings of the 12th ACM Conference on Computer and Communications Security*, CCS'05, New York, ACM, pp. 36–45, 2005.

[IRW 09] IRWIN C.S., TAYLOR D.C., "Identity, credential, and access management at NASA, from Zachman to attributes", *Proceedings of the 8th Symposium on Identity and Trust on the Internet*, IDtrust'09, New York, ACM, pp. 1–14, 2009.

[IWA 08] IWAIHARA M., MURAKAMI K., AHN G. *et al.*, "Risk evaluation for personal identity management based on privacy attribute ontology", *Proceedings of Conceptual Modeling – ER 2008, 27th International Conference on Conceptual Modeling*, Barcelona, Spain, pp. 183–198, 20–24 October 2008.

[JAC 14] JACOB E., MATIAS J., MENDIOLA A. *et al.*, "Deploying a virtual network function over a software defined network infrastructure: experiences deploying an access control VNF in the University of Basque Countrys OpenFlow enabled facility", Technical report, 2014.

[JAI 08] JAIN S., SHAFIQUE F., DJERIC V. *et al.*, "Application-level isolation and recovery with solitude", *Proceedings of the 3rd ACM SIGOPS/EuroSys European Conference on Computer Systems 2008*, Eurosys'08, New York, ACM, pp. 95–107, 2008.

[JAI 13] JAIN R., PAUL S., "Network virtualization and software defined networking for cloud computing: a survey", *Communications Magazine, IEEE*, vol. 51, no. 11, pp. 24–31, 2013.

[JAM 12] JAMSHED M.A., LEE J., MOON S. *et al.*, "Kargus: a highly-scalable software-based intrusion detection system", *Proceedings of the 2012 ACM Conference on Computer and Communications Security*, CCS'12, New York, ACM, pp. 317–328, 2012.

[JIN 12] JIN X., KRISHNAN R., SANDHU R., "A unified attribute-based access control model covering DAC, MAC and RBAC", *Proceedings of the 26th Annual IFIP WG 11.3 Conference on Data and Applications Security and Privacy*, DBSec'12, Berlin, Heidelberg, Springer-Verlag, pp. 41–55, 2012.

[JUB 14] JUBA Y., HUANG H.-H., KAWAGOE K., "POSTER: Security Control System Enabling to Keep an Intra-LAN in a Secure State Using Security-and-Performance Ratio Control Policies", *Proceedings of the 2014 ACM SIGSAC Conference on Computer and Communications Security*, CCS'14, New York, ACM, pp. 1442–1444, 2014.

[JUN 15] JUNIPER, "QFX5100 Ethernet Switch", available at: http://www. juniper.net/assets/jp/jp/local/pdf/datasheets/1000480-en.pdf, 2015.

[KER 03] KERN A., SCHAAD A., MOFFETT J., "An administration concept for the enterprise role-based access control model", *Proceedings of the Eighth ACM Symposium on Access Control Models and Technologies*, SACMAT'03, New York, ACM, pp. 3–11, 2003.

[KER 05] KERN A., WALHORN C., "Rule support for role-based access control", *Proceedings of the Tenth ACM Symposium on Access Control Models and Technologies*, SACMAT'05, New York, ACM, pp. 130–138, 2005.

[KIN 06] KING S., CHEN P., "SubVirt: implementing malware with virtual machines", *2006 IEEE Symposium on Security and Privacy*, pp. 14–327, May 2006.

[KIR 07] KIRCH J., "Virtual Machine Security Guidelines: Version 1.0", available at: http://ht.transparencytoolkit.org/FileServer/FileServer/ whitepapers/hardening/CIS_VM_Benchmark_v1.0.pdf, 2007.

[KOW 09] KOWTARAPU C., ANAND C., GURUPRASAD K. *et al.*, "Network separation and IPsec CA certificates-based security management for 4G networks", *Bell Labs Technical Journal*, vol. 13, no. 4, pp. 245–255, 2009.

[KYR 13] KYRIAZIS D., "Cloud computing service level agreements: exploitation of research results", available at: http://ec.europa.eu/ information_society/newsroom/cf/dae/document.cfm?doc_id=2496, 2013.

[LAB 15] LABS A.C., "NFVOps Orchestration Framework", available at: http://sdn.calsoftlabs.com/downloads/Brochures/NFVOps.pdf, 2015.

[LAU 12] LAUTER K.E., "Practical applications of homomorphic encryption", *Proceedings of the 2012 ACM Workshop on Cloud Computing Security Workshop*, CCSW'12, New York, ACM, pp. 57–58, 2012.

[LEE 08] LEE A.J., WINSLETT M., BASNEY J. *et al.*, "The trust authorization service", *ACM Transactions on Information and System Security*, vol. 11, no. 1, pp. 2:1–2:33, 2008.

[LEM 14] LEMKE A., "How to manage security in NFV environments", available at: https://techzine.alcatel-lucent.com/how-manage-security-nfv-environments, 2014.

[LIU 16] LIU V., "Analytic framework for NFV orchestrator", available at: https://tools.ietf.org/html/draft-liu-nfvrg-analytic-framework-00, 2016.

[LOG 14] LOGIC R., "Toward a federated identity service based on virutalization: a Buyer's guide to identity integration solution, from meta and virtual directories to a federated identity service based on virtualization", available at: http://www.ciosummits.com/ Online_Asset_Radiant_Logic_Buyers_Guide.pdf, 2014.

[LUC 13] LUCENT A., "Network functions virtualization – challenges and solution: strategic white paper", available at: http://www.tmcnet.com/ tmc/whitepapers/documents/whitepapers/2013/9377-network-functions-virtualization-challenges-solutions.pdf, 2013.

[LXC 14] LXC, "Linux containers", available at: https://linuxcontainers.org/, 2014.

[MAC 13] MACAULAY T., "The 7 Deadly Threats to 4G: 4G LTE Security Roadmap and Reference Design", available at: http://www.mcafee. com/in/resources/white-papers/wp-the-7-deadly-threats-4g.pdf, 2013.

[MAH 14] MAHALINGAM M., DUTT D., DUDA K. et al., "Virtual eXtensible Local Area Network (VXLAN): a framework for overlaying virtualized layer 2 over layer 3 networks", available at: https://tools.ietf.org/pdf/rfc7348.pdf, 2014.

[MAL 08] MALEK B., MIRI A., KARMOUCH A., "A framework for context-aware authentication", *2008 IET 4th International Conference on Intelligent Environments*, pp. 1–8, July 2008.

[MAN 10] MANCHANDA N., ANAND K., "Non-uniform memory access (NUMA)", available at: http://cs.nyu.edu/lerner/spring10/projects/NUMA. pdf, 2010.

[MAR 07] MARKATOS E., "Large scale attacks on the internet lessons learned from the LOBSTER project", available at: https://www.ist-lobster.org/publications/presentations/markatos-attacks.pdf, 2007.

[MAT 14] MATIAS J., GARAY J., MENDIOLA A. et al., "FlowNAC: flow-based network access control", *Proceedings of the 2014 Third European Workshop on Software Defined Networks*, EWSDN'14, Washington, DC, IEEE Computer Society, pp. 79–84, 2014.

[MCD 14] MCDOWALL J., "Inherent security design patterns for SDN/NFV deployments", available at: http://events.linuxfoundation.org/ sites/events/files/slides/Design_Patterns_submitted.pdf, 2014.

[MCK 08] MCKEOWN N., ANDERSON T., BALAKRISHNAN H. *et al.*, "Openflow: enabling innovation in campus networks", *SIGCOMM Computer Communication Review*, vol. 38, no. 2, pp. 69–74, 2008.

[MEN 96] MENEZES A.J., VANSTONE S.A., OORSCHOT P.C.V., *Handbook of Applied Cryptography*, 1st edition, CRC Press, Inc., Boca Raton, 1996.

[MEN 13] MENG S., LIU L., "Monitoring-as-a-service in the Cloud: Spec Phd Award (Invited Abstract)", *Proceedings of the 4th ACM/SPEC International Conference on Performance Engineering*, ICPE'13, New York, ACM, pp. 373–374, 2013.

[MEY 13] MEYER C., SCHWENK J., "Lessons learned from previous SSL/TLS attacks – A brief chronology of attacks and weaknesses", *IACR Cryptology ePrint Archive*, vol. 2013, p. 49, 2013.

[MIC 05] MICROSOFT, Microsoft baseline security analyzer V1.2, White paper, available at: https://technet.microsoft.com/en-us/library/dd277467.aspx, July 2005.

[MIC 10] MICROSOFT, "Hyper-V Update List for Windows Server 2008", available at: https://technet.microsoft.com/en-us/library/dd430893 (WS.10).aspx, September 2010.

[MIJ 16] MIJUMBI R., SERRAT J., GORRICHO J.L. *et al.*, "Network function virtualization: state-of-the-art and research challenges", *IEEE Communications Surveys Tutorials*, vol. 18, no. 1, pp. 236–262, February 2016.

[MOD 12] MODI C., PATEL D., BORISANYA B. *et al.*, "A novel framework for intrusion detection in cloud", *Proceedings of the Fifth International Conference on Security of Information and Networks*, SIN'12, New York, ACM, pp. 67–74, 2012.

[MON 14] MONASCA, "Project Monasca: Monitoring as a Service", available at: https://wiki. openstack.org/wiki/Monasca, 2014.

[MON 15] MONTERO D., YANNUZZI M., SHAW A. *et al.*, "Virtualized security at the network edge: a user-centric approach", *Communications Magazine, IEEE*, vol. 53, no. 4, pp. 176–186, April 2015.

[MOR 12] MORAIS A., CAVALLI A., "A distributed intrusion detection scheme for wireless ad hoc networks", *Proceedings of the 27th Annual ACM Symposium on Applied Computing*, SAC'12, New York, ACM, pp. 556–562, 2012.

[MUN 11] MUNDADA Y., RAMACHANDRAN A., FEAMSTER N., "Silverline: Data and network isolation for cloud services", *Proceedings of the 3rd USENIX Conference on Hot Topics in Cloud Computing*, HotCloud'11, Berkeley, USENIX Association, pp. 13–13, 2011.

[MYE 14] MYERSON J., "Protect a PaaS from Hackers with Four Phases of Defense", available at: http://www.techrepublic.com/article/protect-a-paas-from-hackers-with-four-phases-of-defense/, November 2014.

[NAR 98] NARTEN T., NORDMARK E., SIMPSON W., "Neighbor Discovery for IP Version 6 (IPv6)", available at: https://www.ietf.org/rfc/rfc2461.txt, December 1998.

[NEC 13] NEC, "NEC Launches World's First Virtualization Mobile Core Network Solution", available at: http://www.nec.com/en/press/201310/global_20131022_03.html, 2013.

[NET 14] NETWORKS C., "Six Vendors Select Certes' Solutions for Encryption in Network Function Virtualization Deployments", available at: http://certesnetworks.com/solutions/cloud-security/, 2014.

[NET 15] NETWORKS N., "Building Secure Telco Clouds", available at: http://networks.nokia.com/sites/default/files/document/nokia_telco_security_white_paper.pdf, 2015.

[NOK 17] NOKIA, "Project CloudBand 3.1: The production platform for NFV", available at: https://networks.nokia.com/products/cloudband, 2017.

[NOX 08] NOX, "NOX", available at: http://www.noxrepo.org/nox/about-nox/, 2008.

[NUN 13] NUNES R., PONTES R., GUEDES D., "Virtualized network isolation using Software Defined Networks", *IEEE 38th Conference on Local Computer Networks (LCN)*, pp. 683–686, October 2013.

[OBE 08] OBERHEIDE J., COOKE E., JAHANIAN F., "CloudAV: N-Version Antivirus in the Network Cloud", *Proceedings of the 17th USENIX Security Symposium*, San Jose, CA, pp. 91–106, July 2008.

[OPE 15a] OPENCONTRAIL, "OpenContrail: An Open Source Network Virtaulization Platform for the Cloud", available at: http://www.opencontrail.org/, 2015.

[OPE 15b] OPENVZ, "OpenVZ Virtuozzo Containers", available at: https://openvz.org/Main_Page, 2015.

[OPE 17] OPENSTACK, "OpenStack", project website: https://www.openstack.org/, 2017.

[OPN 15] OPNFV, "OPNFV: Linux Foundation Collaborative Projects", available at: https://www.opnfv.org/, 2015.

[ORA 12] ORACLE, "Network Isolation in Private Database Clouds", available at: http://www.oracle.com/technetwork/database/database-cloud/ntwk-isolation-pvt-db-cloud-1587225.pdf, 2012.

[PAG 13] PAGANINI P., "Hardware attacks, backdoors, and electronic component qualification", available at: http://resources.infosecinstitute.com/hardware-attacks-backdoors-and-electronic-component-qualification/, 2013.

[PAT 17] PATTARANANTAKUL M., TSENG Y., HE R. et al., "A First Step Towards Security Extension for NFV orchestrator", SDN-NFV Security Workshop'17, March 2017.

[PAX 99] PAXSON V., "Bro: a system for detecting network intruders in real-time", Computer Networks, vol. 31, no. 23–24, pp. 2435–2463, December 1999.

[PÉK 13] PÉK G., BUTTYÁN L., BENCSÁTH B., "A survey of security issues in hardware virtualization", ACM Computing Surveys, vol. 45, no. 3, pp. 40:1–40:34, 2013.

[PET 04] PETRONI N.L., TIMOTHY J., JESUS F. et al., "Copilot – a coprocessor-based kernel runtime integrity monitor", Proceedings of the 13th USENIX Security Symposium, pp. 179–194, 2004.

[PLA 15] PLANET C.B., "Blue Planet Streamlines the Definition and Creation of NFV based Services", available at: http://www.blueplanet.com/products/nfv-orchestration.html, 2015.

[POX 08] POX, "POX", available at: http://www.noxrepo.org/pox/about-pox/, 2008.

[PRI 14] PRIEBE C., MUTHUKUMARAN D., O' KEEFFE D. et al., "Cloudsafetynet: detecting data leakage between cloud tenants", Proceedings of the 6th Edition of the ACM Workshop on Cloud Computing Security, CCSW'14, New York, ACM, pp. 117–128, 2014.

[QAZ 13] QAZI Z.A., TU C.-C., CHIANG L. et al., "SIMPLE-fying middlebox policy enforcement using SDN", SIGCOMM Computer Communication Review, vol. 43, no. 4, pp. 27–38, August 2013.

[RAB 05] RABIN M.O., "How to exchange secrets with oblivious transfer", 2005, Harvard University, Technical Report 81, 2005.

[RAN 07] RANGA G., FLOWERDAY S., "Identity and access management for the distribution of social grants in South Africa", *Proceedings of the 2007 Annual Research Conference of the South African Institute of Computer Scientists and Information Technologists on IT Research in Developing Countries*, SAICSIT'07, New York, ACM, pp. 125–131, 2007.

[RIG 15] RIGGIO R., SCHULZ-ZANDER J., BRADAI A., "Virtual network function orchestration with Scylla", *Proceedings of the 2015 ACM Conference on Special Interest Group on Data Communication*, SIGCOMM'15, New York, ACM, pp. 375–376, 2015.

[ROE 13] ROESCH M., "Snort", available at: https://www.snort.org/, 2013.

[ROU 06] ROUILLER S.A., "Virtual LAN Security: Weaknesses and countermeasures", available at: https://www.sans.org/reading-room/ whitepapers/networkdevs/virtual-lan-security-weaknesses-countermeasu res-1090, 2006.

[RUB 13] RUBENS P., "Secure SSL Against Today's Threats", available at: http://www.enterprisenetworkingplanet.com/netsecur/secure-ssl-against-todays-threats.html, 2013.

[RUB 15] RUBIO-MEDRANO C.E., ZHAO Z., DOUPE A. *et al.*, "Federated access management for collaborative network environments: framework and case study", *Proceedings of the 20th ACM Symposium on Access Control Models and Technologies*, SACMAT'15, New York, ACM, pp. 125–134, 2015.

[SAI 05] SAILER R., VALDEZ E., JAEGER T. *et al.*, "sHype: Secure Hypervisor Approach to Trusted Virtualized Systems", *IBM Research Report RC23511*, 2005.

[SAM 08] SAML O., "Security Assertion Markup Language (SAML) V2.0 Technical Overview", available at: https://www.oasis-open.org/committees/download.php/27819/sstc-saml-tech-overview-2.0-cd-02.pdf, 2008.

[SAN 09] SANTOS N., GUMMADI K.P., RODRIGUES R., "Towards trusted cloud computing", *Proceedings of the 2009 Conference on Hot Topics in Cloud Computing*, HotCloud'09, Berkeley, CA, USENIX Association, pp. 1–5, 2009.

[SEC 16] SECURED, "Security at the network edge", available at: https://www.secured-fp7.eu/, 2016.

[SEK 12] SEKAR V., EGI N., RATNASAMY S. *et al.*, "Design and implementation of a consolidated middlebox architecture", *Proceedings of the 9th USENIX Conference on Networked Systems Design and Implementation, NSDI'12*, USENIX Association, Berkeley, pp. 24–24, 2012.

[SHA 05] SHAFIQ B., BERTINO E., GHAFOOR A., "Access control management in a distributed environment supporting dynamic collaboration", *Proceedings of the 2005 Workshop on Digital Identity Management, DIM'05*, ACM, New York, pp. 104–112, 2005.

[SHA 11] SHAN Z., WANG X., CHIUEH T.-C., "Tracer: enforcing mandatory access control in commodity OS with the support of light-weight intrusion detection and tracing", *Proceedings of the 6th ACM Symposium on Information, Computer and Communications Security, ASIACCS'11*, ACM, New York, pp. 135–144, 2011.

[SHA 14] SHANMUGAM P.K., SUBRAMANYAM N.D., BREEN J. *et al.*, "DEIDtect: towards distributed elastic intrusion detection", *Proceedings of the 2014 ACM SIGCOMM Workshop on Distributed Cloud Computing, DCC'14*, ACM, New York, pp. 17–24, 2014.

[SHE 12] SHERRY J., HASAN S., SCOTT C. *et al.*, "Making middleboxes someone else's problem: network processing as a cloud service", *ACM SIGCOMM Computer Communication Review*, vol. 42, no. 4, pp. 13–24, 2012.

[SHE 15] SHERRY J., LAN C., POPA R.A. *et al.*, "BlindBox: deep packet inspection over encrypted traffic", *Proceedings of the 2015 ACM Conference on Special Interest Group on Data Communication, SIGCOMM'15*, ACM, New York, pp. 213–226, 2015.

[SHI 15] SHIN S., WANG H., GU G., "A first step toward network security virtualization: from concept to prototype", *IEEE Transactions on Information Forensics and Security*, vol. 10, no. 10, pp. 2236–2249, 2015.

[SOL 12] SOLUTIONS NETWORKS, "Core network virtualization: a proof of concept", available at: http://networks.nokia.com/system/files/document/nsn_core_network_virtualization_proof_of_concept_brochure.pdf, 2012.

[SON 00] SONG D.X., WAGNER D., PERRIG A., "Practical techniques for searches on encrypted data", *Proceedings of the 2000 IEEE Symposium on Security and Privacy, SP'00*, IEEE Computer Society, Washington, DC, pp. 44–55, 2000.

[SON 14] SONG Y., KIM H., MOHAISEN A., "A private walk in the clouds: using end-to-end encryption between cloud applications in a personal domain", in ECKERT C., KATSIKAS S., PERNUL G. (eds.), *Trust, Privacy, and Security in Digital Business, Lecture Notes in Computer Science*, Springer International Publishing, 2014.

[STA 10] STALLINGS W., *Cryptography and Network Security: Principles and Practice*, 5th edition, Prentice Hall Press, Upper Saddle River, 2010.

[SUZ 05] SUZUKI S., KONDO S., "Dynamic network separation for IPv6 network security enhancement", *The 2005 Saint Workshops 2005. Symposium on Applications and the Internet Workshops, 2005*, pp. 22–25, January 2005.

[SWE 02] SWEENEY L., "K-anonymity: a model for protecting privacy", *International Journal of Uncertainty, Fuzziness and Knowledge-Based Systems*, vol. 10, no. 5, pp. 557–570, World Scientific Publishing Co., Inc., October 2002.

[TAK 14] TAKABI H., "Privacy aware access control for data sharing in cloud computing environments", *Proceedings of the 2nd International Workshop on Security in Cloud Computing, SCC'14*, ACM, New York, pp. 27–34, 2014.

[TAY 15] TAYLOR M., "Elastic scalability in network functions virtualization", available at: http://info.metaswitch.com/hs-fs/hub/415294/ file-2519013034-pdf/PDFs/Elastic_Scalability_in_NFV.pdf?t=144727916 1132, February 2015.

[TEE 10] TEERAKANOK S., VORAKULPIPAT C., KAMOLPHIWONG S., "Anonymity preserving framework for location-based information services", *Proceedings of the International Conference on Management of Emergent Digital EcoSystems, MEDES'10*, ACM, New York, pp. 107–113, 2010.

[THO 15] THOMSON S., NARTEN T., JINMEI T., "IPv6 stateless address autoconfiguration", available at: https://tools.ietf.org/pdf/rfc3315.pdf, 2015.

[TNO 14] T-NOVA, "T-NOVA", available at: http://www.t-nova.eu/ overview/, 2014.

[VMW 15] VMWARE, "VMware patches download", available at: https://www.vmware.com/patchmgr/findPatchByReleaseName.portal, 2015.

[VMW 16] VMWARE, "VMware vShield", available at: https://www.vmware. com/files/pdf/vmware-vshield_br-en.pdf, 2016.

[VSE 17] VSERVER L., "Linux-VServer", available at: http://linux-vserver.org/Welcome_to_Linux-VServer.org, 2017.

[WAN 11] WANG Q., JIN H., "Data leakage mitigation for discretionary access control in collaboration clouds", *Proceedings of the 16th ACM Symposium on Access Control Models and Technologies, SACMAT'11*, ACM, New York, pp. 103–112, 2011.

[WAT 11] WATERS B., "Ciphertext-policy attribute-based encryption: an expressive, efficient, and provably secure realization", *Proceedings of the 14th International Conference on Practice and Theory in Public Key Cryptography, PKC'11*, Italy, pp. 53–70, March 2011.

[WPA 12] WPA, "Linux WPA/WPA2/IEEE 802.1X supplicant", available at: http://w1.fi/wpa_supplicant/, 2012.

[WRA 10] WRAIGHT C., "White paper: content-aware identity & access management in a virtual environment", available at: http://marketing. computerworld.com/content_aware_iam_june2010.pdf, 2010.

[XIL 14] XILOURIS G., "T-NOVA: overall system architecture and interfaces", available at: http://www.t-nova.eu/wp-content/uploads/2014/01/TNOVA_D2.21_Overall_System_Architecture_and_Interfaces_ v.1.0.pdf, 2014.

[XIO 13] XIONG J., YAO Z., MA J. *et al.*, "PRAM: privacy preserving access management scheme in cloud services", *Proceedings of the 2013 International Workshop on Security in Cloud Computing, Cloud Computing'13*, ACM, New York, pp. 41–46, 2013.

[YAN 13] YANG K., JIA X., REN K., "Attribute-based fine-grained access control with efficient revocation in cloud storage systems", *Proceedings of the 8th ACM SIGSAC Symposium on Information, Computer and Communications Security, ASIA CCS'13*, ACM, New York, pp. 523–528, 2013.

[YAN 14] YANG Y., CHEN X., WANG G. *et al.*, "An identity and access management architecture in cloud", *Seventh International Symposium on Computational Intelligence and Design (ISCID) 2014*, vol. 2, pp. 200–203, December 2014.

[YAO 86] YAO A.C.-C., "How to generate and exchange secrets", *27th Annual Symposium on Foundations of Computer Science*, pp. 162–167, October 1986.

[YAO 14] YAO F., SPRABERY R., CAMPBELL R.H., "CryptVMI: a flexible and encrypted virtual machine introspection system in the cloud", *Proceedings of the 2nd International Workshop on Security in Cloud Computing, SCC'14*, ACM, New York, pp. 11–18, 2014.

[YAU 10] YAU S.S., AN H.G., "Protection of users' data confidentiality in cloud computing", *Proceedings of the Second Asia-Pacific Symposium on Internetware, Internetware'10*, ACM, New York, pp. 11:1–11:6, 2010.

[YEH 05] YEH H.-T., SUN H.-M., "Password authenticated key exchange protocols among diverse network domains", *Computers & Electrical Engineering*, vol. 31, no. 3, pp. 175–189, 2005.

[YEO 95] YEONG W., HOWES T., KILLE S., "Lightweight directory access protocol", https://tools.ietf.org/pdf/rfc1777.pdf, 1995.

[ZHA 03] ZHANG Y., LEE W., HUANG Y.-A., "Intrusion detection techniques for mobile wireless networks", *Wireless Networks*, vol. 9, no. 5, pp. 545–556, 2003.

[ZHA 14] ZHANG Y., JUELS A., REITER M.K. *et al.*, "Cross-tenant side-channel attacks in PaaS clouds", *Proceedings of the 2014 ACM SIGSAC Conference on Computer and Communications Security, CCS'14*, ACM, New York, pp. 990–1003, 2014.

[ZHA 15] ZHANG T., LEE R.B., "CloudMonatt: an architecture for security health monitoring and attestation of virtual machines in cloud computing", *Proceedings of the 42nd Annual International Symposium on Computer Architecture, ISCA'15*, ACM, New York, pp. 362–374, 2015.

[ZHO 08] ZHONG G., HENGARTNER U., "Toward a distributed K-anonymity protocol for location privacy", *Proceedings of the 7th ACM Workshop on Privacy in the Electronic Society, WPES'08*, ACM, New York, pp. 33–38, 2008.

[ZON 14] Zong N., Dunbar L., Lopez D. *et al.*, "Virtualized network function (VNF) pool, problem statement", available at: https://tools.ietf.org/html/draft-zong-vnfpool-problem-statement-06, 2014.

[ZOU 13] Zou D., Zhang W., Qiang W. *et al.*, "Design and implementation of a trusted monitoring framework for cloud platforms", *Future Generation Computer Systems*, vol. 29, no. 8, pp. 2092–2102, 2013.

[ZUC 15] Zuccaro L., Cimorelli F., Priscoli F.D. *et al.*, "Distributed control in virtualized networks", *Proceedings of the 10th International Conference on Future Networks and Communications (FNC 2015) / The 12th International Conference on Mobile Systems and Pervasive Computing (MobiSPC 2015)*, vol. 56, pp. 276–283, 2015.

Index

mobile
  devices, 46, 92, 94, 139, 160,
    176, 201
  networks, 5, 40, 87, 88, 91–95,
    158, 203

N, P, R, S

network isolation, 86, 108, 134,
    173, 174, 181, 182, 185–187,
    190–192, 216
NFVIaaS, 45–49, 52, 55, 56, 81,
public clouds, 141, 142, 162, 179,
    204
reference points, 2, 3, 7
scaling, 6, 7, 9, 10, 15, 17, 18, 21,
    23, 27, 128, 172
scenarios, 55, 75, 76, 103, 104,
    117, 138, 139, 144, 157, 158,
    160, 163, 173, 174, 176, 197,
    201, 207, 216
security
  analysis, 101
  management, 8, 49, 86, 107,
    108, 121, 126, 127, 131,
    133, 177, 191, 216
  management platforms, 126
  requirements, 45, 54, 56, 60,
    63, 83, 94, 101, 105, 106,

108, 109, 111, 113, 184,
    191, 215
service orchestration, 119, 121
threats, 48, 50–52, 56, 60, 63,
    80–83, 92, 94, 96, 101, 104,
    106, 108, 169, 171, 174,
    181
specifications, 14
standardization, 34, 173
status, 17, 23, 84, 123, 132, 137,
    164, 165

T, U, V

telco scenarios, 139, 160, 176, 201
trusted environments, 95, 183, 190
typical frameworks, 122
use cases, 42, 45, 61, 63, 70,
    83–86, 104, 105, 108, 119
vCDN, 68, 74, 86
vCPE, 68, 69, 86, 91
VIM, 4, 8–10, 13–16, 20–22,
    24–28, 51, 82, 130
virtualization
  of mobile networks, 87, 92, 95
VNFaaS, 59, 60, 63, 67–69, 71, 74,
    80, 81, 83, 84, 86
VNFM, 8–11, 13–15, 17, 19,
    21–25, 82, 110
VNPaaS, 58–67, 84, 86, 104

Printed in the United States
By Bookmasters